GATEKEEPER

Also by John F. Sullivan

Of Spies and Lies:
A CIA Lie Detector Remembers Vietnam

GATEKEEPER

Memoirs of a
CIA Polygraph Examiner

JOHN F. SULLIVAN

Potomac Books, Inc.
Washington, D.C.

Library of Congress Cataloging-in-Publication Data

Sullivan, John F., 1939-
  Gatekeeper : memoirs of a CIA polygraph examiner / John F. Sullivan. — 1st ed.
    p. cm.
  Includes index.
  ISBN-13: 978-1-59797-045-7 (hardcover : alk. paper)
  ISBN-10: 1-59797-045-X (hardcover : alk. paper)
  1. Sullivan, John F., 1939- 2. Polygraph operators—United States—Biography.
3. United States. Central Intelligence Agency—Officials and employees—Biog-
raphy. 4. Intelligence service—United States. I. Title.
  JK468.I6S85 2007
  327.730092—dc22
  [B]
                              2006018101

(alk. paper)

Printed in the United States of America on acid-free paper that meets the American National Standards Institute Z39-48 Standard.

Potomac Books, Inc.
22841 Quicksilver Drive
Dulles, Virginia 20166

First Edition

10 9 8 7 6 5 4 3 2 1

CONTENTS

ACKNOWLEDGMENTS

One of my purposes in writing *Gatekeeper* was to correct what I see as misconceptions about polygraph; at least as practiced in the CIA. In the process, I have cited numerous examples of CIA polygraph examiners' successes as well as their failures. Many of my former colleagues have been generous with their time in discussing some of their successes and failures, and I am most appreciative.

Lisa Camner, my editor at Potomac Books, Inc., has been a delight with whom to work, and whatever success *Gatekeeper* has much will be owing to Ms. Camner's efforts. An author's ego is a fragile thing, and Ms. Camner's sensitivity is not something I will soon forget.

As was the case when I wrote my first book, my wife, Lee, played a paramount role in *Gatekeeper*. Lee's attention to detail is only surpassed by her skill as a typist; both of which helped turn my manuscript into acceptable copy for a publisher. Saying "Thank you" to Lee is almost trite, but I have never said those two words with more sincerity.

A final acknowledgement is to the CIA's Publications Review Board (PRB). Of late, there has been some criticism of the PRB from Agency authors and charges of censorship made against the Board. My experience has been quite the opposite in that I have found the PRB to have been very accommodating. Redactions from manuscripts, articles, speeches, and lectures have been minimal, and I am most appreciative.

Any success that *Gatekeeper* has will be due in large part to the efforts of Michie Shaw, Julie Kimmel, and Lisa Camner, members of the editorial staff at Potomac Books Inc. Their professionalism and competence are impressive and their sensitivity to my ego is deeply appreciated.

AUTHOR'S NOTE

In writing *Gatekeeper*, I have included much dialogue. As I did not record the conversations I cite, I submit that the dialogues herein are accurate to the best of my ability.

Many of my former colleagues have asked that I not use their true names in *Gatekeeper*. To comply with this request, I have used pseudonyms enclosed in quotation marks at first mention.

GLOSSARY

A/COPS	acting chief of operations
ADDS	assistant deputy director of support
AF	Africa Division
APA	American Polygraph Association
AVH	Allamvedelmi Hatosag (Hungarian intelligence service)
BI	background investigation
BNDD	Bureau of Narcotics and Dangerous Drugs
CD	Clearance Division
CIA	Central Intelligence Agency (the Agency)
CIARDS	Central Intelligence Agency Retirement and Disability System
CID	Criminal Investigations Division
CIG	Central Intelligence Group
COD	chief of the overt operations desk
COG	Cuban Operations Group
COS	chief of station
CT	career trainee
DA	director of administration
DCI	director central intelligence
DCOS	deputy chief of station
DDA	deputy director of administration
DDO	deputy director of operations
DGI	Direccion General de Inteligencia (Cuban intelligence service)
DI	deception indicated
DI	Directorate of Intelligence
DIA	Defense Intelligence Agency

DO	Directorate of Operations
DODPI	Department of Defense Polygraph Institute
DOE	Department of Energy
DOJ	Department of Justice
D/OS	director of (the Office of) Security
DP	Directorate of Plans
DS&T	Directorate of Science and Technology
EB	Employee Branch
EEO	equal employment opportunity
EOD	enter on duty
EPA	Exceptional Performance Award
FOI	Foreign Operations Intelligence
GRU	Soviet military intelligence
HUMINT	human intelligence
IG	Inspector General
IRB	Interrogation Research Branch (precursor to IRD)
IRD	Interrogation Research Division
IS	intelligence service
KGB	Soviet intelligence service
LA	Latin America Division
MfS	Ministerium fur Staatsicherheit, East German intelligence service
MI	military intelligence
MI6	British foreign intelligence service
NAS	National Academies of Sciences
NCO	noncommissioned officer: enlisted ranks from corporal through sergeant major
NDI	no deception indicated
NOC	nonofficial cover
NSA	National Security Agency
OGA	other government agencies
OGC	Office of General Counsel
OMS	Office of Medical Services
Ops Fam	Operations Familiarization Course
OS	Office of Security
PAR	performance appraisal review
PATB	professional aptitude test battery
PD	Polygraph Division
PHS	personal history statement
POW	prisoner of war
QAS	Quality Assurance Staff
QC	quality control

QSI	quality step increase
R/I test	relevant/irrelevant test
RIP	reinvestigation polygraph
SAD	Special Activities Division
SIP	specific issue polygraph
SOG	Special Operations Group
SORT	Security Officer Recruit Trainee
SPO	security protective officer
STASI	East German Ministry of State Security (MfS)
SWAG	scientific wild ass guess
TDY	temporary duty
TRIP	trial period polygraph test
VC	Viet Cong
VSA	Voice Stress Analyzer
WMD	weapons of mass destruction

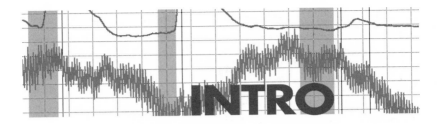

THE ART OF THE POLYGRAPH

In September 1947, when the Central Intelligence Agency (CIA) came into being, its primary function was to collect intelligence on the intentions and capabilities of America's enemies from both open and clandestine sources. It was hoped that the analysis of this intelligence would provide information about our enemies that would be of value to the U.S. executive branch in formulating policy.

Much of the intelligence collected during the early years of the CIA came from human sources—e.g., spies, refugee debriefings, and open sources such as newspapers and radio broadcasts—and was thus called human intelligence (HUMINT). The Directorate of Science and Technology (DS&T) and satellites didn't exist.

Verifying the information provided by human sources was a problem. Rarely, if ever, were CIA case officers able to independently corroborate information that their assets provided. In 1950 it was suggested that polygraph might be of some use in determining the veracity of the agents and assets who were providing information.

Depending on one's point of view, polygraph may or may not have had some success. Polygraph examiners succeeded in identifying and obtaining admissions from numerous agents who were fabricators, and this was not good news for case officers who thought they had been running good agents. As polygraph examiners uncovered more and more bad operations, case officers began to view polygraph examinations of their agents as hurdles to be overcome. A pattern was evident in the case officers' responses to tests. Those resulting in a "no deception indicated" (NDI) call were applauded, and the examiner was congratulated on a job well done. For tests in which the examiner concluded that the subject had been deceptive, particularly if no admissions were obtained, the results were often challenged and the examiners were given the cold shoulder or worse.

On occasion, the challenges became heated and the polygraph's validity was challenged, as was the competence of the examiner. Even when challenged calls were not overturned, the unfavorable results of the examination were often disregarded. The Directorate of Plans (DP) was under no obligation to accept the results of a polygraph test, and the Office of Security (OS) had no input into how the DP dealt with assets who had failed their polygraph tests.

There are many questions about the validity and reliability of polygraph. After thirty-one years as a polygraph examiner I have concluded that polygraph is much more effective in determining that a person is being deceptive than it is in verifying that a person has been or is being honest. In my discussions with case officers, I tried to make the point that if they accepted examiners' conclusions when we called their agents good, they should also accept them when we called their agents bad, not just because it was the fair thing to do but because a "bad" call is more accurate. A "deception indicated" (DI) call is based on unexplained reactions and what the examiner assesses as bad behavior on the part of the subject, whereas an NDI call is based on a lack of reaction to relevant questions. On the occasions when a subject has "beaten" me, it was because I called the subject, who turned out to be deceptive, nondeceptive. My rule of thumb for case officers was "If an agent's polygraph test is deemed DI, take it to the bank. If the test is deemed NDI, have a healthy skepticism."

Polygraph examiners' successes are defined by the admissions that they obtain, and Agency case officers' successes are defined by the number of good assets they recruit. What is often seen as a success for a polygraph examiner can be, and often is, interpreted as a failure for a case officer. This phenomenon is part of the historic antipathy that Agency case officers have toward the polygraph.

If detecting lies or identifying liars can be seen as a part of determining truth—and I think it can—polygraph examiners using "lie detectors" are by definition searchers for truth. I considered many of my colleagues and myself as very active participants in a quest for truth. In the course of our quest, we were often vilified when we failed and ignored when we succeeded.

From the day that polygraph was introduced to the Central Intelligence Agency in 1948 until today, it has been a source of controversy. The Agency is the U.S. government's primary user of the polygraph, and the focus of the following pages will be on polygraph use in the Agency. In the Agency, polygraph is used to screen applicants for employment, to test staff and contract employees as part of periodic security reviews, and to test operational assets to verify information they have provided as well as to determine if they are double agents.

As a screening device for applicants, polygraph has demonstrated its utility over and over; examiners have obtained admissions of every type of criminal activity. Employee testing has resulted in admissions of espionage, malfeasance, and security breaches. In the operational arena, double agents have been exposed, fabricators have been identified, and significant data provided by assets have been verified. This is the plus side.

On the downside, Agency examiners have made significant "misses." Subjects have concealed significant derogatory information, which polygraph examiners and background investigators have, in turn, failed to uncover, causing the Agency serious problems. Staff employee Aldrich "Rick" Ames was a mole working for the Soviets, who beat the polygraph and severely damaged the Agency. Operational assets have also beaten the polygraph and have led many an Agency case officer down the primrose path.

Another downside is the "false positive." False positives in the polygraph context are tests that, according to the examiner, indicate deception, when in fact the examinee has been truthful. False positives are the Achilles heel of polygraph and a legitimate reason to attack polygraph. Innocent people have been unjustly accused of wrongdoing, have been denied employment, and have been traumatized as a result of a false positive polygraph test. As an examiner, the most difficult part of my job was dealing with a polygraph subject who I strongly felt was being truthful but who was producing polygraph charts that were indicative of deception. Still, false positives are rare.

Opponents of polygraph claim that the damage polygraph does negates any of its perceived benefits. In the Agency, at least during my career, this was not the case, and the unpublicized successes outweigh the trumpeted failures by a wide margin.

In the applicant-testing venue, the overwhelming majority of security disapprovals come about as a result of polygraph-derived information. If obtaining admissions that result in security disapprovals can be considered success, the Agency's polygraph program, especially when compared with other parts of the security-screening process, has been very successful.

Polygraph's detractors usually argue that too many innocent applicants are denied employment as a result of polygraph testing and that that is too high a price to pay. What many of these critics don't know is that until 1979 no Agency applicant was denied a job based on a polygraph test unless that person had made an admission. Between 1979 and 1999, when I retired, the CIA rarely denied employment based solely on polygraph test results, and I can't recall testing an applicant who was denied employment without an admission.

More frequently polygraph opponents argue that the polygraph process lacks scientific validity. I agree, and this is where many of my former colleagues and I disagree. Many extraneous factors that impact a polygraph test cannot be quantified or scientifically measured, and this, I posit, seriously weakens any argument promoting polygraphy as a science. Among these extraneous factors are the examiner's ability and experience, the subject's fear or lack of fear of detection, the chemistry between the examiner and the examinee, the subject's mindset, the test's importance to the subject (i.e., does the subject have a great deal to gain by passing the test or a great deal to lose by not passing?), the subject's intelligence, etc. I could cite many more.

Of these factors, none is more important than the examiner's ability and experience. This above all is what makes polygraph more art than science. In none of the attacks on polygraph that I have read do I recall any mention of the examiner's ability as a factor in assessing the validity or reliability of a test. In failing to acknowledge the examiner, polygraph opponents weaken their arguments.

The examiner's ability is what makes a polygraph work; the subject's fear of detection is why it works. Several years ago, on CBS's *60 Minutes*, Diane Sawyer moderated a piece on polygraph. In her presentation, Ms. Sawyer set up a scenario in which a store hired a polygraph examiner to try to determine which of its employees committed a theft. The store manager told the examiner which employee was suspected, and after testing several employees, the examiner concluded that the employee the store manager had identified as a suspect was the thief. But after the examinations Ms. Sawyer revealed that there had been no theft. She cited this experiment as evidence that the polygraph was flawed. Ms. Sawyer failed to note that none of the employees being tested had anything to lose by being detected. Polygraph is flawed, but using the *60 Minutes* experiment to make this point is intellectually dishonest and unscientific.

Shortly after my book *Of Spies and Lies* came out, I went back to Long Island, New York, for a class reunion. The brightest guy in my class offered to bet me that he could "beat" me on a polygraph test. My usual answer to such queries is, "Polygraph isn't a parlor game and running tests as part of a bet trivializes my work." But this time, I made him the following offer: "I'll run a test on you, but we will do it the way it is really done. What that means is that you put up some serious money. If I can catch you in a lie, the money is mine." In a real test an examiner's ego may be bruised if he is beaten on a test, but the subject has the most to lose.

"Here is the test I will conduct. On a sheet of paper, I will write the numbers from 1 through 10, and ask you to circle one of the numbers between 3 and 8, without telling me which number you circled. I will then ask you ten questions, each beginning with have you circled number 1, 2, 3, 4, 5, etc.? Number 1, 2, 9 and 10 are 'dead' numbers. You are to answer each of my questions with a 'No.' One answer will be a lie. If I identify the number you circled, you have to pay me the money. That's the way it is in the real world of polygraph. The pressure is on you, not me." My classmate declined to take me up on my offer.

When arguing against the charge that the Agency relies too heavily on a process that lacks scientific validity, the Agency's most used response is to point out that the polygraph examination is only one part of the screening process; the background investigation, medical examination, psychological assessment, and personal interviews are also factored into personnel decisions. This is true, but a polygraph subject's admission of serious wrongdoing has more impact on a decision to disapprove an applicant than all of the other parts of the process combined. When a polygraph subject admits ongoing felonious activity, recent use of illegal drugs, or other disqualifying information, an adjudicator's decision is objective and easy to defend. All other parts of the clearance/adjudication process, with the exception of disqualifying medical information, are much more open to interpretation and challenge.

In June 1968, when I entered the CIA, 92 percent of all applicants who were security disapproved were disapproved based on polygraph-derived information. If a person passed his or her polygraph test, and unless a disqualifying medical condition was found, an applicant's security approval was an almost foregone conclusion. In trying to recall instances in which applicants who passed their polygraph tests were subsequently denied employment, I can only recall two.

Polygraph opponents use the claim of a lack of scientific evidence validating the polygraph as a club with which to batter the test, and thus they ignore polygraph's demonstrated utility. For every false positive, hundreds of applicants who are concealing criminal activity and personal vulnerabilities are uncovered. Most polygraph opponents claim that better background investigations (BI) will eliminate the need for the polygraph. My experience has been that BIs rarely develop enough derogatory information to generate a security disapproval; I can recall only three cases in which they did. If one takes into consideration how long it takes to conduct a good BI, the cost of a BI, and the amount of information that is missed in a BI, increasing the reliance on BIs is not only impractical but dangerous. Polygraph examiners, in hours, develop information that BI investigators fail to uncover in weeks and months. Conducting a good BI is a difficult task, and it takes years to become a good investigator. The pool of experienced investigators is drying up, and this, in conjunction with the increasing numbers of BIs the investigators have to do, negatively impacts the quality of the BIs. Many BIs that I have read are "canned," bland, and lacking in substance. Just as there are good and bad polygraphers, there are good and bad investigators too. A good example of a bad BI is the investigation conducted to verify CIA turncoat Rick Ames's claim that his in-laws were wealthy. The investigator who was sent to Bogota, Columbia, to verify that Ames' in-laws were wealthy did just that. Unfortunately, he was wrong. Ames' mother-in-law was a leftist academician and his father-in-law a judge. They were genteel, of modest means and not in a position to provide Ames with financial support as he had claimed. Apparently, the investigator had only checked with people in the American embassy about the social status or wealth of Ames' in-laws, and did not check with any Columbians who actually knew the family.

A more recent example is the last BI the CIA ran on me. In the spring of 2003 I filled out a Questionnaire for National Security Position (Standard Form 86) in conjunction with an update of my security clearances. The SF 86 was given to the investigator who conducted my BI. As soon as the investigator completed the BI, I was scheduled to take a polygraph test, which was also part of the security clearance update.

Two years later, in March 2005, I read my investigative file and noted that the 2003 BI contained information from an informant who claimed that I had met and married a *foreign national* during my tour in Vietnam. I have been married only one time—on August 29, 1970, eighteen months before I left for Vietnam—to Leonor "Lee" Tijerina, an American citizen of American parents who was born in Laredo, Texas. This information was in the SF 86 given to the investigator; yet no note accompained his report to say that the informant's information may not have been correct. (Lee, who was an Agency employee when we married, accompanied me to Vietnam.)

A private firm specializing in government agency clearance BIs had conducted my 2003 BI. I had known the supervisor of the investigator who did my BI for many years and decided to call him to discuss what I had read in my file. To my surprise, he told me that informant interviews are presented to the adjudicators as obtained at the time of the interview. I pointed out that information in my SF 86 contradicted the information the informant provided and suggested that the investigator's report should have noted that. "John, that's not the way we do it," he replied. These two examples should raise some questions about the reliability of BIs.

Time is also a critical factor in screening CIA applicants. Consider the hypothetical case of a U.S. citizen who is uniquely qualified for a position at the Agency that needs to be filled immediately. This person has worked overseas for years and is returning to the United States only to take a position with the Agency. Completing a BI of this person will take a long time and will be very expensive. Polygraph is the most practical way to address this problem.

Many critics of polygraph claim that the fear of and lack of faith in the polygraph discourages many qualified people from applying for positions that require a polygraph test as a part of the clearance procedure. My experience in the Agency has been that more people don't apply or withdraw their applications because of the time that it takes to complete security processing.

I have been told that BIs cost as much as $10,000 to conduct and can take up to a year to complete. Given the volume of applicants and employees whom the Agency has to process for security clearances and the time and money a polygraph examination can save, polygraph is essential to the security-screening process. There should be no doubt as to how critical the information developed during polygraph examinations is, and until a better, less intrusive means of obtaining it comes along, polygraph is and should be here to stay.

My perception is that the anti-polygraph faction is for "anything but polygraph," regardless of how ineffective their "anything" is.

Several times each day Agency polygraph examiners obtain information that a BI failed to uncover. Most derogatory information developed in a BI is hearsay, and corroborating information is seldom found. References given by subjects usually request confidentiality, and the BI subjects in most cases cannot be told who made an allegation against them. What defense does the subject have against false allegations a colleague or a neighbor has made?

In attacking polygraph, opponents focus on the technical aspects of the process and seem to ignore the nontechnical side of the process. In making a polygraph call, examiners analyze the subject's charts, assess the subject's behavior, and consider the facts of the case.

Most parents don't need a polygraph to determine when their children are lying and most of us feel that we can recognize when a politician tells a lie because when people lie, they do and/or say things that they don't do when they tell the truth. People who are lying avoid eye contact, answer questions with questions, are evasive, feign righteous indignation, and so on.

The phrase "facts of the case" in the context of a polygraph test means "Does what the subject says make sense?" The best way that I can explain this is to give an example. Before I left for Vietnam, one applicant in five whom I tested and who was between the ages of eighteen and twenty-five admitted to some illegal drug use. When I came back from Vietnam, almost four out of five applicants in that same age group admitted to some illegal drug use. During a post-Vietnam polygraph examination, a young man whom I was testing told me that he had worked his last two years in college and two subsequent years as a bartender at a ski resort. During the pretest, in response to the question, "Since the age of eighteen, have you tried marijuana or drugs for nonmedicinal purposes?" his answer was "I don't even know anyone who uses drugs." Not, "no," but "I don't even know anyone who uses drugs." In terms of probability, I doubted his response was true. Also, the young man had not answered the question I had asked him; this is bad behavior. At that point, I did not challenge him or even suggest that I was skeptical about his reply as I did not want to overstimulate him to the question. (Spending too much time on or actually interrogating a subject about a question during the pretest can sensitize a subject to a question and cause him to react to the question.)

During subsequent testing the strongest reaction on the test was to his "no" answer to the question regarding his drug use. Posttest, when I asked him, "Did you feel yourself react to any of those questions?" he answered, "They all felt the same to me." Again, the subject didn't answer with a direct "no" but with an evasive disclaimer. This to me was suspicious behavior. The subject may not have lied during the test, but as strong and consistent as his reaction was, I was certain that he knew which question he was reacting most strongly to. Of course, the subject may have had good reasons for not wanting to tell me about his sensitivity to the drug question, but at this point in the interview, the one thing I knew was that the subject was being evasive.

When I finally confronted the young man, I didn't accuse him of lying. I said, "You are reacting to the drug question more than to any other question on the test. What I need from you is an explanation as to why you are reacting to that question that I can verify polygraphically. Whatever explanation you give me, I am going to test you on."

His response: "You've got to be kidding me!"

He and I went round and round for over an hour, and I was not able to get an admission from him. I took my charts to "Frank Cross," who was my supervisor at the time, and told him that I was sure that my subject was lying and that I hadn't been able to get an admission out of him. Cross went in to talk to the young man. Within a half hour the young man admitted significant use and sales of illegal drugs. In this particular case, I found the subject's behavior and the facts of the case to be every bit as germane to my conclusion that he had been practicing deception as were the polygraph charts.

Regardless of how convinced I was that the subject had been deceitful, without an admission, my conclusion lacked proof. Interrogation is the means by which polygraphers get proof. Few, if any, would claim that interrogation is any kind of science, and even fewer would discount the effectiveness of a good interrogator in getting at the truth.

Interrogations in the polygraph context come about when an examiner believes that a subject is lying and elicitation fails to get an admission.

When all parts of the polygraph process are applied, the probability of false positives is lessened but not eliminated. If no admission is obtained, a call has to be made and often this call is deception indicated. The process may lack scientific validity, but based on the number of admissions Agency examiners have obtained, I believe a case for the reliability of the process can be made.

Polygraph opponents would have us believe that examiners run some charts, analyze the charts, and conclude that a subject is either deceptive or nondeceptive. In the Agency's polygraph program, nothing could be farther from the truth, and in the following pages, I will argue three points: First, a lack of evidence supporting the scientific validity of polygraph testing does not invalidate the polygraph as a security-screening device. Second, comparing polygraph testing as practiced in the Agency with testing elsewhere is comparing apples and oranges. The Agency has been conducting polygraph tests longer than the other government agencies, and until 1995 it had the best training program for examiners in the federal government. I know of no incident in which another agency's examiner has obtained an admission of espionage from an employee. I have heard Agency examiners obtain several such admissions. Many of the criticisms of polygraph made by the anti-polygraph faction don't apply to polygraph testing as it is conducted in the Agency. Third, as many problems with and valid criticisms of polygraph as there are, it is the best security-screening device available.

Nothing I can say or write will assuage the victims of false positive polygraph examinations or change their minds about the polygraph. This also applies to those who, even if polygraph testing were 100 percent reliable and valid, would recommend its being abolished. However, I hope those who read this book with an open mind will pause before they jump on the anti-polygraph bandwagon.

Truths that my former colleagues and I have uncovered have made positive contributions to the Agency's intelligence product. In identifying applicants and employees who have engaged in criminal activities, my colleagues and I have made the Agency a safer place to work.

In their attacks on polygraph, anti-polygraph factions have used distortions, misrepresentations, and lies to try and make their points and have callously disregarded the efforts and accomplishments of a highly dedicated group of professionals.

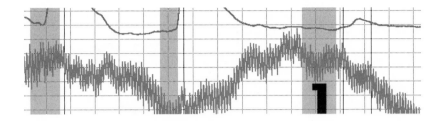

THE PATH LESS TRAVELED

When I, a first-generation Irish American, was growing up in Greenport, a small town on the eastern end of Long Island, working for the CIA was not on my list of career options. I was raised to believe that the way one paid one's dues for living in America was by serving in the military, and after graduating from Albany State Teachers College in 1961 and teaching high school for a year, I enlisted in the U.S. Army in July 1962. Three of my five years in the army were spent in military intelligence (MI). My MI experience sparked an interest in the CIA.

When I was discharged from the army in 1967, I enrolled in graduate school at Michigan State University to pursue a master's degree in German. While at Michigan State, I interviewed with a CIA recruiter. That interview and the subsequent interviews with the CIA in Langley, Virginia, led me to conclude that as a polygraph examiner I would be traveling down a unique and very interesting career path, and in June 1968 I entered on duty at the CIA. My career as a polygraph examiner lasted thirty-one years—full of boredom and excitement, success and failure, joy and sorrow, and again, borrowing from the poet Robert Frost, choosing the path I did made a difference to me, particularly in terms of how I would view the world. My career path afforded me opportunities to participate in, rather than be an observer of, history.

My first boss at the CIA was William "Bill" Osborne. During my initial interview with him in May 1968, I noticed a picture of DCI Allen Dulles on his office wall with an inscription that read, "Polygraph is our first line of defense. —Allen Dulles." After thirty-one years as a polygraph examiner in the CIA, I came to the conclusion that my colleagues in CIA's Polygraph Division (PD) and I were, in essence, gatekeepers. Our job was to keep the bad guys out, while letting some good guys in. The bad guys included agents from other intelligence services who were trying to penetrate the Agency and CIA applicants who were concealing

11

vulnerabilities that could lead to blackmail or criminal activity, making them unsuitable for Agency employment.

In the early years of CIA's polygraph program, polygraph tests focused on detecting Communists and homosexuals. Early tests had more questions dealing with Communism than any other issue, but the homosexuality issue was pursued equally vigorously. In the early years the Office of Security and the Interrogation Research Branch (IRB), the branch responsible for the Agency's polygraph program, were very homophobic. In part, this was a knee-jerk reaction to the 1960 defections of two National Security Agency (NSA) cryptographers, Bernon F. Mitchell and William H. Martin, who turned out to be homosexuals.

At the time I entered on duty, my training officer said that no examiner had ever obtained an admission from a subject that he or she was a Communist. He also said, "If you ever get a subject to hand over a Communist Party membership card, I guarantee you will be promoted to GS-13 on the spot." Rarely were any significant admissions obtained during interrogations on the Communism issue. Examiners were much more successful in pursuing the homosexual issue.

When they interrogated a subject on the homosexual activity issue, some examiners stepped over the line by delving into heterosexual relationships. This practice significantly contributed to the negative image Agency employees had of polygraph.

The Communism issue was dropped from the questions covered in applicant testing because we rarely developed any information from subjects on this issue. This issue was subsequently replaced with a question dealing with a subject's involvement in any subversive or terrorist activity. The asking of the question on homosexuality was discontinued because it was no longer seen as a vulnerability to blackmail. I surmise that the CIA's examiners over the years probably obtained more disqualifying information regarding homosexual activity than any other issue covered during applicant testing with the exception of criminal activity. The overwhelming majority of security disapprovals recommended by the Office of Security are based on polygraph-derived information. Between 1952 and 1979, not one of the security disapprovas was based on a test result; rather they were based on admissions obtained. Subjects could produce polygraph charts that examiners felt indicated deception, but unless the subjects made admissions, for all intents and purposes they passed their tests.

The polygraph examiners' role in working with the Agency's clandestine service is different from the role they play in employment and security reviews. The clandestine service asks examiners to identify double agents and fabricators. The emotional high that comes with getting subjects to admit that they are double agents is hard to describe, and such an admission is rare. Admissions of fabricating information are much more common and, thus, not nearly as satisfying. The commonality between the two types of admission is the case officers' disappointment upon hearing the news that they are dealing with bad agents. In many cases, when I delivered the news of an admission, the case officer's initial reaction was "kill the messenger."

In the ensuing pages, I will cite cases in which Agency examiners have obtained admissions of espionage from CIA staff, a contract employee, an applicant, and a military detailee. Examiners have obtained disqualifying admissions of criminal activity in thousands of tests, and I will cite several that stand out.

Regardless of how many spies, criminals, and other miscreants the gatekeepers have uncovered, whenever polygraph is discussed, the Rick Ames case is often cited to show that the tests are ineffective. Ames beat the polygraph in 1986 and 1991, and his treachery led to the deaths of ten agents. Much of the blame for the Ames disaster fell on polygraph. When confronted with this argument, I like to point out that the gatekeepers let Ames in when he was "good." He turned "bad" only after he had entered on duty. It should be noted that 90 percent of the damage Ames did came before his 1986 polygraph test.

Ames and Harold James Nicholson are the only two Agency moles who have been caught and prosecuted. Beginning in October 1995, a year after he had begun working for the Soviets, Nicholson failed three polygraph tests that dealt with the issue of working for a foreign intelligence service. He made no admissions, and to my knowledge, no action was taken against him until his arrest.

We gatekeepers have taken much criticism for our failures and have received very little recognition for our successes. I hope the following pages address that slight.

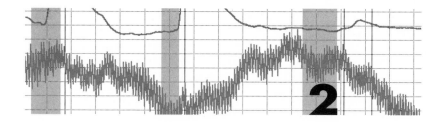

IN THE BEGINNING

On May 1, 1947, Roscoe Henry Hillenkoetter replaced Gen. Hoyt Sanford Vandenburg as director of the Central Intelligence Group (CIG), and when the National Security Act was passed later that year, Hillenkoetter became the first director of central intelligence (DCI). During Hillenkoetter's tenure, it was suggested that polygraph be made part of the Agency's personnel security process, and in August 1948 Hillenkoetter authorized the use of polygraph on an experimental and voluntary basis.

At that time polygraph testing was not widespread, and the process was not well known. The idea that physiological changes occur in people when they lie was not new, but the idea that these changes could be measured and used as a basis for determining truth or deception was only beginning to gain acceptance.

Cesare Lombroso is the first person known to have used a physiological measurement as a determinant of deception. In 1895 Lombroso conducted a study in which he claimed success in identifying deceptive responses by measuring blood pressure fluctuations in the criminal suspects he was questioning. In 1914 Vittorio Benussi conducted a study on changes in respiration that could be interpreted as indications of deception, and in 1915 William Marston used three measurements—blood pressure, rate of respiration, and fluctuations in skin resistance taken during testing—to determine deception. These measurements are used in today's polygraph testing. John A. Larson developed the first instrument that would simultaneously record all three measurements.

Leonarde Keeler subsequently built a better instrument that was the forerunner of the polygraph instruments examiners use today. Keeler also developed the relevant/irrelevant (R/I) test. In this test, a person's physiological reaction to a relevant question (i.e., a question germane to the issue at hand) is compared with his or her physiological reaction to an irrelevant question (i.e., a nonemotionally loaded or nonthreatening question, such as "Are you sitting down?"). In addition to being nonemotionally loaded and nonthreatening, the irrelevant question had to be a question that the examiner knew the answer to.

Polygraph technique (or an examiner's modus operandi), question construction, and chart interpretation as we know them today are for the most part the products of the efforts of John E. Reid, the person considered the father of modern polygraph. His "Reid test" eventually replaced Keeler's R/I test in the Agency, and the Reid School became the Harvard of polygraph training facilities. *Truth and Deception: The Polygraph (Lie-Detector) Technique*, the book Reid wrote in collaboration with Fred E. Inbau, is the polygraph examiner's bible and the number-one reference source for all questions about polygraph.

Before Hillenkoetter could give the go-ahead to begin polygraph testing of Agency employees, he had to find someone to run the program. Grover Cleveland Backster Jr. (or G. Cleve Backster, as he likes to be called), an interrogation instructor at the U.S. Army's counterintelligence school at Fort Holabird, Maryland, was selected, and he entered on duty on April 12, 1948. At the time Backster entered on duty, he was not a trained polygraph examiner, but during his first few months at the CIA, he underwent polygraph training and was certified by Leonarde Keeler. In August 1948 Robert B. Bannerman, the Agency's deputy director of support, underwent the first CIA polygraph examination, and between August 1948 and January 1949 the CIA conducted a total of 123 polygraph examinations.

An article that appeared in the Sunday, December 4, 1949, *Washington Post*, regarding the CIA's polygraph program stated, "No one has been dismissed except on the basis of information obtained from individuals questioned during field investigations." The "field investigations" were polygraph examinations. The article also noted that three examiners who had been trained by Leonarde Keeler had administered the tests.

As a result of the "successes" early examiners had in obtaining admissions from deceptive subjects, a proposal was made in 1949 to use the polygraph on operational assets, agents recruited by the CIA's clandestine service case officers. Testing operational assets is so different from testing employees and applicants that a new type of examiner was needed—specifically, one who spoke a foreign language, was culturally attuned to living and working in foreign countries, was amenable to travel around the world, and was familiar with clandestine operations. In 1949 such an examiner could be found only in the ranks of DP case officers. Several DP officers were recruited, afforded polygraph training, and sent overseas to test assets. New guidelines were established for testing operational assets: they were required to take the test if asked and refusal to participate in a polygraph exam was grounds for dismissal.

One of the many problems with the Keeler R/I tests that the early polygraph examiners used on operational assets was the difficulty of finding valid irrelevant questions. In applicant and staff tests, questions regarding a subject's place and date of birth were used as irrelevant questions. In the operational arena, much of the biographic data CIA subjects provided were not verifiable, and many times all the CIA knew about the subjects was what they told us. Even so, operational examiners identified many fabricators, and polygraph gained a higher degree of respect within the DP than it had within the CIA population in general.

By 1950 polygraph was beginning to catch on, and the future antipathy to polygraph testing had not shown itself to any notable degree. Backster was in the midst of building a good CIA polygraph program when he was made an offer that was too good to turn down: when Leonarde Keeler died in 1949, Backster was asked to head the Keeler Polygraph Institute, a job he readily accepted.

When Backster left, "Ray Ormond," a security officer with no polygraph experience, was selected to take over the Agency's polygraph program. My sense is that Ormond was selected to maintain the status quo until a more suitable replacement could be found. Still, the use of polygraph increased during Ormond's tenure, and by this time polygraph was becoming a permanent fixture in the Agency. That being the case, in September 1951 Ormond established a list of criteria for polygraph examiners:

1.   Must be between the ages of twenty-five and forty-five;
2.   Should have a college degree in law, pre-medicine, or applied science;
3.   Must be at least a GS-11;
4.   Must have experience in investigations, interrogation, or intelligence;
5.   Must demonstrate personality traits indicative of stability, discretion, maturity, and the ability to handle subjects in polygraph examinations;
6.   Must have a foreign language capability.

Of these, number two was the most unrealistic. In my thirty-one years with the CIA, I met two polygraph examiners with law degrees and none with pre-med or applied science degrees.

Ormond successfully maintained the status quo, had no major flaps on his watch, and, in 1952, was succeeded by Chester C. "Chet" Crawford.

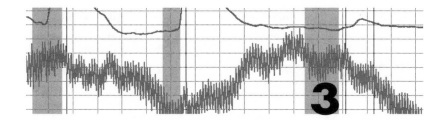

THE CRAWFORD ERA

Cleve Backster may have been the first polygraph examiner to conduct a polygraph test in the CIA, but Chet Crawford, who ran the program from 1952 to 1965, was the father of the CIA's modern polygraph program. During Crawford's tenure, polygraph's role in the CIA was defined and its utility in the personnel security arena was established. Examiners had much success identifying unsuitable employees and applicants, and the aggressive interrogations used to obtain admissions began to give rise to a negative image of polygraph. In-house training was necessary in part because Crawford believed the polygraph test format and procedures espoused by Reid and Keeler were not applicable to the multiple-issue test that Crawford deemed necessary to get a complete picture of the subjects tested by the CIA.

Much of the negative image was the result of employees' admissions, made during their polygraph examinations, that resulted in dismissal from the CIA or loss of security clearance. Agency employees, who at the time *volunteered* for the polygraph tests, were never told why their colleagues were being fired and, thus, were left to draw their own conclusions, e.g., that taking a polygraph examination might not be worthwhile. It was one thing to deny a security clearance to applicants, who in many cases were not risking their future CIA employment by taking the polygraph test. It was quite another to fire current employees, who were voluntarily risking their careers and financial security by taking the polygraph test. The pressure on the examiners, as well as on the subjects, was intense. As the number of employees who lost their jobs grew, polygraph examiners were deemed the CIA's "wearers of the black hats" and the number of employees who volunteered to take the polygraph test decreased.

Eventually, the staff testing was phased out. Though it had had some success in terms of identifying problem employees, the hostility employee testing generated among the staff began to outweigh any perceived benefits. At the same time he eliminated employee testing, Crawford proposed making applicant polygraphs a requirement for employment. Testing all applicants meant the CIA required more examiners, and over the next year, the Interrogation Research Branch doubled in size.

In late 1952 Crawford proposed that the CIA maintain a cadre of career polygraph examiners. As part of his proposal, Crawford recommended that the new CIA examiners be recruited from and trained in the CIA, not hired from the pool of examiners who had been commercially trained. Polygraph tests were originally designed to resolve one issue, whereas the early CIA screening tests contained as many as sixteen relevant questions. The biggest difference between the CIA approach to polygraph and the private sector philosophy was that, in the CIA, unless subjects admitted or acknowledged wrongdoing, their tests were deemed "favorable." In the private sector, an examiner who concluded that a subject was practicing deception could call the subject "deceptive" and the test "unfavorable" without an admission.

When Crawford took over the program, polygraph was still on trial, and making calls of unfavorable or deception indicated (DI) without admissions was a risk Crawford was unwilling to take. The fact that Crawford was unwilling to risk the program's viability by allowing such calls without admissions spoke well to Crawford's political astuteness, as well as his attitude toward polygraph. The first deception indicated/unfavorable call without an admission was not made until 1979. On that occasion, an applicant was denied a security clearance. That applicant's test was deemed deception indicated on the issue of involvement in terrorist activity. An extensive postpolygraph investigation uncovered the applicant's involvement with the Students for a Democratic Society.

In conjunction with Crawford's proposal to establish a cadre of CIA examiners was his proposal that polygraph examiners be made part of the Office of Security. In 1952 and 1953 most polygraph testing fell under the Directorate of Plans, and many of the examiners were former DP case officers. The DP strongly objected to Crawford's proposal and countered with a recommendation that polygraph examiners come under the aegis of the DP. This was Crawford's first turf war, and for a comparative newcomer, he fared very well. DCI Allen Welsh Dulles signed off on Crawford's proposal, and the Office of Security was given the responsibility for recruiting, training, and managing the CIA's polygraph cadre. Polygraph examiners became members of OS's Interrogation Research Branch. Note that the word "polygraph" was not used in the name of the office to which polygraph examiners were assigned.

Having lost that battle and perhaps in an attempt to recover some prestige, the DP then proposed that when testing operational assets examiners should conduct the polygraphs and DP case officers should complete any required interrogations. Crawford objected to this proposal and again prevailed. With the backing of DCI Dulles, Crawford established the policy that polygraph examiners would handle all aspects of any tests that they conducted.

Crawford may have won this battle, but in so doing he set the stage for the antipathy that still exists between the Office of Security and the clandestine service or DP, which later became the Directorate of Operations (DO) and today is the National Clandestine Service. The DP/DO looks at OS much in the same way that the CIA views the FBI and vice versa. Many of the case officers with whom I worked over the years saw me as a "cop" who was out to bust their agents and not as a safeguard against double agents and fabricators.

The private sector polygraph community viewed the testing formats and procedures Crawford instituted in IRB as aberrations. It wasn't that Crawford saw private sector polygraph as inferior to what he was promoting in the CIA—although he may have—but rather that he saw it as irrelevant to the CIA program. In essence, Crawford cannibalized private sector polygraph procedures to fit the CIA's polygraph program.

Early successes on the part of IRB examiners generated some hubris, which presaged IRB's isolation from the polygraph mainstream. Crawford eschewed outside training for examiners and discouraged examiners from joining the American Polygraph Association (APA). Training, such as it was, was conducted by the IRB training officer and was unstructured. The training course lasted six weeks and was one-on-one with never more than two candidates undergoing training at one time. Crawford did not aggressively recruit commercially trained examiners and depended on recruiting from within OS to meet IRB staffing needs.

One of the commercial examiners Crawford did hire was "Greg Milenski," who, at the time Crawford recruited him, was a training officer at John E. Reid and Associates. Milenski was a former marine and an alumnus of Michigan State University. At Reid, he had an outstanding reputation, and at the time he entered on duty, he knew more about polygraph than anyone in IRB. Milenski was the first examiner to become chief of the Polygraph Division without having completed a tour outside of polygraph. He instituted some changes in the CIA polygraph program that, in my opinion, made it the best of all the U.S. government polygraph programs.

Crawford's IRB was perceived by some as a "rogue elephant." The hubris that Crawford and some of his minions at times showed didn't help, but the bottom line was that his examiners were getting the job done. The great majority of security disapprovals issued by the Office of Security's Clearance Division continued to come as a direct result of polygraph-derived information.

The polygraph tests administered by IRB during the Crawford era were very cumbersome, and as mentioned previously, their primary focus was the subjects' possible Communist affiliations. Every relevant aspect of the Communism issue was covered in depth: membership in the Communist Party, association with friends who were or who might be Communists, knowledge of anyone who was sympathetic to Communism, and participation in any type of Communist activity (attending rallies, signing petitions, contributing money, and so on). A report that I read from this era was twenty-nine pages long and dealt only with the subject's "Possible Communist Sympathies," as the report was titled. The subject was hired.

To my knowledge, no CIA subject ever admitted to being a current member of the Communist Party, and unless specific admissions of participation in or sympathies for Communism and Communist activities were made, no adverse actions were taken.

Only one question relating to homosexual activity was included in the early version of the applicant polygraph test, but no issue was pursued more vigorously. "Homophobic" seems an appropriate adjective to describe the attitude of OS/IRB toward homosexuals during the Crawford era. In the process of ferreting out homosexuals, some IRB examiners used questions regarding heterosexual activities, such as "How often do you date?" "Are you a virgin?" "Are you cohabiting?" "Do you date foreigners?" etc., as lead-ins to elicit information on homosexual activity. Unfortunately, and to this day I don't know why, much of the information obtained regarding heterosexual activity of females was reported.

Regarding the reporting of heterosexual activity, in all the reports I read from this era, I rarely saw a comment on the heterosexual activities of a male. A case could be made that the Office of Security was not only homophobic but sexist, with a tinge of racism thrown in. On one memorable occasion, I picked up a file for my morning case and in reading the BI saw the notation, "Subject dates blacks!" underlined. When I went to pick up this female subject, I was rather surprised to find that she was an African American.

Admissions of security breaches were regularly obtained, but no spies were caught and rarely was an employee dismissed because of an admission of a security breach. Most employees who lost their clearances lost them as a result of admissions of homosexual activity, whereas most applicants were denied clearances as a result of admissions of criminal activity.

Many applicants were disqualified when they admitted to falsifying their personal history statements (PHS). Occasionally, acknowledgement of an alcohol problem had negative consequences, such as the denial of a security clearance. During the Crawford era, illegal drug use was not on the Office of Security's radar, and admissions of illegal drug use were rare.

By the end of Crawford's tenure, the Interrogation Research Branch had become his fiefdom, and he ruled it like a feudal lord. On one occasion, DCI Dulles asked Crawford to allow him to monitor a polygraph test. Crawford denied Dulles's request and made his denial stick. Under Crawford's leadership, IRB examiners might not have made a lot of friends, but they kept some bad people out of the CIA, identified employees who should not have been in the CIA, and made themselves indispensable to the Clearance Division's adjudicators.

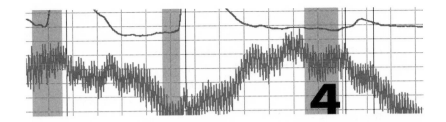

FIRST IMPRESSIONS

By the end of the Crawford era in 1965, the Interrogation Research Branch had slowed its hiring spree, but in the previous ten years the number of examiners had grown to the point that the office no longer was a branch but a division and the office designation became Interrogation Research Division (IRD). Crawford had taken IRB out of mainstream polygraph, and there had been no changes in testing techniques or training during his tenure. Greg Milenski, who entered on duty in 1964, was the last "outside" examiner to be brought into IRD, and turnover was very low. Many of the examiners were over fifty, and none was under thirty-five years old. For many, the assignment to IRB was the last stop on the career train; they had no bigger or better assignments to anticipate—only retirement.

When I entered on duty in June 1968, IRD was one of the smaller offices in the Office of Security. Two-thirds of the examiners were assigned to CIA headquarters and the other third was assigned to overseas posts. Bill Osborne was the chief of IRD, and he had one deputy. There were two IRD supervisors: a chief of overt operations who supervised all applicant and employee testing and a chief of covert operations who was in charge of all operational testing. "Ray Fox," the chief of overt operations, was the supervisor I had the most contact with. He was very paternalistic and one of the nicest men I have ever met.

On my first day as a CIA employee, I had an experience that showed me early on that polygraph examiners could be beaten, that BIs are flawed, and that the CIA's personnel standards might not be as high as I thought. As part of the OS checking-in process, the director of the Office of Security gave a welcoming address to all new employees. When three new employees and I showed up in his office, his secretary told us that he was busy and suggested that we go to the cafeteria for a cup of coffee and come back in about half an hour.

Twenty minutes later I was on my way out of the cafeteria when I heard a familiar voice say, "John, what are you doing here?" I turned to see "Larry Chester," a guy I had been stationed with in Germany while I was in the army. Chester told me that he had been recruited by the Agency's Office of Communications. I liked Chester and had been his friend, but he was a complete foul ball. He had a drinking problem and financial problems (mainly the products of stupid bets). On two occasions I caught him stealing money from the unit coffee fund. On several occasions I bought him meals because he had run out of money. On another occasion he got drunk and attacked a German female. If two of our friends hadn't been there to pull him off the girl, Chester could have been arrested. Two questions immediately came to mind. "How did he get through the polygraph?" and "Who did his BI?" Then another thought occurred to me: IRD wasn't the only office that was not getting the best and the brightest. After exchanging phone numbers with Chester, I went back to the D/OS's office with the other new OS employees.

After the director's welcome address, I returned to IRD and mentioned my concerns about Chester to one of the more senior examiners. I said that I couldn't believe that a BI hadn't uncovered enough information to keep Chester out of the CIA or that he had gotten through the polygraph. We pulled Chester's polygraph file and looked at the results of the test: no reportable information.

Milenski had administered Chester's test. When I discussed the case with him, he said, "I got a lot of little stuff from him but nothing serious." I had thought that the question, "Since the age of eighteen, have you committed a serious crime?" would have done Chester in on his polygraph test. After talking with Milenski, I concluded that Chester hadn't viewed the transgressions I knew he had committed as "serious crimes" and didn't consider his "no" answer a lie.

Coming up with a rationale for how Chester made it through the background investigation was more difficult. For the part of Chester's BI completed in Germany the investigator seemed to have checked only with the military and local police to see if he had a police record. It also seemed as though the investigator didn't talk with anyone who had been stationed with Chester, as I can't imagine Chester's colleagues would have offered anything but derogatory information.

This incident did not significantly lessen my faith in polygraph or BIs, but it was disconcerting and a less than positive way to begin my career in the Agency. Also, as I soon learned, no examiner likes to be told that he "missed" a subject, that is, passed someone who should have been caught. And here I was, the new kid on the block, telling a future legend that he had probably made a bad call.

Another surprise on that first day was in regard to my salary. During my first interview with the CIA, I had been told that I would be brought on board as a GS-9. I was very pleased, and during my interviews with PD management, the question of salary never came up. As I was settling in on that first day, an OS personnel officer brought me a letter welcoming me into OS as a GS-7. Thinking there had been a mistake, I went to Bill Osborne, who told me nothing could be done about it. Next I went to the training officer. He said that had I asked, "We would have given you anything you asked for," adding that I had been a goddamn fool. Naive, yes, and possibly a fool, but I had been lied to, and I never forgot it.

My new colleagues made me feel very much at home, but being the youngest, as well as the only single guy in the office, limited my social interaction with them. Training began almost immediately. My first assignment was to read two books: *Truth and Deception* by John Reid and Fred Inbau and a paperback on the human body with a title I cannot recall. I spent the next few days learning how to operate the Stoelting instrument that IRD used at the time. As I became more proficient in operating the instrument, we moved on to reviewing the three types of questions that we would ask CIA applicants: norm, relevant, and control.

A norm question was one that the examiner knew the answer to and that was not emotionally weighted; thus a subject had no reason to lie in answering it. A relevant question is one with an unknown answer, and thus the subject's likelihood of lying in response is greater: for example, "Since the age of eighteen, have you tried marijuana or drugs for nonmedicinal purposes?" A control question is one that the examiner hopes will evoke a significant reaction. A known lie is the best of all control questions, the theory being that if a subject does not show any reaction when lying in response to a question, the test is invalid. Norm questions are usually based on information in the subject's personal history statement, and there are two sets of relevant questions: one set of counterintelligence questions and a second set about lifestyle issues. IRD also recommended a number of suitable control questions.

When I wasn't in a one-on-one training session with the training officer, I would pore over polygraph files and reports, paying particular attention to the charts that had been run. Trying to identify the chart reaction that indicated deception was one of the more beneficial training exercises. Often I took the charts to the examiner who had run the test to discuss how he had interpreted them. This reinforced what I had been reading in *Truth and Deception* about chart interpretation and also helped me build rapport with my colleagues. But there was a downside: in discussing charts with my colleagues, I came to realize that some of them had never read *Truth and Deception*, didn't know much about chart interpretation, and didn't have much faith in polygraph. Milenski was the exception. He not only knew the book by heart, but he also could impart the knowledge therein and believed in what he was doing. He became my go-to guy for any and all questions about polygraph.

During my third week on the job, I was given a break from class to attend an Office of Training course, Introduction to the CIA. This was a five-day course during which each of the CIA's four directorates—the Directorate of Science and Technology, the Directorate of Plans (clandestine services), the Directorate of Intelligence, and the Directorate of Support—made presentations on their functions.

I found the course to be informative and enlightening, but it was also my first experience with collective, as well as individual, anti-polygraph sentiment. On the first day, when I introduced myself, I heard some hisses and boos from my classmates. None of these seemed malicious, but during class breaks, I could always count on someone to relate a story of how he or a friend had had a bad experience with polygraph.

During the DP's presentation, the class was asked to review the Runge case and make a decision as to whether or not Lt. Col. Evgeny Runge, a KGB illegal—that is, a deep-cover, sleeper asset of a foreign intelligence service—who defected in Berlin in 1967, had been a double agent. Runge had identified a KGB penetration of the West German Foreign Ministry, Leonore Sutterlin, who had committed suicide, and her husband Heinz, who was also an illegal. The fact that he had given up a penetration and an illegal indicated, at least in my mind, that Runge wasn't all bad.

My first question to the presenter was, "How did he do on his polygraph test?"

Her answer: "It doesn't make any difference because Russian spies are trained to beat it."

My brilliant retort: "That's not what I asked you. I repeat, how did he do on his polygraph test?" At this point, the presenter actually became a little hostile, and I dropped it after saying, "If you don't know, just say so. But I think you should know."

The DP presenter was the first CIA operations officer I had ever met, and I was not impressed. She had not done her homework on the Runge case, and when challenged, she reacted defensively. I remember thinking, "If she's a case officer, I hope she is better than this."

That day after class I went back to IRD to check on Runge's polygraph test and spoke with the examiner who had tested Runge. He told me that Runge had passed his test and that STASI, the East German intelligence service, had flooded West Berlin with agents in an attempt to find him. "Take it to the bank. Runge was no double agent," the examiner said. In the years since Runge's defection, there have been no indications that he was an illegitimate defector. But the "spies are trained to beat the polygraph" comment is one I heard throughout my career, as well as after I retired.

When I returned to IRD the following Monday, I started doing mock tests. I would go through the entire test procedure, using one of PD's secretaries as a subject. That week I was given the only written test I took during my training: a five-question test on physiology.

During this time my belief in the CIA's omniscience took another blow. The Chester incident on my first day had raised questions about the Agency's security processing, but the Russian invasion of Czechoslovakia in August 1968 raised some serious doubts.

"How in hell did we miss this one?" I asked Ray Fox the morning that we found out about the invasion. Clearly, the Agency had been caught flatfooted.

"John, this is why we have a CIA," answered Fox.

My thought was, "Gee, Ray, I thought we had a CIA to find out about these things before they happen." With that thought in mind, I prepared to conduct my first examination.

For my last training exercise, I memorized my pretest presentation. Once my training officer was satisfied that I had my pretest down, he handed me the file of an applicant whom I would test the following Tuesday. He told me to read the file and prepare some norm questions; the day before the test, he would quiz me on the information in the file.

There was no ceremony, celebration, or congratulations at the end of my training, nor should there have been. The training was cursory and, frankly, not much more challenging than the training I underwent to become an altar boy. But in the context of the polygraph tests of the time, it was adequate. The fact that I saw my training as adequate to qualify me to run tests speaks volumes to the state of polygraph in the CIA in 1968. The lack of structure, written tests, lectures on the theoretical aspects of polygraph, etc., raised a question in my mind: "If this is how seriously they take training, how serious can they be about testing?"

My first test was somewhat anticlimactic. The person I tested was a twenty-year-old female who was applying for a clerical position. She was much more nervous than I was, and the test went very well.

In the late 1960s polygraph interviews were not recorded. Fox and Osborne monitored each testing room, but that was the extent of the control over the sessions. The chiefs monitored the interviews in part because the Office of Security and IRD were very sensitive to female subjects' occasional complaints that examiners unnecessarily pried into their sex lives. As an added measure to head off complaints, every female who was polygraphed was also afforded a posttest interview with a female security officer, during which each female applicant was asked if anything untoward had happened during her polygraph interview, as well as whether or not she had any comments about the examiner who had conducted her test. Initially, I felt a little offended by this, but I became used to it. The woman who conducted the posttest interviews was very classy. Some of the examiners saw her as someone who was "out to get them," but she never seemed that way to me.

On one occasion, I tested a nice young woman and had problems getting readable charts from her. I couldn't identify any particular question as a problem, so with Ray Fox's blessing, I sent her for her posttest interview. When I got back from lunch, the interviewer and my subject were waiting for me. "I think Miss X has something to tell you," said the interviewer. I brought Miss X back into my office, where she said that she had lied to me that morning about not using drugs. Miss X went on to tell me that she had tried marijuana on one occasion. Additional testing went well, and Miss X was hired.

Once I began testing, it became apparent that many OS/IRD managers saw the polygraph instrument as a prop that examiners used to set subjects up for elicitation and interrogation. There was no greater proof of the CIA's distrust of polygraph than the fact that, unless admissions were obtained, subjects passed their tests. The Moore case makes this point.

Edwin G. "Ed" Moore II was a CIA employee whom I had met in Vietnam. In 1976, after he retired, he threw a bag of classified documents over the wall of the Soviet embassy in Washington, D.C. and, in the same bag, left a note offering to sell classified documents to the Soviets. Vitaly Yurchenko, the Soviet security officer, called the police and fire departments, suspecting that the package was a bomb. When the package was opened, some classified documents were found, along with instructions for contacting the unidentified sender. The FBI loaded the dead drop near Moore's house, as directed in the note, and monitored the site. When Moore serviced the drop, the FBI arrested him. Although financial gain was a strong motivation, Moore was also a disgruntled employee, having been passed over for promotion on numerous occasions.

While a CIA employee, Moore had been arrested and charged with arson. His trial resulted in a hung jury, and the prosecutor declined to retry him. On his return to the CIA, he was afforded a polygraph test, which he failed on the issue of having committed a serious crime. "Rob Creed," who had tested Moore, confronted him but could not get an admission out of him, and Moore was reinstated.

In August 1968, when I did my first test, an examiner could make only three calls to characterize the results of an applicant test: report, no report, or inconclusive. If significant information had been developed or an admission was obtained during the interview, the examiner would call "reportable information" and write up a report detailing the information developed. If no reportable information had been developed, the examiner would call "no reportable information," which, for all practical purposes, was a favorable call. In the absence of an admission of disqualifying behavior, no adverse actions were taken against a subject, and if no medical or psychological disqualifiers were found, most applicants were offered jobs. In 1968, according to Osborne, 92 percent of all applicants who underwent polygraph testing were offered positions. Osborne also pointed out that 92 percent of the 8 percent of disqualified applicants had been disqualified as a direct result of polygraph-derived information.

The third call that IRD examiners could use was inconclusive. According to the American Polygraph Association, about 5 percent of any given population is physiologically or psychologically unsuited for polygraph testing. During my first three years in IRD, I tested several subjects who I felt were unsuited for testing. The charts I obtained from these subjects were unreadable, and the call for each of these tests was no reportable information. OS management was very reluctant to allow IRD to submit an inconclusive call as the result of a polygraph test. Inconclusive meant "we don't know," and OS did not like to say that it didn't know. Another factor was that Clearance Division had grown accustomed to making security decisions based on polygraph input and were very reluctant to do so without that input.

Regardless of how indicative of deception subjects' polygraph charts were, how poor their verbal and nonverbal behavior was, or how illogical or even nonsensical subjects' "stories" were, these elements were neither mentioned in the examiners' reports nor did they factor into the examiners' calls. No admission meant no report. This, more than any other aspect of the CIA's polygraph program, set it apart from private-sector polygraph.

Examiners were very limited as to what we could say to subjects during an elicitation or interrogation. For example, we could not specifically tell employees that they would be fired if they didn't pass their tests, and we couldn't tell applicants that they wouldn't be hired unless they passed their tests. We could and did allow our subjects to think that might happen but were enjoined from specifically stating it. It is difficult for anyone who has never been a polygraph examiner to understand what a handicap this is. For the polygraph to be effective, it is important that there be benefits (being offered a job) for passing the test and consequences (being denied a job) for failing. More simply put, successfully completing a polygraph test should be in a subject's best interest. The more a subject has to gain by successfully completing a polygraph test or the more a subject has to lose by not successfully completing the test, the more effective the test.

Whether or not an actual lie detector exists is debatable, but no polygraph examiner has run at least one hundred tests without concluding with certainty that a subject he or she has tested was lying. In the approximately six thousand tests that I have conducted, I have not accused more than one hundred subjects of lying, but on the occasions when I did, I was never proved wrong.

Getting an admission is partly a function of ego. No examiner wants to get "beat," and every examiner wants the kudos and self-satisfaction that can come with catching a liar. Examiners may experience a kind of high after a lengthy interrogation in which they succeed in getting a subject to admit that he or she has lied. Obtaining admissions defines examiners; it is what they are paid to do. My former colleagues and I have obtained admissions of every type of criminal activity imaginable: theft, arson, drug use, rape, incest, child molestation, spousal abuse, etc. Knowing that unless an admission was obtained no adverse action would ensue drove some examiners to be overly aggressive in their pursuit of an admission.

About six weeks after completing training, I conducted my first interrogation. Much, if not most, of the information obtained during a polygraph test is obtained during the pretest. In the case of my first interrogation, I developed little information during the pretest, and during testing, the subject's reactions to the question regarding falsification of his CIA application stood out. I reviewed every part of the application with the subject and did not get an admission, but I did observe a lot of bad behavior. As the elicitation turned into an interrogation, I began to realize that this subject was working very hard to beat me. I had no doubt that he was lying to me, and I just had to get it out of him.

When I reviewed his application, I noticed that when I was going over his educational background, he seemed particularly nervous. When I focused my interrogation on his education, the subject's behavior, indicating deception, worsened. After about two hours the subject told me that he had failed to report on his application that he had flunked out of college. Subsequent to flunking out, he had obtained his BA from another college, but he hadn't indicated this on his application either. Subsequent testing supported that that was his only falsification/omission. The man was hired.

This case illustrates a very sore point with many CIA polygraphers: in adjudicating their suitability, subjects are not punished for lying or withholding information for hours before making an admission. In so many cases the admission that is obtained is insignificant, but the extent to which a subject goes to avoid making the admission is, or should be, factored into the adjudication.

The lack of quality control (QC) was a serious deficiency in IRD testing in 1968. When I began interviewing applicants, my instructions were to run a test and bring the charts that I obtained to Ray Fox. I was the rookie in the office and the only examiner in IRD whose charts were being reviewed. Fox would look over the charts, and if he saw any reactions that he felt were unresolved, he would send me back to continue the interview. If he felt that no issues needed to be resolved, he would tell me to let the subject go and sign off on the results of the test.

I had been out of training less than three weeks when I conducted a test on an individual who I concluded was at least withholding information, if not actually lying, about having committed a serious crime. My efforts to elicit an admission from him were unsuccessful, and after about an hour of butting heads with the subject, I took the charts to Fox. I told Fox that I was sure the guy was lying but I couldn't get an admission. Fox looked at my charts and said that he didn't see any reactions that concerned him and told me to let the subject go. Fox was my supervisor and I debated my interpretation of the charts with him, but ultimately, he held sway and I let the subject go.

That afternoon I went to Milenski and told him what had happened. Milenski then told me about the first test he did as a CIA examiner, on a young man who had just finished college and was applying for a job with the Agency as an accountant. At the end of the test Milenski concluded that his subject was concealing information about homosexual activity. "I was the new kid on the block, and I wanted to check with Fox before interrogating this kid," Milenski said. Milenski went on to say that he took his charts to Fox, and Fox, after looking at them said, "He's thinking about something he did in high school. Let him go." Milenski let the young man go.

The next morning, when Milenski arrived in the office, a secretary told him that the young man he had tested the previous day was in the lobby and wanted to see him. The young man apologized to Milenski for having lied to him during his test and said that he was a homosexual who had engaged in a homosexual act the night before his test. Milenski was in no way critical of Fox, commenting only that I would have to learn to deal with Fox's poor chart interpretation.

About two weeks later Fox came into my office, showed me a polygraph file, and asked me if I remembered the case. It was the file of the

man whom I had been reluctant to let go because I believed he was concealing information about a crime. When I told Fox that I remembered
the case, he said, "He was just arrested for insurance fraud." I didn't say,
"I told you so," but did comment, "Ray, I didn't want to let that guy go."

After another, similar incident I stopped bringing my charts to
Fox. No one else reviewed charts, and so I was essentially doing my own
quality control. From that point on, I ran my tests, made my decisions,
and signed off on the results. Not once, over the next two years, did
anyone come to me and suggest that I had missed any of the applicants I
had tested.

When I told my training officer that I had stopped taking my charts
to Fox, he said, "I wondered when you were going to figure out that Ray
can't read a chart." My impression was that Fox could identify reactions
but didn't see them as indications of deception; simply put, Fox didn't
believe in polygraph. It is very difficult for me to be critical of Fox now, as
he was very kind to me when I first started at the Agency.

Fox never commented when I stopped bringing my charts to him,
and we got along very well, but we did have one serious confrontation.
About two months after I started reviewing my own charts, I tested an
applicant who, from the outset of the interview, came across as a jerk.
The subject came into the interview a bit disheveled and slightly hung
over. He told me that he had been out drinking the night before and had
had a few too many. When I suggested to him that he might have been
better off calling in and postponing the test, he said that he just wanted
to get it over with. During testing he reacted consistently and strongly to
the crime question. Ultimately, he admitted to me that he had been in
numerous barroom brawls and had had his fair share of traffic tickets
but denied committing any felonies. I did some additional testing and
concluded that this subject was concealing something more serious. With
that in mind, I picked up the pace, and the subject soon admitted that he
and some friends had recently gang raped a seventeen-year-old girl. This
wasn't the first time that I had caught a liar, but it was one of the more
serious admissions that I had obtained and I was feeling pretty good about
the job I had done.

Fox hadn't reviewed my charts, but he did read my report. After
reading my report, he told me that I couldn't report what the subject
admitted because the subject was under eighteen when the rape had occurred. That simply wasn't true, and I said, "I don't know where you got
that information, but according to his PHS, he was nineteen." I also said,
"Ray, I asked the question, 'Since eighteen, have you committed a serious
crime?'" Fox then said that the incident qualified as "kid stuff" and reiterated that I would have to take the information regarding the rape out of
the report. "I don't care if this guy was fifteen when he did what he did.

I don't want him working here. He is one of the assholes I was hired to keep out of here," I said. Fox replied that it wasn't my job to make such decisions, and that was that.

Each morning Fox was the first one in the office. Shortly after Fox arrived, Osborne would show up, and he and Fox would have a cup of coffee. The day after Fox told me to change my report, I interrupted his morning conversation with Osborne. "Ray, if you want that report changed, you're going to have to sign it, because I won't." As I had thought he would, Osborne asked, "What's the problem?" I told him, and he said, "Of course you report it."

Although the man was denied a security clearance, I'll remember this incident as another case of winning a battle and losing the war. I was glad I had done it, but unfortunately, it was not the only time a supervisor directed me not to report what I viewed as a serious admission.

Once Fox assigned me to test a very senior noncommissioned officer (NCO) who was being detailed to the Agency. The man was highly decorated, stood six feet six inches tall, and was very imposing. In testing subjects I was always deferential without being obsequious. My deferential attitude worked well with the NCO, and we hit it off immediately. Unfortunately, he had some serious problems with his test, namely, his reactions to the question about homosexuality. My initial thought, based on my knowledge that he had been stationed in Thailand, was that he had engaged in sexual activity with a female impersonator and had found out, after the fact, that his partner was a male.

Not this time. After about a half hour of trying to elicit an explanation for the reactions to the homosexuality question, the subject broke down and cried. "I have been having sex with dogs for the last twenty years," he blurted out. During my youth in a very Irish Catholic household, sex with girls was never discussed, sex with boys was considered something only abnormal people did, and sex with animals was something I had never heard about. The subject went on to say that he had tried to stop but couldn't, and during a trip to visit his in-laws the previous week, he had had sex with the family dog. I was briefing Fox on what the subject had told me when, much to my surprise, Osborne interjected and said, "John, that's not reportable." To me, sex with animals is cruel and aberrant behavior, and any person who would engage in this type of activity in all probability has other problems. I found it mind-boggling that Osborne didn't see it that way. But my anger wasn't such that I tried to go around or over Osborne to get the information reported, and I just chalked the incident up as a learning experience.

In those early years it never ceased to amaze me what some subjects would voluntarily tell me during tests. Some would divulge highly personal information that often took me by surprise. For example, one subject I tested was a stunning young woman who was applying for a position as a secretary. Being the youngest and only single examiner in IRD, it often fell to me to test younger applicants. This test was a bonus. In reading her personal history statement, I found out that she was a Sephardic Jew with a degree in international relations, spoke Spanish fluently, and claimed to have some capability in Russian. During the pre-test, I spoke a little Russian with her and became a bit enthralled. My initial impression was that this was the kind of person I wanted working at the CIA.

During initial testing, the subject reacted consistently and strongly to the question, "Has anyone ever attempted or threatened to blackmail you?" As soon as I suggested that she was having a problem with this question, she said, "You have to understand, I'm Jewish." I hadn't ex-pected this, but she followed that up with, "And I'm having an affair with an Arab." To make matters more interesting, this young lady then told me that her boyfriend had impregnated her and sent her to Juarez, Mexico, for an abortion. "If my parents ever found out about this, they would be devastated. I couldn't let that happen," she said. The young lady also acknowledged that her boyfriend was married and currently in London on business and that he knew she was applying for a job with the CIA. She also advised that she planned to continue her affair with him. When I said that I would need the name of her boyfriend, she readily provided it. The CIA traced his name and learned that he worked as a travel agent for his country's airline and was suspected of being an intel-ligence officer. This lovely young lady was not hired.

I had a similar experience when interviewing a twenty-nine-year-old female Ph.D. who was applying for a position as an analyst in the Directorate of Intelligence (DI). Again, during the pretest, when asked about blackmail, the subject said that earlier that year a "biker" had picked her up in a laundromat and subsequently he had moved in with her. The subject went on to say that she found out that, while this biker was living with her, he was engaging in criminal activity (burglaries, car break-ins, etc.) and that because of that, she moved out without telling him. The subject volunteered, "I guess I am just not lucky with men." She fol-lowed that by telling me that while in graduate school she had an affair with one of her professors. "He told me that he was single and wanted to marry me," she said. "I lent him $10,000 and had to sue him to get it back," she added. This woman was denied a clearance based on her "lack of maturity."

Even more surprising was the applicant who told me that his KGB case officer had told him to apply for a job with the State Department and not the CIA because the State Department didn't use the lie detector.

At the time I tested him, the young man had not accepted the KGB pitch, but he had reported it to the FBI and was cooperating with them. There was no mention of this in the subject's file.

Another applicant told me that she had attempted to commit suicide. I hadn't been looking for this type of admission when I began the interview, but when I asked her about any medication she was taking, her behavior changed. Initially, she acknowledged taking some of her mother's headache medication, but ultimately said that on an occasion when she and her mother had a fight, she took several of her mother's sleeping pills in an attempt to kill herself. Subsequently, a memorandum came down from the Office of Security's management dictating that the issue of attempted suicide be pursued and that any information developed was to be reported.

Personally, things were going well, but my first Christmas as an Agency employee proved to be very enlightening. At that time, security officers were required to do after-hours security checks once every five or six weeks. These involved checking safes to make sure they had been locked and the check sheets initialed. Each officer was assigned specific safes in specific offices.

At about 5:00 p.m. on December 22 or 23, I began my check. When I started my check on the ground floor, I noticed employees in various stages of inebriation, staggering out of offices. I saw one man throwing up in a wastebasket, another passed out on a desk, and a couple kissing under mistletoe. When I opened the door of an inner office in the suite of offices that I was checking, I came upon a man removing a woman's bra. Both were drunk; neither seemed embarrassed, and I checked the safe and left. In another office, I found a couple half-naked and totally wrapped up in each other. This was my first exposure to the Agency's "party-hearty" mentality, and over the years, at headquarters and overseas, it was a constant.

That same week I logged my first security disapproval based on homosexual activity. The subject was the son of an OS employee who during the test admitted that he had picked up an older man in a bowling alley, taken him home, and engaged in homosexual activity. Once again Fox tried to kill the report, claiming that the young man was only seventeen when the incident occurred. I showed Fox the PHS in which the subject's listed date of birth showed him to be eighteen. The young man's parent was assigned to the Clearance Division, and IRD went to some lengths to make sure that the parent didn't see the report. The young man was not hired.

My tests continued to go well, but I felt that the absence of a quality control process was a fatal flaw in the IRD. We were supposed to be professionals, but I knew of no business or organization that did not have a quality control process in place to monitor its employees' performances. Without a QC process, performance standards were set arbitrarily if at all, and evaluating examiners' performances was quite subjective. As a more insidious result of not having a QC process in place, some of my colleagues and I became imbued with a false sense of omnipotence. Every day we made serious decisions about our subjects' fates, and no one ever told us that we might have been making mistakes. The mistakes I am sure we were making were in our failures to identify deceptive subjects. At that time, there was no reinvestigation polygraph program, and the chances of a miss coming to light in a subsequent exam were minimal.

The lack of QC also allowed examiners more subjectivity in making polygraph calls. In some cases, if an examiner liked the subject and the subject sounded good, the examiner would make a no reportable information call with little fear of it being overturned. A quality control process would have made that much more difficult.

Still, even a good QC program would have done little to overcome OS's institutional antipathy toward polygraph. Allowing marginal employees to nest in IRD was one of the main manifestations of OS's antipathy. A case in point: "Bo Mooney" was the worst examiner in the history of CIA's polygraph program. He had been summarily kicked out of the DP for incompetence and had applied for a job in IRD in an attempt to resurrect his career. The training officer told me that Mooney was the only student he had who didn't pass the training course, but Osborne didn't have the heart to drop him. Everyone in IRD knew that Mooney was totally incompetent. After a tour overseas with PD, Mooney took a job with OS's support staff. In his new job Mooney traveled around the world with a one- or two-man team conducting security surveys.

While conducting a survey in Europe, Mooney took off on his own, went to Amsterdam, and got in a bit of trouble. He got drunk at a party thrown by some Agency people, pinched a senior officer's wife in the butt, and ran up a $900 tab in a whorehouse. The team leader sent Mooney home. As punishment Mooney was allowed to choose between returning to IRD, where he would never be promoted or allowed to travel overseas again, and looking for another job in OS. Mooney opted for the latter and for the rest of his career he continued to perform substandard work. I couldn't believe that Mooney was given the choice to remain in PD and saw this as another example of the low esteem in which OS management held polygraph examiners.

That low esteem wasn't limited to the Office of Security. On one occasion I was traveling overseas and was asked by a senior officer, "Do you know Bo Mooney?" When I told him that I did, he said, "He applied for an assignment with us. When I read his personnel file, I couldn't believe what I was reading. In my twenty-eight years in CIA Personnel, I have never seen a worse file. How could Security keep a disaster like him around?" I had no answer.

A quality-control process would have made it much easier for Osborne to fire Mooney. Even the most basic QC process would have identified Mooney as a problem early on and forced Osborne to take action. A QC process would have included regular reviews of Mooney's work and forced management to acknowledge his deficiencies as an examiner.

Bill Osborne was the face of and spokesman for IRD, and in both roles he performed poorly. He showed his disdain for Director of Security Howard Osborne in part by remaining stone-faced and silent during the weekly Office of Security staff meetings. A regular attendee at these staff meetings told me that he never heard Bill say a word at any of the meetings. In alienating himself from OS, Bill also cut IRD off from OS.

On a daily basis IRD had more grist for the Office of Security's public relations mill than all other branches of OS combined. Osborne's refusal to promote IRD in any way denied examiners recognition that they deserved and inhibited their chances of getting promoted. Although I had nothing to compare the morale in IRD with at the time, I recognized that it was very bad. I didn't rethink my decision to come into IRD, but I did have some doubts and hoped that things would improve.

Despite IRD's problems, I liked my job and knew some good work was being done to resolve disputes and uncover criminal activity. About six months after I began testing, Milenski conducted a high-profile test that raised the bar for performance in the division by conducting one of the more significant tests done in IRD up until that time. On the day of that test, an employee walked in to Howard Osborne's office and told him that a CIA colleague had molested his young daughter that morning. Why he hadn't called the police, I don't know, but he told Osborne, "Either you do something about this guy or I will." Osborne had the accused brought into his office where he confronted him with the allegation. The man denied having molested the little girl, and Osborne asked him if he would take a polygraph test. Surprisingly, the man readily agreed.

I was talking to Fox when Bill Osborne came into the office and said that Howard Osborne wanted an alleged child molester tested immediately. Osborne also told Fox that Howard Osborne would be coming down to monitor the case. Milenski was taken off a case that he had been assigned and briefed on the allegation.

Fox panicked. He started straightening up desks, running around like the proverbial chicken with his head cut off, and reminding everyone that, "Mr. Osborne is coming down." I had never seen Howard Osborne in IRD, and my impression was that this would be his first visit.

Milenski was relaxed and seemed to be looking forward to the test. I think this disconcerted Fox almost as much as the fact that Howard Osborne was coming down to monitor the test.

Within an hour Milenski had a written confession from the molester. Howard Osborne was very impressed and gave Milenski a quality step increase (QSI) on the spot. I think Fox was more surprised than he was impressed. That was the first time he had ever seen how effective a good examiner conducting a good test could be. This case was a career maker for Milenski. In IRD, we knew Milenski was superb at his job. He was the best trained, most experienced, and most knowledgeable examiner in IRD. In some ways he was a deaf man in a room full of blind men. After this case Milenski's reputation spread throughout OS. As isolated as IRD was from OS, this was a good thing, and for a little while, IRD basked in the reflected glow of Milenski's success.

One great case does not an image change, and it wasn't long before IRD was once again the bastard child of Security. As much as I think Osborne's lack of leadership contributed to the poor image of IRD, I know another factor was at play. Background investigations (BIs) were the bread and butter of the Office of Security, and many in OS saw polygraph as a threat to BIs. Investigators were the sacred cows of OS, and if they had to be protected at the expense of IRD, so be it.

Investigators conducted background investigations on all CIA applicants before the applicants were invited in for a polygraph examination. The theory was that if enough derogatory information was developed during the background investigation, processing on the applicant could be cancelled, and the cost of bringing an applicant in for a polygraph test could be saved. In reality, a BI rarely resulted in an application's cancellation. I can't recall more than five occasions during my career in which a BI resulted in a security disapproval.

The cost of a polygraph in terms of both time and money was significantly less than that of a BI, and polygraph was a much more effective technique in terms of obtaining disqualifying information. Polygraph examiners developed information that had been missed during the BIs, and to me it seemed logical to do the polygraph test before the BI—logical, perhaps, but acceptable, no.

I was present when one of Howard Osborne's deputies brought the assistant deputy director of support (ADDS) into IRD for a tour of the office. During the walk-through I heard the ADDS ask, "If most people are disqualified based on polygraph information, why do we need the BI?" Osborne's deputy delivered his answer with a straight face: "You have to remember, BIs give the examiners the leads they need to do their tests."

The Office of Security's ambivalence toward polygraph was also reflected in the way it discouraged promising young security officers from applying for positions with IRD, while at the same time pushing some of the less qualified security officer recruit trainee (SORT) candidates into polygraph. "Grant Rollins," a very fine security officer who rose to become chief of the Polygraph Division, as well as director of OS, said that when he applied to become a polygraph examiner, "Will Rump," a very senior OS manager, tried very hard to talk him out of it. In a further example, when I was the PD recruiter, a candidate failed the Professional Aptitude Test Battery (PATB). Passing the PATB was a requirement for being accepted into PD. Rump interceded and requested that I have the candidate retake the test. He again failed. Rump waived the PATB for this candidate, and PD ended up with a poor examiner.

Nascent security officers going through SORT received a welcoming speech by Rump during which he invariably said, "I don't want to offend any of you polygraph examiners in the class, but no polygraph test will ever be as good as a BI." Rump wasn't the sharpest knife in the drawer, but I knew that he knew better than that. In my opinion, he was just quoting OS's "put down polygraph" line.

Os's antipathy notwithstanding, I obtained my share of admissions, did not feel inferior to many of my colleagues, enjoyed the interaction I had with subjects, and felt that I had pretty much found a home. What cemented my decision to stay in IRD was my training trip and subsequent entry into the world of operational polygraph.

Before I could be certified to conduct operational tests, I had to take a training trip with an experienced examiner. In March 1969 Bill Osborne and IRD managers came to the conclusion that I was ready to start conducting operational tests. One of the criteria for examiners selected to perform ops tests was that they must have administered at least five hundred polygraph tests. By March 1969 I had administered about two hundred tests and was pleasantly surprised when told that I would be taking my training trip in April.

Milenski took me on the trip, and it could not have gone better. I didn't catch any double agents, but I did work on some good cases. I interpreted for a test in which Milenski identified a double agent who had been working for the East Germans. What I remember most about that test was that when Milenski and I told the case officer that his agent was lying when he denied cooperating with the East Germans, the case officer's first words were, "That goddamn box!" The case officer then said, "His roommate was arrested by STASI six weeks ago."

"I didn't see that anywhere in the file," I said.

"I forgot to put it in," said the case officer.

"What do you want us to do?" Milenski asked.

"Let him go. Don't interrogate him," the case officer said.

That test served as a great introduction to the world of operational polygraph in the sense that it taught me that case officers, for the most part, saw polygraph as a necessary evil. Working with spies overseas was what had attracted me to the CIA. My training trip surpassed my expectations, and I was hooked.

Less than two days after returning from the training trip, I was asked to take an extended trip to Laos. Without hesitating, I said, "Yes," and for the next two years I was constantly on the road.

My trip to Laos introduced me to the world of Agency paramilitary operations, which were conducted by the Agency's Special Operations Group (SOG). SOG people were on the front lines in the Cold War, and my admiration for them knows no bounds.

On one of my two trips to Vientiane, the capital of Laos, Rob Creed, a legendary examiner, introduced me to "Tony Fitzpaldi." Fitzpaldi was an ops officer in Vientiane and struck me as a bit of a wild man. About a month after returning from Laos, "Lee Jensen," who was working in OS's Special Activities Division (OS), approached me and asked me if I knew Fitzpaldi. When I told Jensen that I had met Fitzpaldi but didn't really know him, Jensen said that Fitzpaldi had just been charged with raping a Laotian woman.

"He denies it, but from the evidence we have, there is no doubt he did it. We want to bring him back for a polygraph test," Jensen said.

"What happens if he passes his test," I asked.

"John, there is no way he is going to pass his test," Jensen replied.

Fitzpaldi returned to headquarters, and during his interview with SAD, he denied all charges. He also refused to take a polygraph test. Fitzpaldi was allowed to take a medical retirement. In my naiveté, I felt Fitzpaldi was let off the hook and my sense of justice was offended. Fitzpaldi was a criminal and should have been treated as such. Fortunately, such incidents were very rare in the CIA, but at the outset of my career, being starry eyed and pure of heart, the Fitzpaldi case was disillusioning.

As much as I liked the travel, I liked the testing more. Operational tests in many ways were better than tests we performed on applicants and employees. Fewer questions were asked, and examiners had more leverage with the subjects. More important (at least to me) these cases were about the CIA's business—clandestine operations. Being a part of that world was important to me.

Many of those I tested for the DO were old agents who had been on the CIA's payroll for years and had outlived their intelligence value.

However, occasionally, I was given a real gem. Not long after I went on the road, I tested a nuclear physicist who was selling the Agency information on his country's nuclear program. My test confirmed some very specific information the man had provided and which was later verified by another source. The sense of accomplishment I derived from this test sustained me through many of the more mundane tests.

Occasionally, a mundane test could get my adrenaline pumping. Just before my first-year anniversary as an examiner, I did such a test. The young man I tested had just been discharged from the U.S. Army and was applying for a job as a mechanic. A little unkempt, he was profane and didn't seem to be particularly intelligent. During the pretest he admitted some petty theft and minor drug use, but nothing that would disqualify him. During initial testing he had suspicious reactions to questions regarding his homosexual activity since the age of eighteen. When I confronted him on this issue, he took immediate and profane umbrage. "You accusing me of being a goddamn fag?" was his denial—not an angry, and more believable, "No!"

Elicitation turned into interrogation, and I went after him. Ultimately, the young man told me that he had awakened a fellow GI by sodomizing him. According to him, the reasons for doing this were, "I was drunk. I hated the guy and thought he was a fag." After the test, as I took the young man back to the reception area, he felt the need to vent and did so: "It takes a real asshole to do your job, and I pity you," he said. "That may be so, but I have a job, and you don't, and won't, at least not with us," was my brilliant rejoinder. After that test, I looked forward to getting back on the road.

For some, the constant travel might have been a problem, but I loved it. On a trip in January 1970 I had an experience that changed my life: I went to a party at which I met my future wife. I arrived in country late on a Friday afternoon and called the office to check in. The voice that answered the phone was mellifluous and intriguing and connected me with the chief of support, who invited me to a party at the ambassador's residence on the following Sunday. He introduced me to the COS secretary, Leonor Estela Tijerina, and eight months later she became Leonor Sullivan. Meeting Lee was the highlight of my career in the CIA.

As busy as I was, I never thought that my work was dangerous. I knew that if I was caught conducting a test overseas, I would probably be arrested and thrown out of the country, but I didn't have any particular fear of being physically harmed. However, a couple of incidents sent my adrenaline into high gear.

On one of my trips to Central and South America, I was scheduled to make five stops. During my second stop I received a cable advising me that a U.S. Navy officer had been stabbed to death in the city that was to be my fourth stop and warning me to be very careful. Shortly after reading the cable, I passed a pawnshop, noticed a rather lethal looking switchblade, and bought it. On reflection, I can't figure out why I bought that knife, but to this day, I thank God that I did.

During the fourth stop, I worked one day on a case until about 12:30 a.m. The case officer, in a rush to get home, dropped me off in the center of the city where I caught a taxi to take me to my hotel. At each street corner en route, the driver stopped to ask men standing around, "Have you seen Jorge? I have to find him." After the third stop, I told the driver in Spanish to get me back to the hotel *now*. When he stopped at the next corner and again asked for Jorge, I took out the knife, flicked it open, and told the driver in Spanish, "I am really in a hurry. Let's get back to the hotel." I think he got the message. He turned the taxi around, and we were at the hotel in less than ten minutes. My sense was that the driver and Jorge might have robbed me or worse had I not had the knife. Back in headquarters, when I related this story to "Ken Haneda," chief of ops, he got upset; I think I gave him the impression that I was some kind of cowboy.

The taxi incident was about as dangerous as it ever was. On another occasion on another trip, I went to a movie, and by the time the movie was over a curfew was in effect and the streets were deserted. It was about 1:00 a.m. when I started walking back to the Sheraton, where I was staying. It was eerie walking through the deserted streets, and I began to get a little nervous. There was a lot of guerilla activity in the city, and on a previous visit to the country I had been awakened by the sound of machine gunfire as an army colonel was assassinated. When I had looked out the window, I had seen the colonel with his arms wrapped around a telephone pole, covered in blood.

My memory of the assassination increased my nervousness as I walked home after the movie, and I was much relieved when a taxi came along. At first the taxi driver ignored my attempt to flag him down, but eventually he turned around and picked me up. When I got in the taxi, the driver told me that it was very dangerous to be out after curfew and that had I been a local he would not have stopped. At the hotel, all the doors were locked, and the desk clerk was reluctant to open the door. He chastised me for being out after the curfew and told me that I had been very lucky.

As the years went on, I came to realize that were anything to happen to me, it would be because I was in the wrong place at the wrong time; I would not be personally targeted. On two occasions I experienced minor earthquakes, and on another I came down with a very bad case of food poisoning that resulted in my losing twenty-three pounds. On the occasion when I got food poisoning, I had eaten breakfast at the hotel, and as soon as I took a bite of the breakfast sausage, I knew there was something wrong with it. Later that morning, in the midst of a test, the diarrhea, nausea, and chills began. I managed to finish the test and asked the case officer I was working with to take the instrument, charts, and notes back to the office. I then returned to the hotel, where I stayed in bed until the following Monday morning. No one called to see how I was doing; it was a pretty miserable weekend.

While danger was not much of a factor, I experienced a lot of tension on the job. On many occasions a case officer told me to go to a hotel room and wait for a subject to show up. I often sat in the hotel considering the possibility that the subject was a double agent and might bring the police with him.

Subjects are not supposed to be told ahead of time about their polygraph tests for many reasons, the most important being to prevent the case officer and examiner from being caught by local authorities in the act of conducting a polygraph test on an agent. Among the other reasons are to prevent the subject from taking drugs or medications to inhibit the test or to give him or her time to come up with an excuse to avoid taking the test. As early as my first operational test, I learned that this was a rule case officers seldom followed. Some case officers told their agents about the test ahead of time to enhance rapport. Other case officers felt that springing a polygraph test on agents without warning made it more difficult for their agents to get through the test, and unfortunately, some case officers tried to coach their agents as to how to beat the test.

Staying on the road was not only a refuge from headquarters bureaucracy but also a money saver. I rarely had to cash a check because I was living on the per diem I earned while traveling. This was one of the better perks of the job.

In the spring of 1970 I went on what was the best of my many temporary duty (TDY) assignments. I spent five weeks traveling all over Europe, conducted some great tests, and came back to headquarters thinking I had a great job. At one of the stops on that trip I worked with a case officer I instantly disliked. When one of his agents admitted to me that he had revealed to a newspaper reporter that he was working with the CIA, I took a bit of pleasure in reporting it to the case officer. As a result, the agent was let go, and the operation was shelved.

In June 1970 I began the longest TDY of my career. In July, while on a stop, Lee and I got engaged. On the tail end of the trip, on August 29, 1970, Lee and I were married. After our honeymoon, Lee went back to her station, and I returned to headquarters. Lee joined me in November.

Shortly after her return to Washington, Lee was assigned to one of the desks in the DP. One day I picked her up to go to lunch, and as we were walking to the cafeteria, three women passed us in the corridor. One of the women stopped, pointed to me, and said, "There's the man who destroyed my life." Incidents like this, i.e., running into someone whose test did not go well, are always at the back of polygraphers' minds. This young lady, whose life I had destroyed, had entered on duty before she was eighteen and was ineligible for polygraph testing. I interviewed her, asked her all the questions that applicants were asked, and told her that as soon as she turned eighteen, she would be given a polygraph test on those questions. She was supposed to be tested in November 1968, but because of a clerical error, she wasn't tested until November 1970. When I tested her she volunteered that she had been using marijuana and a stimulant once a week since the previous December. Then she said, "You're not going to tell anyone, are you?" I told her that I would have to report what she told me, and she said, "Oh, Lord, there goes my job." On the day when she saw Lee and me in the corridor, she had just been terminated. I felt bad, but that's part of the job.

In April 1971 Lee and I began a four-year assignment in South Vietnam. During our four years in Vietnam, I don't remember receiving one piece of communication from IRD. I was out of sight and out of mind.

In early 1972 we received word that Richard McGarrah Helms had resigned as DCI. He had not submitted his resignation at the beginning of President Nixon's second term, but rather two weeks after Nixon took the oath of office. The word from headquarters, via new assignees and those returning from leave, was that Helms had refused to help Nixon cover up the Watergate scandal and was forced out. I remember thinking at the time I heard this, "If this is true, Helms just went up a notch in my estimation."

On February 2, 1973, James Rodney Schlesinger was appointed director of central intelligence to replace Helms. In his five-month tenure (the shortest of any DCI), he wreaked a good deal of havoc in the Agency. Schlesinger ordered the DP to put together a list of all its misdeeds. This alarmed many. I don't know if it had been his intention to present this list to Congress or not, but he resigned to become secretary of defense before doing so.

When I visited headquarters during an emergency leave to attend Lee's father's funeral in February 1972, Ray Fox warned me not to hang around the cafeteria or library because Schlesinger was monitoring those places to find employees who were goofing off. This typified the aura of fear and uncertainty during Schlesinger's reign. I can think of no contribution he made to the Agency, but on March 1, 1973, he did change the name of the Directorate of Plans (DP) to the Directorate of Operations (DO). The title for the director of the Directorate of Operations became deputy director for operations (DDO).

Bill Osborne retired in 1972. None of the three men who succeeded Osborne lasted more than a year, and IRD was in a state of flux. I knew two of the three new chiefs, but I never met the third. In early 1973 an examiner assigned to Vietnam with another U.S. government agency offered to sponsor me for membership in the American Polygraph Association. I sent a cable back to IRD asking for guidance. I wanted to join APA but knew that membership in APA had been discouraged in the past. My request went unanswered.

In 1974 "Les Knoll" was named chief of IRD. When I entered on duty in 1968, Knoll was the "fair-haired boy" in the Office of Security. He had been promoted to GS-14 at a comparatively young age and was a rising star. Knoll had been a very good polygraph examiner and was running a test overseas when he was arrested. He spent thirty days in jail. That ended his career as a polygraph examiner, and after the CIA paid $1 million to get him out of jail, he embarked on a new career path in OS.[1]

I hadn't had a lot of contact with Knoll, but the interactions that I had were favorable and I looked forward to working with him. The contrast between Knoll and Osborne could not have been greater, and at least for the moment, I was elated. Although I didn't see it as such at the time, the beginning of Knoll's term as chief of IRD marked the end of what I term IRD's Dark Ages.

Looking at the history of polygraph in the CIA, the period from about 1963 until 1974 was a time of stagnation and ignorance. At a time when advances in polygraph were being made in the private sector, Chet Crawford was alienating IRD from what was mainstream polygraph. Osborne continued the Crawford policy. What polygraph tenets there were were disregarded by IRD examiners. Polygraph examiners were most often referred to as "operators" instead of examiners and were seen as technicians, not professionals. IRD wasn't getting the best and brightest candidates, as evidenced by my acceptance into the program after a poor evaluation by my recruiter. Security officers were not beating a path to IRD, and the primary criterion for acceptance into IRD seemed to be a desire to get the job. One security officer who wanted an overseas assignment applied to IRD. He was accepted for training,

---

1. The subject Knoll had been testing when he was arrested was told in advance of his impending test. Another service had learned that the local service was planning to break in during the test and arrest the examiner. The other service's representative called in the local CIA chief, left a cable reporting the local service's intentions, excused himself, and left the CIA chief alone in his office. The CIA chief did not read the cable.

underwent a two-week training period, ran fifty cases, and was sent to Vietnam. Another security officer, looking for an overseas assignment, ran one test before he was assigned to Laos.

Crawford's hubris combined with Bill Osborne's antipathy toward Howard Osborne in particular and OS in general helped create an "us against them," "circle the wagons" atmosphere in IRD that did not serve IRD or the CIA well. During Crawford's tenure IRD had a comparatively high profile. Under Bill Osborne, IRD moved into the shadows and stayed there.

On a regular basis, legislation was introduced in Congress to abolish the use of polygraph testing on U.S. government employees. This only added to IRD's defensive posture. These bills died in committee, but the threat was always there.

Much gloom and doom marked my first year in IRD. Polygraph's utility was established but so, too, was the perception that polygraph was a "necessary evil." Office of Security managers paid lip service to supporting the CIA polygraph program, but in reality they practiced a policy of benign neglect toward IRD.

On a personal level I became imbued with the idea that polygraph could be much better than it was, but I didn't see much hope of that happening as long as Osborne was running IRD. More important, those days were dark because I believed that my colleagues and I may have missed many of the subjects we had tested. I had a nagging, although not constant, anxiety that at some time in the future some of our misses would come back to haunt us.

Lee's and my tour in Vietnam was an escape from IRD's depressing atmosphere, and most of my memories of that time are good. My skills as an examiner improved, and I earned the respect of many of my DO colleagues. My first son was born in Vietnam, Lee and I had saved enough money to buy a house, and life was looking pretty good. I saw Knoll's arrival as the beginning of a new and brighter day in IRD.

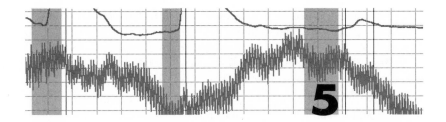

A NEW DAY

Les Knoll, especially when compared with Bill Osborne, had a good reputation in the Office of Security, and he was clearly picked to bring IRD back into OS. Knoll's arrival in IRD coincided with the retirement of Howard Osborne as director of OS. Osborne had thought very highly of Greg Milenski but not much of polygraph, and I saw his departure as another plus.

Unfortunately for me, the man who succeeded Osborne, Charles W. "Charlie" Kane, and I had some history. In July 1970, during a flight from the Caribbean to Central America, I became ill. I was taken off the plane in Miami and to a hospital. While I was in the hospital, Kane visited me. He told me that he had called headquarters and arranged for me to do some testing for him in Miami. By that time I hadn't seen Lee in almost three months, and we had arranged to meet over the Fourth of July holiday. I called headquarters, had Kane's request overruled, and went on to see Lee. Kane was not happy.

Despite Kane's displeasure, the trip was worth it. Lee and I were engaged that Fourth of July and married six weeks later. Thirty-six years later we are still together. When Kane and I ran into each other in Vietnam in 1973, Kane was less than cordial. Fortunately, he retired before I finished my tour in Vietnam.

My tour, with Lee, in Vietnam proved to be a mixed blessing. We made money and I loved the work, but while abroad, as far as OS/IRD was concerned, I was gone as well as forgotten. Before going to Vietnam I was much more oriented to the operational environment than to the headquarters environment. In Vietnam, I became more enamored of the operational environment, and by the time I returned I knew more people in the DO than in the Office of Security. Back in headquarters I was essentially an unknown quantity in the Office of Security, and this proved detrimental to my career.

My operational orientation negatively affected my status in the Office of Security, but more damaging was the whistle-blowing, on Bo Mooney, I had done while in Vietnam. Mooney had been my predecessor in Vietnam and had been sent there because no other examiner in IRD was willing to go. Upon replacing Mooney in Vietnam, I discovered that I had inherited a train wreck. Mooney had passed every subject he tested, and undoing his damage proved to be a Herculean task.

After Vietnam Mooney was assigned to another Asian station. During that assignment he sent me a personal letter, asking that I request his assistance so that he could return to Vietnam on a TDY. I didn't want him back in Vietnam. I conferred with my two colleagues, "Mark Verity" and Rob Creed, and the three of us rejected Mooney's offer. Mooney subsequently sent an official cable offering his assistance to the Vietnam station. Again we rejected his offer. Two weeks later Mooney's boss showed up in Saigon and confronted me: "Why don't you want Bo Mooney here?" he asked. In retrospect, I realize I should not have told him, chapter and verse, exactly why we didn't want Mooney in Vietnam. My whistle-blowing had more negative consequences for me than it did for Mooney. On my first day back in IRD after Vietnam, I was told that I was in the Office of Security's doghouse because of my comments to Mooney's boss. But as bad as things seemed, I had hopes off getting back on track with Knoll's appointment.

Knoll had been in office less than a year when I returned from Vietnam. He welcomed me back, and I resumed testing immediately. I also began to travel a great deal. The operational work I did was more challenging than the testing I did in headquarters, and I thrived on it.

A lot happened during my first year back from Vietnam. Within a year of Knoll's taking over IRD, the Church and Pike committees were empanelled: the Church Committee in January 1975 and the Pike Committee in July of the same year. The focus of the Church Committee was alleged abuses by the CIA, domestic spying, assassinations, etc. The focus of the Pike Committee was determining whether the CIA was worth the money Congress appropriated for it.

In December 1975, shortly after I returned from an overseas trip, Richard Welch, the chief of station in Athens, was assassinated by a Greek terrorist group. The murder signaled that as U.S. government officials working abroad we needed to be aware of not only the local police or security services but also terrorists. The former might arrest, embarrass, and kick us out of their countries; the latter were out to kill us. Working abroad suddenly became a little more stressful than it had been; regardless, it was the environment in which I functioned best.

On the heels of Welch's assassination, in January 1976, President Gerald R. Ford asked for DCI William E. Colby's resignation. Colby, in response to the Church Committee's investigation, had given up what many refer to as the Agency's family jewels (assassinations, drug testing, domestic operations, and so on) in his testimony. Many in the DO strongly criticized Colby for having been so forthcoming, and many said that Colby's openness was naive and did not bode well for covert operations in an extremely dangerous world. Richard Helms, Colby's predecessor as DCI, was particularly critical of Colby. In his testimony before the Senate Foreign Relations Committee, Helms withheld information and was subsequently indicted for having done so. Leaving the courthouse after his plea, Helms was quoted as saying that he would wear his conviction as a badge of honor. In the Agency, the Old Guard rallied to Helms's defense; there were clearly Helms and Colby factions. At the time all of this was going on, I felt that Colby had done the right thing and that had he not been forthcoming Congress might have turned CIA headquarters into a home for the Peace Corps. At a recent Association of Former Intelligence Officers (AFIO) function, I had the pleasure of sitting next to Mr. Colby's ex-wife, and when I mentioned my Peace Corps thought, she laughed and agreed with me. Another AFIO colleague who had worked with Colby offered this idea: "Bill was first and foremost a Constitutionalist and believed that lying to Congress was not only immoral but also impractical."

Regardless of who was right or wrong, in January 1976 President Ford named George H. W. Bush as DCI. At the time Bush was appointed, he didn't want the job because he saw it as a political dead-end. It seems Bush learned to love his work, however; he became one of the most popular DCIs I can remember.

After Bush's appointment the Agency continued in a state of suspended animation, waiting to see what else was going to happen. Frank Snepp, a colleague of mine from Vietnam, screamed for an investigation of what he saw as the Vietnam debacle, and he quit the Agency to write his book, *Decent Interval: An Inside Account of Saigon's Indecent End*. Recovery from and recriminations about Vietnam caused some morale problems, and most of us were wondering how Bush was going to handle his new job. Thankfully, he had a calming effect. His mission seemed to be to get the Agency through a very bad time without any more harm being done, and his tenure gave the Agency a much-needed respite. In rating Bush as DCI, the best I can say is that he did no harm. He was very popular, but he didn't seem to leave any footprints. When he left, many in the Agency felt a genuine sadness.

Bush's "don't rock the boat" style meant less operational work was available for me, but still, I had enough DO cases to keep me content. The Office of Security had little input or vested interest in the operational world, and as a senior Office of Security supervisor once told me,

"Security would rather have you get a kid to admit a couple of extra uses of marijuana than catch a double agent." During my first year back after the tour in Vietnam, I tested two DO assets, or ops agents, whose answers to the questions dealing with working with an intelligence service other than the CIA showed indications of deception. Interrogation of the first of these subjects didn't go anywhere until I said, "Either we resolve this issue here and now or we cannot go on." The agent immediately admitted that he was working for another service. This scenario was repeated with the second agent, and the threat I used with them became a part of my modus operandi in dealing with operational agents. The overwhelming number of operational agents were in it for the money, and fear of losing that source of income was usually enough to inspire forthrightness. We didn't threaten to kill or physically abuse subjects who failed their tests, instead using whatever leverage was available. Most of the time, that leverage was money.

While I was in Vietnam, the face of IRD had dramatically changed. Four supervisors and seven examiners had left the division, and I was in the odd position of being one of the most experienced examiners left as well as the new kid on the block. In addition to the changes in personnel, the focus of our tests had changed. Before I left for Vietnam, fewer than one in five of the applicants I tested acknowledged illegal drug use. Within six months of my return, almost four out of every five applicants I tested admitted some involvement with drugs, and admissions of illegal drug use became the most frequently obtained admission.

As much as I liked Knoll, I was disappointed in him as a boss. I soon learned that Les Knoll saw IRD as the "Siberia of Security." During his tenure he had two mantras, "What have you done today to help me get my GS-16?" and "Don't rock the boat." Knoll did forge a better relationship between IRD and OS, but he was not very proactive regarding change.

One thing that Knoll did for which I am very grateful was send me to the Agency's language school to study Spanish. I had taken two years of Spanish in college, and my pre-Vietnam trips to Latin America had improved my fluency. The four months I spent in language school got me to the point where I could get around pretty well, but still I was not fluent enough to conduct an interrogation.

Shortly after Knoll took over IRD in 1974, the CIA decided to begin a reinvestigation program for its employees. Although CIA employees were told when they entered on duty that they would be subject to periodic security reinvestigations, which included a BI and a polygraph test, the practice of actually performing the reinvestigations didn't begin until 1975. The Office of Security originally proposed that the questions covered during EOD testing be re-covered during the reinvestigation polygraph (RIP) tests. That proposal met with tremendous resistance particularly from the DO, and ultimately the decision was made to address only counterintelligence questions on the reinvestigation tests.

In the summer of 1975 RIP testing of IRD examiners began. Once all the examiners were tested, staff testing began. The most senior people in the CIA were tested first, i.e., all GS-18s, then all GS-17s, and down through the GS-14s. When all of the GS-14s had been tested, other employees were randomly selected for testing. Compared with entering on duty tests, these were much easier, and I enjoyed doing them. They allowed me to meet many of the CIA's managers; this proved enlightening. The only downside to RIP testing was that IRD's new responsibility stretched the division's resources to the breaking point.

A more fortuitous event that occurred at the time Knoll took over IRD was the naming of Robert W. Gambino to replace Charlie Kane as D/OS. Gambino called me to his office to welcome me back from Vietnam, and I found him to be impressive.

My tour in Vietnam had coincided with Milenski's tour in Europe. Milenski returned to IRD in May 1975. Fox had retired while Milenski and I were overseas, and no decision had been made as to who would take over as chief of the overt desk (C/OD). Milenski had done well in Europe, and the Directorate of Operations management was trying hard to recruit him as an operations officer. I don't think Milenski delivered an ultimatum, but the word was that if he didn't get the C/OD job, he would leave IRD.

Milenski got the job and changed CIA polygraph forever. As chief of the overt desk, Milenski monitored the work of every examiner in the division. After a couple of months on the job, Milenski initiated weekly meetings during which he led discussions on various aspects of polygraph testing. More important, once Milenski took over the overt desk, he made mandatory a review of all charts. Initially, Milenski did most of the chart reviews, but as the size of the division grew, it became necessary to delegate this task. Eventually, he designated four full-time chart reviewers. Resistance to outside training was still in vogue when Milenski returned from overseas, and Milenski didn't push it with Knoll. However, when Lee Jensen replaced Les Knoll in 1976, Milenski found a sympathetic ear and began to push for outside training.

Lee Jensen was, in my opinion, the best chief IRD ever had. In Germany and in some Jewish neighborhoods in which I have spent time, I have heard the term "mensch" used in referring to men like Jensen. He was a gentleman of the first order, a gifted painter, a wonderful family man, and a great boss. Jensen had been an examiner when I entered on duty, and I had a good but not close relationship with him. About a year after I entered on duty Jensen left PD to go to the Special Activities Division. (SAD was referred to as OS's Green Berets. Officers in SAD had to bail Agency people out of jail when they got into trouble. SAD officers also conducted many of the more sensitive investigations of Agency people.)

When I decided to stay in polygraph, Jensen made it a point to come down to PD and give me some advice. "John, you are a really good guy and a good examiner," he said. "Polygraph is probably the right place for you, but if you decide to stay here, you are going to have to accept the fact that a lot of guys who are not nearly as qualified as you are going to get promoted ahead of you."

"Somehow or other, I have incurred the wrath of the powers that be in OS, and no matter where I go, I doubt I will get promoted, so I might as well stay here doing what I like to do," I told him.

"You may think that you can live with it, but about the fourth time it happens, you are going to remember this conversation," said Jensen. I never forgot that Jensen had taken the time to have that conversation with me nor did I forget how right he had been.

Morale during Jensen's tenure was the best I can remember it being over the course of my thirty-one years in the office, primarily because Jensen was willing to stick up for us in front of OS management. He fought management's attempts to overload IRD with cases, and he was very proactive in getting examiners promoted. He also resisted cosmetic interference from OS, which was a very conservative office. Two examiners in IRD during Jensen's tenure grew heavy beards, a la the Smith Brothers of cough drop fame. At a weekly staff meeting "Jonas Ewal," one of the real powers in OS, commented to Jensen that he was letting things get out of hand in PD by allowing examiners to grow beards. Jensen told me that he had responded, "Jonas, as long as they do their job, I don't care if they grow hair down to their asses." Jensen retired without ever reaching OS's upper echelons.

A more significant example of Jensen's willingness to back his examiners is the case of examiner "Paul Maxon." Maxon often yanked management's chain, growing a beard being but one example of his rebelliousness. At Bob Gambino's retirement party, before getting into the reception line, Maxon shaved off his beard and put all the hair in a paper bag. As Maxon shook hands with Gambino and congratulated him on his retirement, he also handed him the bag of facial hair—amusing, yes; career enhancing, no.

In the late 1970s minorities were not well represented in OS. There was one African American in IRD, and I can recall only three others in OS. At the time there was a move afoot to attract more African Americans, and one young African American who applied for a position in OS appeared to be an ideal candidate. A very senior OS officer interviewed him, and in his write-up of the interview he commented, "This is the best SORT candidate I have ever seen."

Maxon was assigned to conduct this stellar candidate's polygraph test and spent most of a Friday testing him. The test results were favorable with no reportable information developed. OS managers were delighted with the test results, and the candidate was sent home to await word as to when he would enter on duty.

Over the weekend Maxon had some second thoughts, came into the office, reviewed the test charts again, and concluded that he may have made a bad call. The following Monday morning he went to Jensen and told him that he wanted to bring the man back for more testing. Jensen told Maxon that it was his call and notified OS management. There was consternation on the fourth floor (the home of OS), but the man, who was from out of state, was brought back. "Flynn Jones," IRD's African-American examiner, conducted the retest and obtained enough information to disqualify the candidate. This was a case that could have come back to haunt us, and if not for Maxon's integrity and Jensen's support, it most likely would have.

My only disagreement with Jensen was over a test that I did not miss but that came back to bite me nonetheless. Shortly before I left for Vietnam I tested a young female applicant. The only question to which the young woman reacted at all was the question on homosexual activity. I confronted her, and she adamantly denied ever engaging in homosexual activity. Ultimately, I constructed a test for her that dealt only with the issue of homosexual activity. I concluded that the young woman had, at least up until that time, not engaged in homosexual activity. In my notes, which I did not include in the report, I commented, "She hasn't done it yet, but she will."

Almost five years later an applicant, during his polygraph test, volunteered that he knew we hired homosexuals because his wife, a CIA employee, worked with one. The "one" to whom he was referring was the young woman I had tested. As it turned out, the young woman had become quite notorious in her office and was openly referred to as the "Bull Dyke."

Jensen called me into his office to discuss the case and also told me that he had told Gambino that I had missed this young woman because I had been inexperienced at the time I tested her. I looked over the file, told Jensen that I didn't think that I had been beaten, and told him that we really didn't know when she had begun her homosexual activity. Jensen didn't seem to buy my argument and closed our discussion by saying, "Don't worry about it, John. Every examiner gets beaten."

Gambino ordered that the young woman be afforded a specific issue polygraph (SIP) test regarding homosexual activity. "Bryan Lout" conducted the test. During Lout's session with her, the young woman admitted that she was a lesbian and also that she had attacked a girl with a knife. She further stated that as a young girl she had refrained from engaging in homosexual activity for religious reasons and that for two years after entering on duty she refrained out of fear of losing her job. Lout came to me and said that my conclusions had been right.

Under Jensen, the reinvestigation program really got off the ground and was going well, but occasionally a staff employee would balk. We had tested most of the high-ranking staff employees, and we were starting on the mid-level managers when Milenski came to me with what he referred to as a problem case. "John, I just got off the phone with a very nasty lady. She is supposed to come in here for an RIP, and she spent the last fifteen minutes bitching about her privacy being invaded. She's just a pain in the ass to deal with. I want you to test her," he said.

Milenski was right. In my thirty-one years with CIA polygraph, this woman, "Bonnie Bruja," was one of the most difficult people I ever tested. In reviewing her file before the test, I noticed that her colleagues, especially her subordinates, had nothing but bad things to say about her; they described her as sour, dour, and bitter. From the minute she came into my office on the test day, she was confrontational and abrasive. She argued about every question in the test preview. When I ran the test, I saw a strong and consistent reaction to the question about providing classified information to an unauthorized person. When I suggested that she was having a problem with this question, she flew into a fit of righteous indignation. We reached an impasse, and I excused myself to discuss the test with Milenski.

I told Milenski that this lady was every bit the problem he said she was and that she was also lying. He had been monitoring the test and agreed with me. He also asked me what I was going to do. I answered, "She is a real pain in the ass and isn't cooperating at all. I want to try and adjust her attitude and go on with the test."

"Good luck!" he replied.

When I went back into the room, Bruja was sitting in the chair, tapping her foot, and glaring at the wall.

"Ms. Bruja, the fact that you are here presupposes that you intend to cooperate. It's obvious to me that you have no intention of cooperating, and unless you do, there is no point in your being here."

"You're right!" She took the instrument attachments off and stormed out of my office.

That afternoon Sid Stembridge, Gambino's deputy, called Bruja into his office. Bruja told Stembridge that she would not ever go back for another test. Stembridge told Bruja that she left him no choice but to recommend her immediate dismissal. He then picked up the phone to call the DCI. Before Stembridge could complete his call, Bruja had a change of heart and agreed to return for more testing. She returned to IRD the next day. Not having me test her again was probably the politically correct thing to do, but the examiner selected to administer the retest had, to my knowledge, never conducted an interrogation or obtained a significant admission. Bruja passed her test.

Many Agency employees during their reinvestigation tests asked me, "What would happen if I refused to take the test?" I told them that I really didn't know but that the only employee whom I knew to have refused to take a test was given the option of taking the test or being fired.

I didn't have much time to dwell on Ms. Bruja, as shortly after I tested her, a case came through the division that gave impetus for IRD's expansion and Milenski's push for outside training: the Boyce–Lee case.

In January 1977 Christopher John Boyce was arrested for espionage. Boyce had been a clerk at aerospace giant TRW in Redondo Beach, California, and had been selling highly classified material to the Soviet Union. Andrew Daulton Lee was the courier in the operation and was arrested outside the Soviet embassy in Mexico City. He subsequently exposed Boyce as the source of the classified material. This case revealed that thousands of Agency contractors were working on very sensitive Agency projects without having undergone adequate security screening. OS upper management, mainly in reaction to the Boyce–Lee case, began pushing to have Agency contractors polygraphed. In 1977 we didn't have sufficient manpower to take on testing contractors, and thus the move to expand IRD came to life.

In an interesting sidelight to the Boyce–Lee case, while Boyce was working for the Soviets, he applied for a position requiring a polygraph test. Bryan Lout had been scheduled to go to California to test Boyce and four others who had applied for the same position. When Boyce found out that he would have to take a polygraph test, he withdrew his application.

In February 1977 President Jimmy Carter nominated Adm. Stansfield Turner as DCI, and on March 9, 1977, Admiral Turner was sworn in as the twelfth DCI. He had been on the job for a month when on April 10, an open letter to him was published in the *Washington Post*. The letter had been written by John Stockwell, a disgruntled DO case officer I had served with in Vietnam. Stockwell's letter excoriated the Agency and was a harbinger of things to come. In particular, Stockwell criticized the Agency's performance in Vietnam citing flawed Agency policy there, case officer incompetence, poor-quality operations, and incomplete intelligence. Turner, in my opinion, handled this situation well. In his response to Stockwell's letter, the new DCI said that he wished that Stockwell had come to him before going public and let it go at that.

Stockwell then wrote *In Search of Enemies: A CIA Story*, a vitriolic diatribe against the Agency. Stockwell's views didn't seem to garner much sympathy or support in the Agency, and Stockwell, after his fifteen minutes of fame, seemed to disappear.

Later that year Frank Snepp, an Agency analyst I had worked with in Vietnam and who had resigned from the Agency in protest over how the Agency had handled the evacuation of Saigon, published his book, *Decent Interval*. Coming on the heels of Stockwell's disaffection, *Decent Interval* gave the Agency some negative exposure that it didn't need. As compared with Stockwell, Snepp and his book had some support in the Agency, but Snepp hadn't cleared his book for publication with the Agency's Publications Review Board (PRB) and the Agency went after him with a vengeance. Ultimately, Snepp was forced to forfeit his royalties.

This negative publicity led to one of the more interesting investigations I participated in during Jensen's tenure. In December 1977 Turner called a meeting of all employees ranking GS-15 and higher in the main auditorium. In the evening, after the meeting, a *Washington Post* reporter called Turner at home and asked him to comment on something he had said at the meeting. The briefing Turner gave at the meeting was classified, and he was incensed that someone had leaked information to the *Post*. Turner called Gambino and ordered an investigation. As part of the investigation, all those who attended the meeting were polygraphed. The task of testing each of the attendees fell to me.

Initially I had no hope of identifying the source of the leak. Many of the attendees actually insisted that they be tested to clear their names and were very cooperative. I met many of the CIA's power brokers during the testing, but I didn't feel as though I was getting any closer to identifying the source of the leak. Then, something strange happened.

One of the people scheduled for a test was Gambino's close friend, "Tom Carney." Carney wrote Gambino a letter decrying the fact that polygraph was being used to conduct a witch hunt. Gambino sent me a copy of the letter with a note: "John, I don't want you to let the fact that Carney is a friend of mine influence how you do the test." I did not know Carney well, but I had met him on two occasions and I liked as well as respected him. He was actually revered by many who had worked for him.

Carney had a tough time on his test. I had no doubt that he was withholding information, and I actually coaxed him to admit that he knew and had talked to the reporter who had reported on the meeting, but he would not admit to having leaked the information. It got to a point at which I was absolutely certain that he had leaked the information, but I just didn't have the heart to really go after him; I liked him too much. I excused myself and went to discuss the test with Milenski. "Greg, I know he did it, but I can't get it out of him." Milenski said, "Let me go in there with you." Milenski returned to the room with me, and within ten minutes he had Carney admit that he had leaked the information. We both went to brief Gambino, and I made a point to tell Gambino that Milenski, not I, had gotten the admission from Carney.

On three subsequent tests that I specifically recall, I obtained significant admissions from subjects during first-session polygraph tests. Each of these subjects was turned over to another examiner to do any additional tests. For better or worse, I acquired the reputation as an examiner who lacked the "killer instinct."

Morale in IRD improved considerably during Jensen's reign, but the same could not be said for morale in the Agency. At the time Jensen became chief of IRD, the Agency was still in a state of shock over the Pike Committee report. President Carter, in naming Turner to be DCI, added insult to injury. Turner never gained the acceptance of Agency professionals nor did they gain his. One of the jokes going around headquarters was that Turner was going to have the seventh floor painted battleship gray. Turner had brought several of his military subordinates with him, and a distinct military air wafted through the corridors during his reign.

My impression was that President Carter had bought into much of the Church and Pike committees' castigation of the Agency and had ordered Turner to clean house. Turner, good sailor that he was, took to the task with zeal. His primary focus was the Directorate of Operations, and in the summer of 1977 he submitted to the director of operations a list of more than eight hundred DO positions to be eliminated. On October 31, 1977, in what became known as the Halloween Massacre, more than two hundred DO officers were fired. Over the next three years more than two thousand DO officers left the Agency. Some were forced into early retirement while many others retired out of frustration and helplessness. As more and more DO officers left, a sense of panic blanketed the Agency. I remember running into friends I had served with in Vietnam and who had been given their pink slips. They were bereft and very bitter. Many saw Turner as the Grim Reaper, and resentment, as well as fear, was pervasive.

When Turner, in referring to those dismissed, was quoted as saying, "None of these men has ever heard a shot fired in anger," there was an uproar in the Agency. When I read that quote, my thought was, "Has

Turner ever heard a shot fired in anger?" He had graduated from Annapolis too late for World War II and might have been on ships that shelled enemy positions during the Korean and Vietnam Wars, but I didn't think that qualified him to make such a statement. In any event, the statement exacerbated the rift between Turner and the Agency. Many of my colleagues and I had certainly heard shots fired in anger. From that moment on, the chance of Turner's gaining the support and loyalty of the Agency was null. Among those let go after the massacre were some incompetent officers but also some very good officers whose departure seriously diminished the DO's effectiveness. For example, E. Henry Knoche, the acting DCI at the time Turner was named DCI, who was, in my opinion, one of the really good guys I met in the Agency, didn't show what Turner felt was the necessary deference to the new DCI and was forced out. Another Agency star who was let go was the legendary Theodore G. "Ted" Shackley. Shackley was destined for greater things. He had been COS in three major posts and at a minimum was on track to be the Deputy Director of Operations.

Shackley represented everything Turner hated about the Agency. If Turner had fired only Shackley to show his displeasure with the DO, the DO might have survived, but Turner's "take no prisoners" attitude regarding the DO amounted to a death knell.

The DCI has the power to fire any Agency employee at any time, but in the previous four years the man in power had done so on only five occasions. Jack Garland, one of my bosses in Vietnam, once mentioned to me that the Agency doesn't fire people, adding, "John, if we were to fire some of these clowns we have working for us and put them out on the street, the CIA mystique and aura of omnipotence would be destroyed."

On a professional level I was too low on the totem pole to have any contact with Turner. Each time a new DCI was appointed, we examiners wondered what his attitude regarding polygraph was. Is he for us or against us? Turner, who came in for his polygraph test, was gracious and cooperative, and some of our fears were assuaged. However, he refused to order one of his staff, whom he had brought with him from the Navy to take a polygraph test. This became a sore point with the Office of Security and many of the senior managers in the Agency. The aide for whom Turner waived the requirement to take a polygraph test was suspected of being a homosexual, and by shielding him, Turner opened himself to a lot of criticism. When pushed on the issue, Turner said, "I will vouch for him personally."

A significant flaw with Turner's leadership was his failure to show support for his employees. On an occasion when an employee, during a polygraph test, admitted working on some highly classified material at home, OS recommended that the offender be given two weeks' leave without pay as punishment. The individual asked for an interview with Turner in order to appeal his punishment. Turner ordered that the man be fired. OS interceded on the man's behalf, and the two weeks' leave without pay was enforced.

Turner was a fish out of water in the Agency, and in retrospect, I can find no positives associated with his reign. His attitude toward the DO was entirely negative, and this had far-reaching effects. Risk-taking is a significant aspect of a case officer's modus operandi. DO officers understood this and were willing to take risks when they knew that the DCI would support them. As it became apparent that Turner was not on their side, their willingness to take risks diminished, as did the number of assets they recruited. Time has healed many of the wounds Turner inflicted on the CIA, but the effects of his preference for technical intelligence collection over HUMINT operations can be seen in the CIA's failure to run effective clandestine operations against the Iraqis today.

Edward Jay Epstein, author of *News from Nowhere: Television and the News* and *Agency of Fear: Opiates and Political Power in America*, summed up Turner's reign in an article he wrote in 1985, titled "Who Killed the CIA? The Confessions of Stansfield Turner." In the article, published in *Commentary* in October 1985, Epstein, who had no agency connections, enumerated many of the mistakes he felt that Turner made while at the CIA and, in particular, took Turner to task for his lack of understanding of HUMINT.

Under Turner, we examiners conducted fewer operational tests and thus, we traveled less frequently, but for the most part during his reign it was business as usual in IRD. Two examiners were in training during the first year of Jensen's tenure, and there had been no real change in the training format—one instructor worked with one or two students. The time was not ripe for Milenski to push to have all new examiners undergo the full six-month Reid training course, but he did push for some outside training: he suggested that IRD send some examiners to John E. Reid and Associates for advanced polygraph training. The two-week Reid course covered all aspects of polygraph testing. Jensen went along with Milenski's idea and convinced Gambino to approve the training. Two examiners at a time were sent to Reid, and in all, I think eight examiners took the advanced course.

Milenski then successfully lobbied for making the Reid Interrogation Course a requirement for all new examiners. This course covered the application of Reid's nine-step interrogation technique. I attended both of the Reid courses and found the interrogation course to be the better of the two. At the time we did five or six interrogations a week in IRD, and what I learned in the Reid class, I put to immediate use.

For me, the main benefit of these courses was the confidence they afforded me: I felt more confident interpreting charts, constructing tests, and interrogating subjects. Another benefit was that once I began applying what I had learned at Reid and saw that these methods worked, my faith in the polygraph process grew. IRD was better because of the Reid training; IRD training was finally emerging from the Dark Ages.

When Jensen announced that he was moving on, a pall covered the office. Three days before Jensen left, he called me into his office. "Before I go, I want to tell you that you have made it a pleasure for me to come in to work every day. You do your job, never complain, and are one of the kinder, more decent people I have met," were the gist of his comments, the nicest any boss ever made to me.

The pall that had been cast when Jensen announced that he was leaving didn't lift when we heard that he would be replaced by "Lou Falcone."

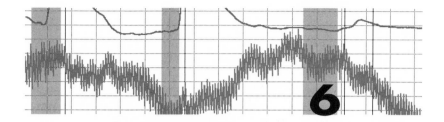

HARD (BUT EXCITING) TIMES

In the summer of 1976 Lou Falcone became Jensen's deputy. Falcone had been in Vietnam when I entered on duty, and I didn't meet him until December 1969, when he was home for Christmas leave. I was the only examiner doing tests during Christmas week and was a little behind on the schedule. On this particular occasion, I hadn't finished a morning case and had brought the subject back in the afternoon to complete the test.

My afternoon subject showed up before I finished with my morning subject, and I was discussing the morning case with Ray Fox when Falcone overheard Fox tell me to try and speed it up. Falcone offered to take my afternoon case. I felt relieved. Fox said, "That's OK, Lou. John can handle it." I didn't understand why Fox would decline Falcone's help, and I felt that neither my subject nor I was being served well. Fox was forcing me to rush a case I was doing and leaving me too little time to prepare for my next case. Though I didn't understand the dynamics between Falcone and the IRD management, this incident gave me the sense that Fox didn't want Falcone doing tests. Later a few examiners in the office told me that Falcone was very unorthodox in his approach to polygraph, very histrionic, and not destined for great things in OS.

According to IRD lore, Falcone had punched out examiner "Amos Spitz" and had told Jonas Ewal, "As long as I am alive, Jonas, know that you will have an enemy." I had worked with Spitz for two years in Vietnam and could understand why Falcone might have punched him. Spitz's personality turned many people off. Examiners who worked with him in IRD disliked him, and case officers refused to let him test their subjects. Ewal was the deputy director of the Office of Security and Falcone's alleged comment to him certainly was not politic, but I admired him for having the courage of his convictions. Before Falcone went back to Vietnam, I had one brief conversation with him. He raved about the station and said that I should think about doing a tour there.

Most of the case officers with whom I worked in Vietnam had arrived after Falcone left, but several interpreters I encountered had worked with him. A test that I often did with the Vietnamese was a "blind numbers" test (described in the introduction). This turned out to be an effective test for me, and I did it often. On one occasion, when I successfully identified the number, the interpreter said, "You know, Mr. Lou would do that test all the time, and I never saw him get the number."

During his tenure as Jensen's deputy, Falcone rarely conducted a test, but if a particularly high-profile test were scheduled, he would do it. One of the high-profile tests he decided to do was that of a new DCI. On the day the DCI was tested, all of the examiners who weren't testing gathered around Milenski's desk to listen to the interview. (Falcone was a rarity in that he wanted an audience for his tests. Most of the IRD chiefs, senior examiners, and experts would not allow their interviews to be monitored.) When Falcone told the new DCI that he was going to do a blind numbers test on him, the entire audience let out a collective, "No! Lou, don't do it!" But Falcone did, and the new DCI beat him. The groan we let out when the DCI told Falcone he had missed the number was almost as intense as the anger many of us felt. Falcone had brought the process into question for the sole purpose of stroking his ego, and he did it with a person whose opinion of polygraph counted.

The next day line examiner "Jim Doom" commented in front of Falcone and several other examiners, "If we are going to give these high-profile people a real test, examiners who test every day should do the tests." Falcone, who took immediate and strong umbrage, jumped on Doom with both feet. I didn't have much use for Doom but felt that Falcone had gone over the line in berating him. Doom was obviously upset over Falcone's comments and retreated to his office. I followed him and misguidedly tried to cheer him up. I told him not to take Falcone's comments personally. One of the things I told Doom was that Falcone was in the Old Guard and saw Doom and the new examiners as a threat. Unfortunately, I also suggested that Falcone might be a little jealous. Doom seemed to be in a slightly better mood when I left his office.

Twenty minutes later Falcone was in my office demanding to know how I dared to suggest to Doom that Falcone felt threatened by or jealous of Doom. Falcone and I had never been warm and fuzzy with each other, and from that moment on, we were much less so.

When Falcone became chief of IRD in 1978, he started off with a bang. One of his first ideas was to have examiners wear white lab coats and be referred to as "doctor." Falcone's deputy, Ken Haneda, took a lab coat, had "Luigi's Pizza Parlor" printed in red on the back, and gave it to Falcone. Without realizing what was printed on the back, Falcone began wearing the coat around the office. When he found out, he was embarrassed and the lab coat/doctor idea died.

Falcone also suggested that examiners occasionally be asked to defend their calls and techniques to their colleagues in a forum format. Falcone's plan, in his words, was to have the examiners "pick each other apart." I don't know how many people tried to talk Falcone out of this, but I know that I told him that the idea was right up there with the Edsel and the Corvair. "Lou, this would absolutely destroy the morale in here and have us at each other's throats," I said. "You're just afraid of being criticized," Falcone said, adding that he thought such sessions would help examiners maintain their edge. I am sure that Falcone paid no attention to me, but Milenski and several others told him that his idea would be ineffective, and he backed off.

To make matters worse, a massive remodeling of the IRD offices was undertaken during Falcone's first year. For six months the cacophony of jackhammers was a constant accompaniment to our polygraph tests. The corridors were dust filled, and debris was everywhere. Subjects and examiners, alike, complained. Falcone complained to Gambino, and Ewal came down to see what the complaining was all about. After a walk through, I heard Ewal say, "This is awful." Subsequently the contractor told us that he would finish as soon as possible.

During Falcone's reign, I did a RIP test on a senior DO officer whom I will call "John Gorgos." I had known Gorgos in Vietnam and liked him. During the interview Gorgos volunteered that he had taken a young officer who had recently entered on duty under his wing. Gorgos went on to say that the young man was having a tough time and was maybe in over his head. I didn't push Gorgos to identify his protégé, but I remember suggesting to him that he might want to talk to someone in OS. Gorgos's protégé turned out to be William P. Kampiles.

Kampiles was a James Bond wannabe who decided that his talents were being wasted as a watch officer in the DO's duty office. Before resigning in November 1977, Kampiles stole a top secret technical manual, flew to Athens, and sold it to the Soviets for $3,000. Unfortunately for Kampiles, the GRU colonel (in Athens), Sergei Bokhan, was a spy for the United States, and he gave the CIA information that led to Kampiles.

I don't know whether Kampiles told Gorgos about what he was about to do before Gorgos went to OS as I advised him, but I do know that Kampiles was arrested and that he claimed his intent had been to run a double agent operation against the Soviets. In November 1978 Kampiles was sentenced to forty years in prison. He was released in 1996.

During Kampiles's EOD test, he had acknowledged some minor shoplifting that the examiner did not report. When the case was reassessed after Kampiles was caught and sentenced, one of the Office of Medical Services (OMS) psychologists commented that had he known about the shoplifting, he would have disqualified Kampiles. I found this comment to be gratuitous grandstanding, which in the long run made examiners' jobs more difficult. In hundreds of other cases examiners had made similar decisions to not report what they saw as minor transgressions. In fact admissions of minor transgressions frequently led to more significant admissions, once examiners informed subjects that minor transgressions would not be reported. After Kampiles, examiners had much less discretion as to what we could withhold from a report.

Fallout from the Kampiles case was widespread and had some long-lasting implications. Kampiles's immediate supervisor in the duty office was fired, control procedures for keeping track of classified documents were tightened, and a new employee "trial period" was introduced. During the trial period, before employees were granted staff status, a BI and RIP were conducted.

As the trial period polygraph test idea took hold, it became apparent that IRD was going to need many more examiners. We were already testing applicants as part of the EOD process and staff as part of the reinvestigation program. An industrial contractor testing program had begun and was about to expand. Adding trial period employees to IRD's list of testing responsibilities would require a large infusion of new examiners. At this point, Milenski began lobbying for new examiners to attend the Reid Basic Polygraph Course.

Falcone agreed that IRD's current training program was inadequate to handle the requirements that were going to be levied with the introduction of the trial period. With Milenski's urging, he recommended that IRD start sending new examiners to Reid for the six-month basic course. In 1979 the first two trainees were sent to Reid, and over the next two years, eighteen other CIA examiners were trained at Reid.

During this time complaints from the DO's Cuban Operations Group (COG) against IRD became strident, in large part because none of its agents could pass their polygraph tests. At one point the chief of COG met with the polygraph examiners. He said to us, essentially, "Guys, not all of our agents can be bad" and "You guys are doing bad tests." Unfortunately, the Cuban assets, with very rare exceptions, *were* all bad. Trying to sell that idea to the chief of COG was an exercise in futility, and the meeting only exacerbated the problematic relationship between the division and his group.

My experience with Cubans, which dated back to the time I was in the army, made me think that, although some of the Cuban agents might not be bad, the overwhelming majority of them probably were. On the occasion of the chief of COG's visit, I didn't think it politic to make my opinion known to him.

When I entered on duty in 1968, almost half of the tests IRD conducted were in support of DP operations. To prepare examiners who had had no previous experience dealing with DP case officers or testing operational assets, IRD sent new examiners to the Farm, the CIA's covert training facility, to take the Operations Familiarization Course (or Ops Fam, as it was known). Ops Fam was my first experience interacting with the DP. Many of my classmates went on to do quite well in their careers, and the interactions I had had with them during our time at the Farm served me well.

During Ops Fam, as in every Agency training course I took, as soon as it was known that I was a polygraph examiner, classmates and instructors alike felt it incumbent on them to share with me a story about polygraph. Most of these stories were fairly benign, but I remember an occasion on which one of the Ops Fam instructors approached me in the student bar one night and said, "Polygraph isn't worth a shit with the Cubans." He went on to tell me that Cubans had been raised in an environment where lying was as natural as screwing and that they felt no guilt when they lied. At that time many Cuban assets were passing their polygraph tests, and I can only assume that this case officer had no faith in polygraph because he believed that the Cubans were beating their tests.

I had yet to test my first Cuban and had had no discussions with my IRD colleagues about testing Cubans. However, a part of the foreign operations intelligence (FOI) curriculum at Fort Holabird was devoted to interrogation/debriefing training, and the subjects used in this training were refugees who had recently fled Castro's Cuba. In November 1964 my FOI classmates and I went to Miami to sit in on the debriefings and interrogations that English-speaking Cubans conducted at the debriefing center. During that week in Miami, I took an immediate liking to the Cubans who were running the debriefing center. They were dedicated, energetic, professional, and from what I could see, honest. That rather limited experience with Cubans didn't qualify me to rebut the instructor's comment, but viscerally, my reaction to him was very negative; I lumped him with all the others whom I had encountered who had nothing but negative comments about polygraph. I thought to myself, "Screw you!" but said out loud, "I guess they are going to be a real challenge," and walked away.

Shortly after completing the Ops Fam course in 1969, I began testing DP assets. During my third overseas trip, I was asked to polygraph a

Cuban seaman who had jumped ship and was seeking asylum in the United States. The man was very nervous when I first met him, and it took the interpreter and me almost forty-five minutes to settle him down. Once he was calm, I explained (through the interpreter) the purpose of the test, i.e., that we wanted to make sure he was telling us the truth about why he was seeking asylum and that he had not been sent to spy on us by the Direccion General de Inteligencia (DGI), the Cuban intelligence service. I also told the man that to be granted asylum he would have to pass the test. He passed the test without any difficulty, and it is my understanding that he was granted asylum.

I had my first experience testing a Cuban operational asset five months later. I was working in Central America, had just met my future wife Lee, and was hoping to prolong my stay. I was writing the report on a test I conducted the night before when Lee brought me a cable ordering me to cut my stay short and get to a country in the Caribbean as soon as possible. I was there by 3:00 the next afternoon.

When I met with the case officer that evening, he told me that the agent I was to test was a Cuban whom the station knew was a double agent working for the DGI. Regardless of how the test came out, he wanted me to tell the agent that he had passed the test—his rationale being, "We want this guy to think we believe and really trust him." I could understand the case officer's thinking but was a little ambivalent about doing the test. Polygraph's effectiveness is very much dependent on fear of detection. Anything that diminishes that fear should be avoided. I could envision this man going back to Havana and telling DGI trainees how he beat a CIA polygraph test, and I saw nothing good in that. My ego was also a factor. If the test indicated deception, I wanted to try to get an admission. Still, in weighing the damage to my ego and the possible lessening of the DGI's fear of a CIA polygraph against the potential benefit of a successful disinformation operation, the dis-information operation won.

Putting my concerns aside, I administered the test. The subject's charts showed clear indications of deception. I told the subject he had passed the test, packed up my equipment, and left.

My next foray into the world of Cuban subjects involved a Cuban foreign service officer, who had shown up at a U.S. embassy, identified himself as a Cuban diplomat, and requested political asylum. His test did not go well. I verified that he had not been a DGI officer and concluded that he had not been truthful about why he was seeking asylum. Elicitation turned into interrogation, and ultimately, the subject admitted that he had been embezzling embassy funds was afraid of being caught, and had defected. It had taken me about four hours to resolve the test, and I felt pretty good about how it had gone.

Of all the tests I conducted on Cuban subjects, one stands out as an example for those who tell me that polygraph doesn't work on Cubans. The subject of the test was code-named Banker, and he had shown up at a U.S. embassy seeking political asylum. He claimed to be a Cuban diplomat, and as a show of good faith, he turned over $25,000 that he claimed to have stolen from the Cuban embassy to which he had been assigned. Banker turned over his passport, and the embassy sent a cable to the country he claimed to have been assigned to. Via the cable, the embassy determined that a man with Banker's name and fitting his description was assigned to the Cuban embassy in that country. COG, back in headquarters, was notified. "Wally D'Ansera," the counterintelligence officer in Cuban Operations, was convinced that Banker had been directed to defect by the DGI and recommended that we not grant him political asylum. "Chris Hermon," who wrote intelligence reports for COG, agreed with D'Ansera, but "Don Ward," chief of COG, overrode the objections, and Banker was taken to the United States for debriefing. "Dick Harris" handled the debriefing and concluded that Banker was not from DGI. I was asked to polygraph Banker and was also invited to sit in on a meeting about Banker.

Ward chaired the meeting. Much of my operational experience had been in Latin America, and I had previously worked with everyone at the meeting. I knew and liked Ward and thought Harris was an outstanding case officer. But D'Ansera and I did not get along at all; there was no love lost between us. I knew and liked Hermon and considered her to be a fine reports officer.

In this case, D'Ansera had a problem believing that anyone, except a DGI agent, would turn over $25,000 as a show of good faith. Harris disagreed: "This guy is as sleazy as they come, but I feel pretty sure that he isn't DGI." Like D'Ansera, Hermon thought the guy was DGI: "This seems like the sort of thing the DGI does," and "He really hasn't given us that much good stuff." Ward commented that Banker had identified DGI officers with whom he had worked and had given COG some pretty good leads on Cuban diplomats who might be vulnerable to an approach. Ward summed up by saying, "John, I guess the ball is in your court. Just make sure he isn't DGI."

Harris and I agreed that the following Monday was a good day to do the test, and he gave me the bio sheet that Banker had filled out. On the way back to my office, I stopped in to see one of the Cuban translators, "Adolfo Uribe," who worked in COG. I had worked with him before and liked as well as respected him. I knew that he had been raised in Havana. I told him about the test I was going to do and asked him if he would look over the bio sheet and tell me if he saw anything wrong with it. Uribe asked if I could leave the bio sheet with him and let him get back to me the next day.

The next day Uribe told me that he thought Banker "smelled" and that he had some reservations about him. Specifically, Uribe pointed out that Banker had to be lying about either his age or where he had gone to school. According to Banker's bio sheet, he had graduated from the Havana School of Business at the age of seventeen, and Uribe felt that this was impossible. Uribe explained that the Havana School of Business was one of the most prestigious schools in Cuba, and to get in, one had to be a graduate of a good high school and have had excellent grades. This gave me two questions: "Were you born on ____?" and "Are you a graduate of the Havana School of Business?"

Based on Harris's comment that Banker was a "sleaze," I had trouble believing that he had turned in $25,000, unless he had taken much more. That suspicion grew when I learned that on his flight to freedom, Banker had stopped in Switzerland rather than taking a direct flight. Question #3: "Did you turn in all the money you took from the embassy?"

During one of his debriefings, Banker told Harris that he had met with a Communist union leader in Spain. Harris wanted that verified. "Did you meet with a Communist union leader in Spain as you said?" became question #4.

And last but not least, "Have you ever been a member of the DGI?"

Harris drove me over to the apartment where COG was keeping Banker and his much younger bride. My initial impression wasn't good. Banker looked and came across like the stereotypical used car dealer. He spoke excellent English and voiced absolute confidence in his ability to get through the polygraph test.

During the preview of the test questions, Banker emphatically denied being DGI and swore that he had turned in all of the money he had taken, was born on the date he claimed, had graduated from the Havana School of Business, and had met with a Communist union leader in Spain. Subsequent testing failed to support four of his claims. The only question he "passed," was his "no" answer to the question, "Have you ever been a member of the DGI?"

Banker's reaction when he answered, "Yes," to the question, "Did you turn in all of the money you took from the embassy?" was the most significant and consistent on the test, and I forcefully confronted him on this issue. For approximately an hour, he held out, but when I told him that I was convinced that he had put some money in a Swiss bank account, he said, "Even if I did, you can't make me give it back." At that point, I knew I had him. I advised him that stealing that money made him a thief and not a political refugee: "If the Cubans ask for you to be extradited, we will send you back."

"You guys would never do that," Banker replied.

We were at loggerheads until Harris took Banker and his wife to Dulles Airport to put them on a plane destined for Canada. At that point Banker admitted to stealing $100,000 and putting $75,000 in a Swiss bank account. Subsequently, Banker admitted to lying about his age because he had told his wife he was ten years younger than he really was. He also admitted that his story about graduating from the Havana School of Business was a lie. He said he had been in the Cuban Merchant Marine, at sea, when Fidel Castro gained power. When he returned to Cuba, he wanted to join the Foreign Service and knew that the Cuban foreign service looked favorably on the Havana School of Business as a source of administrators. After Castro's takeover, the school had closed, and most of the faculty had fled to the United States. Thus, Banker thought (and was right) that the Castro government, which was hard-pressed to staff its foreign embassies, would not be able to verify his claim of having graduated from the Havana School of Business. I was unable to get Banker to recant his story about meeting the Communist union official in Spain.

Ward was pleased with the results of the test. Wally D'Ansera wasn't. COG did make use of Banker for several years, until he was arrested for income tax evasion.

Banker had lived a lie for most of his life, and according to the lore about Cubans and polygraph, he should not have had significant reactions to his polygraph questions. He was also an amoral person and certainly felt no guilt about lying to us. But he was afraid of what might happen if he were caught in a lie and so the test worked on him as it does on most people.

Tests usually wouldn't be challenged if a subject made an admission, but the overwhelming majority of Cuban assets failed their polygraph tests without making admissions. One of the more prominent Cuban agents, whom I will call "Foul Ball," walked into a U.S. embassy, claimed to be DGI, and offered to work for the CIA. Dick Harris interviewed him, concluded that the DGI was directing the man, and recommended that the CIA not use him. John Weir, a highly regarded case officer, was asked to handle Foul Ball—who turned out to be a real foul ball. Foul Ball failed three polygraph tests, and on one occasion, Weir confronted me and asked me why his asset kept failing his tests. "Because he is a double agent and lying," I answered. I found it interesting that Weir was given a $10,000 cash award for handling Foul Ball, and Harris, who had recommended that we not take Foul Ball (and was subsequently proved to be right), was given no recognition.

Mainly because of Foul Ball, the Cuban Operations Group invited Milenski; "Al Tremayne," an excellent examiner who had been named

Polygraph Division's chief of ops; and "Al Serrano" to attend a COG conference held at the Farm. Milenski, Tremayne, and Serrano thought that they were being invited to the conference to discuss polygraph and come up with ways to improve Cuban asset testing. They were wrong.

COG used the meeting to blindside and viciously attack polygraph, repeating the mantra that the examiners "had to be wrong" because "not all of their agents could be bad." They charged that polygraph examiners were "headhunters," looking to make a name for themselves, that the examiners knew next to nothing about Cubans or DO operations, and that the examiners' incompetence was doing serious damage to COG's mission, as well as to the morale of its case officers. This was the most serious attack DO ever mounted against polygraph, and it colored relations between examiners and DO case officers for years. The "they can't all be bad" refrain was repeated after 90 percent of the assets recruited by the Iranian task force formed after the 1979 embassy takeover in Tehran failed their polygraph tests.

COG attacked polygraph after Foul Ball in part because some of their Cuban assets were providing very good information. It is one thing to call an asset who isn't providing any worthwhile information bad, and quite another to claim that an asset who is providing good information is bad. The DGI was very smart in that it was giving its double agents good and even damaging information to pass to the CIA in order to establish bona fides. Examiners who tested the Cubans, for the most part, acknowledged that bad agents don't give good information but stuck to their guns regarding the calls they made on their tests. My impression was that Falcone was actually sympathetic to the DO case officers, and because of that, he stayed away from the fray between IRD and COG.

Falcone was a bit puritanical, and if he found out during a test that his subject was an adulterer, the subject most likely would not pass his or her test. On one occasion, Falcone actually got down on his knees and prayed with a subject in order to get a confession. It worked. He railed against birth control (he had had eight kids; two had died in infancy) and would get apoplectic about abortion.

My travel helped keep me out of Falcone's line of fire but, occasionally, even that didn't help. One of the DO desk officers I had worked with in Vietnam requested that IRD send me to a denied area—that is, a country considered hostile and in which we have no embassy—to conduct a test. A local had contacted a CIA officer there, telling him that he had information about a planned assassination. No polygraph test had ever been run in this country, and thus some logistical problems needed to be worked out before the subject could be tested. When Falcone showed me the request, I jumped at the opportunity. Before I left, Falcone took me into his office and offered me a chance to back out of going.

"I'll go, John. You don't have to go. You can just stay home with your family," said Falcone.

"Lou, this is what I came here to do, and I want to go," I answered.

To be fair to Falcone, I think it was a case of his not having much faith in me as an examiner as much as it was his wanting what could have been a high-profile case.

I arrived in country on a Friday night and left the next Friday. In the interim, I tested the man and concluded that the assassination plot was actually in the works. My report ended up on the president's desk.

At 7:00 the following Monday morning, I walked into my office to find Ken Haneda waiting for me. He seemed upset, and his first words to me were, "Didn't you see Gambino's cable?"

"No. What cable?" I asked.

"Gambino sent a cable ordering you not to do the test. He thought this was some kind of trap and that you were going to get wrapped up," Haneda answered.

"I never saw the cable," I answered.

I had the impression that Haneda didn't believe me, probably because of the switchblade incident (described in chapter 4), and thought I had taken an unnecessary risk. After reviewing the charts I had run during the test, Falcone verified my no deception call, but didn't offer a "Welcome home, John! Good job!"

Not to be outdone, Falcone jumped on the very next high-profile case. An American ambassador had been slain, and his chauffeur was a suspect. The local police asked for the CIA's help, and it was suggested that the chauffeur be polygraphed. Falcone did the test and cleared the chauffeur. When I saw the charts, I couldn't believe that Falcone had passed the man. The charts were "flat," i.e., they didn't show any reactions, and I would have called the test inconclusive.

While in country for the chauffeur's test, Falcone worked with a female case officer, "Freda Karl," who apparently made a great impression on him. Falcone came back from that trip raving about her, describing her as very tough and competent. Less than two months after Falcone's return, Karl's boss sent her home for misconduct. Her division chief in headquarters wanted to fire her, but Karl claimed that she had been falsely accused and agreed to take a polygraph test.

I had a reputation in IRD for being an easygoing examiner, and that's what Falcone wanted for this test. When he assigned me the case, he told me that he would be surprised if I had any problems with Karl.

I had no doubt that Falcone was trying to influence my call, and I resented it, but I also decided that if Karl lied during the test, I would get an admission from her.

The charts I ran for Karl's initial testing were very erratic and hard to read, and her behavior was terrible. I was convinced that she was lying and excused myself from the room to discuss the case with Falcone and Milenski. I told them that I wanted to interrogate Karl, and Milenski said, "Go to it." Falcone didn't say anything.

Discounting operational tests, my interrogation of Karl was one of the more intense I had ever conducted. I told her that I believed that she was lying and that if she thought she was going to lie to me and get away with it, she had another think coming. Karl tried to stare me down and then asked to go to the ladies room. A female examiner who had been monitoring the test followed her into the ladies room and found her crying. When she returned, she made a complete confession.

When I left the room to inform Milenski and Falcone of the test results, I saw Milenski waiting in the corridor. He had a big grin on his face and was telling me what a great job I had done. I briefed Falcone, who made no comment. My impression was that he was sorry that he had assigned the case to me. Milenski's praise let me know that the hard line, when successful, is the way to do tests. Approximately one year later, I took a junior examiner on his training trip to Latin America. Karl met the plane, and although I recognized her immediately, she introduced herself to me as if it were the first time we had ever met. Karl was to be our chauffeur while we were in country and would drive us to and from our test sites.

On our second day in country, she picked me up at the hotel, and on the way to the test site, she stopped at a butcher shop owned by two Lebanese refugees. I went into the shop with her and was more than a little surprised by the way she gave her order.

"Guys, tonight, Senator Tower [Senator John Tower of Texas], the ambassador, and a congressional delegation are coming to my house for a cookout. Make sure the meat you send over is good," she said to the butcher.

Back in the car, I said, "Freda, why in hell did you tell them who was going to be at your house tonight?"

"Oh, John, those guys aren't bad guys. Relax."

It was hard for me to believe that a supposedly experienced case officer would do what I had just seen Karl do. There were frequent terrorist acts in the city as well as anti-American sentiment, and Karl's party would have been a very inviting target.

A few years later Karl applied for a position as a polygraph examiner. At the time she applied, I was not aware that she was applying and gave no input to the panel that interviewed her. But, one afternoon I was walking through the reception area as Karl was leaving. We exchanged greetings, and I asked her, "Freda, what are you doing here?"

"I just interviewed for a job with you guys," she answered.

When I talked to Al Tremayne, who had chaired the panel that had interviewed Karl, he said, "She was, without a doubt, the worst candidate I have ever interviewed." Karl was not hired.

Two weeks later "Mike Krohl" came into my office and asked, "John, what in hell is going on here? I just put you in for a QSI, and Lou told me that I would have to put 'Tom Dennis' in for an award before I put you in for one. I don't know Tom very well and don't know what I could cite to put him in for an award." (Recently, I was speaking with Dennis and mentioned this incident. Dennis commented that he had always wondered why he had gotten that award and went on to say that Falcone had recruited him and that "Lou felt responsible for me and took good care of me.")

Krohl was a GS-14 who had come to IRD to do much of the division's administrative work: scheduling tests, compiling statistics, and reviewing reports before they were released. He was having a little trouble scheduling tests, and I took over the task for him. I would read the files, match the subject with an examiner, and assign the next day's tests. My help and the Freda Karl test were the reasons Krohl had decided to pursue an award for me. After Dennis was awarded, Krohl put me in for one, which I received.

Because of my success with Karl I was asked to conduct other specific issue polygraph tests on employees. On one occasion Dennis came to me, saying, "John, a case officer whom I know has been accused of having a sexual relationship with one of his agents. He denies it, and his boss wants him polygraphed. Would you mind doing it?" This was not the kind of test I liked to do, but I told Dennis I would take the case. During the test the case officer admitted that he had had a sexual relationship with his agent. The case officer was not happy with me for having gotten the admission from him and left IRD in a foul mood.

Gambino, for some reason, had taken an interest in this case, and when he read the results of my test, he called me into his office. Apparently, two very senior DO officers had wanted the Office of Security to take action against the case officer if the allegation made against him proved to be true. "John, I want you to go brief these two guys, and what I want you to tell them is that this is a management problem and not a security problem," Gambino said. There had been no indication that the case officer had compromised anything but his integrity, and Gambino felt that didn't come within OS's purview. When I briefed the two men, both were upset but had no choice but to accept Gambino's dictum.

Falcone continued to be a cross to bear, but one of the things that made working with him bearable was that in 1978 he hired "Sara Friend" as a polygraph instrument technician. He sent her to Stoelting in Chicago to be trained in the maintenance of the Stoelting instruments the examiners were using. Sara had been a former CIA secretary who resigned when she began raising a family. When her sixth child started school, she came back to work. I found her to be competent, caring, and classy. Each year she hosted a Christmas party for IRD that drew well-deserved raves. I dubbed Sara "the Hostess with the Mostest," a la Perle Mesta, and it was an appropriate appellation. Sara knew more people in OS than anyone and was very gracious in helping me get to know many of OS's power brokers. When I retired, I numbered Sara among my dearest friends.

In the summer of 1979 Milenski had asked me to retest an applicant whom another examiner had tested. The original examiner was sent out of the office while I did the test. During the test I got enough information to disqualify the applicant and coincidentally found out that the original examiner had fabricated his report. That examiner was never told that his subject was retested, and to my knowledge he was never confronted about the fact that he had fabricated a report. The incident didn't seem to hurt his career as evidenced by the fact that he eventually became a supervisor and a GS-15 in IRD.

That incident made me wonder if any of my tests were being redone. With as much traveling as I did at the time, retesting my subjects while I was on the road would have been easy. I had to find some reason why Falcone was so down on me, and this seemed to be a possibility. I went to Milenski with my concern, asking, "Greg, am I getting beat?" and "Are you having my tests redone like the test you asked me to do over?" Milenski answered "no" to both questions, and I believed him only because, given my less than cordial relationship with Falcone, I felt that he would have welcomed the chance to find an excuse to get rid of me.

No matter what I did, Falcone found fault. On one occasion a good friend in SOG, "Eamon Dailey," came in for his RIP test. Dailey was in his sixties, a typical Irish bachelor (religious, celibate, devoted to his mother, etc.), and a nice man. "Bob Fester" tested him on a Friday morning, and Dailey had some problems. The following Monday morning "Caesar Cervone," a good friend from Vietnam and a member of SOG, approached me in the cafeteria. "John, we're kind of worried about Eamon. He came back from his test on Friday very upset and left for the day. He hasn't come in this morning." I told Cervone that I would look into it.

As soon as I got back to the office, I went to see Fester. Just as he and I decided that we had better brief Falcone, Falcone came down the corridor, asking in a loud voice, "What's the story on this guy Eamon Dailey?" Apparently, the chief of SOG had called Gambino regarding his concern about Dailey, and Gambino had called Falcone. I told Falcone what Cervone had told me, and Falcone became angry. "You can't discuss a polygraph test with anyone outside this office," he almost shouted. Without waiting for an explanation, Falcone stormed back to his office. He then called the chief of SOG and blistered Cervone for asking me about Dailey.

Later that day Cervone came to see me. "John, I just got chewed out for asking you about Eamon," he said. He also said that he thought he had done the right thing. He had. I was embarrassed and apologized to him. Falcone's temper had once again gotten the better of him.

Shortly after the Dailey incident, Milenski asked me to test a woman for the third time because during her first two RIP tests, each with a different examiner, she had produced very erratic charts. As I previously noted, I had a reputation in IRD for lacking the killer instinct and going too easy on subjects. In police or criminal testing venues, my method surely wouldn't cut it, but the CIA clientele was a little different and, in many of the tests I conducted, a softer approach was more effective, as this case demonstrated. The woman, whom I will call "Stella Hodek," had been with the Agency for more than ten years. Before testing her, I took a look at her EOD charts, which were of very poor quality and at best inconclusive. Fox had signed off on them—in the era before quality control.

When I brought Hodek into the testing room, she was very nervous, but when I began speaking to her in Russian, she visibly relaxed and, when she found out that one of my Russian teachers was a good friend of hers, she started to talk to me as if I were a long lost son. After about a half hour of pleasantries, I said, "Ms. Hodek, clearly when you came in for your first two tests, you were very nervous. What's the problem?"

"Vanya [Russian for Johnny], when I came into the Agency, I lied about who I was. I completely falsified my application," she began. Hodek then told me that she had used a phony name and had lied about her place and date of birth. She had been born in Russia, not in Poland as she claimed, and she had concealed that she had been a member of the Communist Party. Hodek's rationale was, "If I told the truth, you never would have hired me."

The charts I ran looked much better than any of her previous charts, and I took them to Milenski. Milenski said that he didn't see anything, and we both went to brief Falcone.

No, "Nice job!" just, "Is she a spy?" said Falcone.

"I don't think so, but I don't know," I answered.

Falcone looked at the charts and said, "Let her go."

(A little over a year ago, I was talking with retired Russian KGB Maj. Gen. Oleg Kalugin, who headed the KGB's worldwide foreign counterintelligence. When I told him that I had studied Russian at the Army Language School in Monterey, California, he said, "We had three of the female instructors on our payroll." I am quite sure that Hodek's friend, my former instructor, was one of them. Did Hodek beat me? I don't think I will ever know.)

Regarding the Hodek case, I am certain that my "nice guy" approach coaxed Hodek to make the admissions that she did. Falcone, Milenski, Dennis, et al. may have thought I was too easy on the subjects in general, but whenever a high-profile case came in and required a gentler, kinder approach, it would most likely be assigned to me.

One of the more memorable of those high-profile cases was a test of a man with considerable political clout who was being hired by the CIA as a consultant. When I tested him, I obtained disqualifying information, wrote up my report, and thought no more about it. The night following the test Gambino called me at home. In my notes from the test, I had written, "I think I have enough, and given who he is, I don't want to push it." My impression was that Gambino had wished that I had gotten more information. In so many words, I told Gambino that anyone else who had admitted what this man had admitted to me would be disqualified. "I didn't want to embarrass him any more than I already had," I said. Gambino denied the man a security clearance, and my reputation of being too nice to get the job done grew.

Admissions such as Hodek's were rare in the RIP venue, and most of the admissions we obtained dealt with security violations—disclosing and removing classified information when not authorized to do so, leaving safes open, working on classified material at home, etc. Because we had admissions of this kind so frequently, random baggage checks were instituted. Security officers were stationed at each headquarters' exit to check departing employees' briefcases and pocketbooks. Employees never knew when a check was going to take place, and during the initial check, over eighty employees were found to be carrying classified material out of the building. On the second occasion, about forty were discovered. The third check was conducted as employees came to work, and I think fifteen or sixteen employees were found to be returning classified material. This program annoyed many people, occupied many security officers, and was shelved.

Every examiner has a list of his or her best tests. I am a bit disappointed to say that I conducted my best test twenty years before I retired.

I described the test in detail in my first book, *Of Spies and Lies*, and won't repeat it here. Let it suffice to say that I caught a Czech double agent who had been trained to beat the polygraph and who had been working for the FBI for four years.

When I brought the charts from that test to Falcone, his only comment was "You'd have gotten a lot better reactions if you hadn't previewed the questions with him." To skip the preview would have been an egregious breach of polygraph procedure; this seemed to have escaped Falcone.

Everything with Falcone was a crisis. One afternoon he called a meeting to announce, as he put it, "one of the most significant events in the history of CIA polygraph." His announcement was that, from that point on, examiners would have to get their reports in within three working days. It was as if someone had let the air out of a balloon when he finished.

Falcone made only one announcement that I felt was important, at a meeting in the summer of 1979. "Today, we just denied an applicant a security clearance based solely on the fact that she failed her polygraph test and made no admissions. This is the first time in the history of CIA polygraph that this has happened." This was a big deal. It had been Gambino's decision to deny the clearance, and based on my knowledge of the case, I had no doubt that it was the correct decision.

In one of the more positive acts of his tenure, Falcone initiated offsite conferences for the examiners. "Offsites" are three-day meetings outside of the headquarters area during which we took a break from testing, discussed polygraph, and listened to guest lecturers discuss common areas of interest. These seminars boosted morale and became annual events. At the very first offsite, held at the Farm, shortly after we finished dinner, we were sitting in the lounge when Falcone announced that he had a surprise for us: a Voice Stress Analyzer (VSA), which some touted as a replacement for the polygraph. Falcone started setting up the VSA, and many of the examiners started to leave. "Where are you guys going?" he asked.

"We're going fishing, Lou," they answered.

Falcone became upset, but no one came back. To those of us who either didn't have the courage to leave or were sincerely interested, Falcone gave a presentation on the use of the VSA. While at Reid, I had seen a demonstration of the machine, and although I was not impressed, I was also willing to be convinced that it worked. Falcone came across as a real proponent of the Voice Stress Analyzer during his presentation, but in the five tests he ran on five examiners, he failed to identify a single deceptive answer. That ended any further discussion about the VSA.

When we returned to headquarters, Falcone, without telling me, recorded one of my interviews and fed the recorded voice of my subject into the VSA. After the test, Falcone told me what he had done and noted that my conclusion, no deception, was the same conclusion he had reached using the VSA.

As a part of the offsites, Falcone invited Office of Security senior management to address examiners and take questions. Falcone knew that IRD was the Office of Security's Siberia, and he felt that having Office of Security managers join us for a few hours might dispel some of the alienation we felt. I enjoyed the offsites, but at one of them, I managed to dig my professional grave a bit deeper. The incident concerned a RIP test conducted several months earlier by "Ken Dorman" on a senior staff employee, "Raymond Beal." Beal had reacted strongly to the question about providing classified material to an unauthorized person. Initially, Beal denied having any problem with the question, and the elicitation turned into an interrogation. Ultimately, Dorman confronted Beal, and Beal admitted that he had shown a Soviet bloc diplomat a classified cable. Beal also admitted that he had had the diplomat as a guest in his house (in the United States) for two days without reporting it, as required.

Dorman did some additional testing, based on Beal's explanation, and concluded that Beal was still withholding information. Dorman confronted Beal, and Beal responded by telling Dorman that Dorman was going to have to find a way other than polygraph to resolve the problem. Beal then removed the attachments, got up out of the chair, and left. Beal's behavior was a rarity, and we all wondered what was going to happen. We fully expected him to be ordered to come back for additional testing, but this never happened.

At the next offsite, when the Office of Security managers asked if there were any questions, I described what had happened with Beal to Gambino and asked, "Why was he allowed to get away with it?" In response, Gambino turned to his deputies who were on the stage with him and said, "Why don't I know about this case?" It was obvious that Gambino had not been informed about Beal, and it became just as obvious that I had embarrassed some people who saw my question to Gambino as evidence not only of my naiveté but also of my disrespect for the chain of command. Making waves was a cardinal sin in the Office of Security, and those whom I had embarrassed were not about to grant me absolution.

Quality control also became an integral part of the CIA's polygraph program during Falcone's tenure. As necessary as I felt having a QC process in place was, it had its downside. QC became the tail that wagged the dog. When Milenski instituted a formalized QC program, his primary guideline to reviewers was, "Don't let the obvious reaction get through or go unchallenged." Somewhere along the way, the process went awry and getting charts that would satisfy a chart reviewer became a serious problem.

Adding to the problem, some of the chart reviewers did not have good reputations as examiners and many felt that they were put in reviewer positions to keep them from testing. "Mark Verity" was the exception. I had worked with Verity in Vietnam, thought he was the best examiner in IRD, and cannot recall one incident of any examiner challenging one of his reviews.

Chart reviewing is an inexact procedure. Some chart reviewers saw respiration tracing as the most significant factor in chart interpretation. Others saw cardio tracing as the most significant. Some reviewers would check charts with a ruler and magnifying glass, while others would just glance at them. Dealing with reviewers became more difficult than dealing with subjects and seriously compromised morale in the office. Knockdown, drag-out confrontations between examiners and chart reviewers became a fact of life in IRD, and on at least two occasions, I thought an examiner and chart reviewer were going to come to blows.

One of the newer examiners came up with a way to avoid such confrontations. During a test, he would ask a norm or irrelevant question and indicate on the chart that a relevant question had been asked. Verity, who had advanced from chart reviewer to team leader, suspected something was wrong with the examiner's tests and started to monitor him more closely. On one occasion when Verity was monitoring him, he wrote down the number of each question as it was asked. When Verity reviewed the charts of the test, he noticed that two relevant questions indicated on the charts had not been asked. Falcone booted the examiner out of IRD. That the examiner was allowed to remain employed by the Agency, let alone in the Office of Security, surprised me. To fire this examiner, the Office of Security would have had to air some dirty laundry and that was something OS didn't do. In OS public image was everything. To go public with the fact that a polygraph examiner had falsified a test would not only give OS a black eye, but could possibly jeopardize the polygraph program. When this incident occurred, I saw it as an aberration and not as a harbinger of things to come. I was wrong.

Outside of IRD and the Office of Security, events took place that, in the grand scheme of things, were far more significant than misconduct on the part of an examiner. Chief among these was the fall of the shah in Iran and the subsequent takeover of the U.S. embassy in Tehran. I had known and worked with two Agency people who had been taken hostage in the embassy, and Lee had worked with one of the communicators. "Cal Malcomson," one of the hostages taken during the takeover, had stopped in to see me just before he left for Tehran. I wished Cal good luck and told him to be careful. As it turned out, Cal had bad luck.

When confronted with the hostage crisis, President Carter blinked. I applauded Carter's decision to try and rescue the hostages but also feel that he should have given the hostage takers an ultimatum: "Release the hostages within 48 hours or face immediate and severe consequences."

Based on what DO colleagues have told me and what I have read, the Agency was caught completely flatfooted by the embassy takeover, mostly because it had no sources in the anti-shah factions. In Iran, the CIA's officers were prohibited from meeting with opposition groups, and I know of no contacts that Agency officers had with the exiled Ayatollah Khomeini or any other expatriate Iranian opposition groups. As a result, after the embassy takeover, the Agency had to play catch up in terms of getting information about the hostage takers. This turned out to be a massive effort that required much polygraph support.

We in IRD had no shortage of work after the embassy takeover, and aside from having to deal with Falcone, I was content. Work life improved even more when Falcone retired later that year. For a while after his retirement, he did some contract work for us, but after IRD's quality controllers overturned several of his tests, he terminated his contract. I last saw Falcone in 1984, at the funeral of a mutual friend at Arlington National Cemetery, and Falcone said hello to me but was rather cool. When Falcone died a few years ago, I was the only CIA person at his memorial service.

As difficult as Faclone's tenure had been for me, it was also a time of introspection and discovery. Falcone made me ask myself, "Is putting up with him worth the grief?" I decided that it was, and in looking inward, I made a few discoveries. I discovered that polygraph works, not as well as I would have liked, but much better than many of its critics claim, and that polygraph is much more an art than a science. I discovered that the CIA did a lot of good work and that most of the CIA people I worked with were good people who more than made up for the miscreants and misfits I encountered. I discovered that, in terms of my professional competence, I was much better at testing operational assets than I was at testing applicants. I had been trained as a case officer in the army, understood the agent handling/intelligence collection process, and was confident working in the operational environment. Along with that discovery came the realization that my abilities and successes in this venue were irrelevant to the Office of Security management. Finally, and perhaps most important, I discovered that the sense of accomplishment and satisfaction I reaped from my work was the only reason I needed to stay in polygraph and that liking what I did was more important than being liked for doing what I did. Lee was not aware of the problems I was having with Falcone but knew that I was not on any fast track for promotion. She also knew how much I liked my work and was very supportive.

With these thoughts in mind, I looked forward to working for Ken Haneda, Falcone's replacement. After Falcone, I needed to decompress and recharge my batteries. Haneda was to Falcone what Lawrence Welk was to Mick Jagger, and at that point in my career, I needed "Tiny Bubbles," not "I Can't Get No Satisfaction."

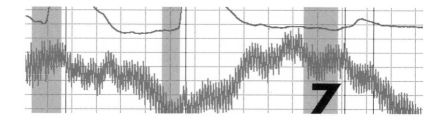

RESPITE

Bill Katopish, who replaced Gambino as the director of the Office of Security, had been a polygraph examiner and was a little more hands-on with the polygraph division than any of his predecessors had been. Katopish regularly read polygraph reports and occasionally made administrative decisions based on information developed during tests.

In one such case, an employee, during RIP testing, offered an explanation for a reaction to the question about contact with foreign nationals, saying that he and his wife would go out looking for hitchhikers with whom his wife could have sex. If necessary, he would pay the hitchhiker to have sex with his wife while he watched. The subject said that he thought some of the men they picked up might have been foreign nationals, but he wasn't sure. This couple would also advertise to find partners for group sex activities. Katopish sent a memo to IRD saying that any acknowledgment of group sex or solicitation for group sex should be pursued and was reportable.

Katopish appointed Ken Haneda to be chief of IRD, an unusual move because Haneda was not an Office of Security careerist. Haneda told me, "It just about killed Katopish to give me the job." Haneda had been a line examiner at the time I entered on duty and was a real gentleman. A Nisei born in American Samoa, Haneda was also a retired U.S. Army lieutenant colonel. Prior to becoming Falcone's deputy, Haneda had been chief of the covert desk.

On a personal level, Haneda and I got along well, but he did have a bone to pick with me. He was a bit of a neatness freak, whereas I wasn't, and my office would not have earned the Good Housekeeping Seal of Approval. Haneda occasionally noted that, as the senior examiner in the office, I should set an example. Haneda never really pushed it, but I recognized that I didn't fit his image of what a manager should be and knew that he never supported me for a promotion.

During Haneda's tour as chief of the covert desk, he and I did have one encounter that influenced our relationship. I had been doing a lot of overseas TDYs, most of which were in Africa. While I prepared for one of these trips to Africa, the deputy chief of IRD announced at a staff meeting that Jim Doom would replace me on the trip. I had pretty much had my fill of West Africa and was even a little relieved upon hearing this news. After the meeting, Doom approached me and said, "I thought you were going to Africa."

"I did too," I said.

"Do you want to go?" Doom asked.

"I don't really care, Jim."

"Will you go?" Doom asked next.

Doom had recently been beaten on an overseas trip. I don't know whether that was his reason for turning down this opportunity, but it was obvious that he didn't want to go. I told him that I'd take the trip, but only if he approached Haneda and told him that he didn't want to take the trip and had asked me to take it. Doom agreed. A few minutes later Haneda's secretary came to my office and said that Haneda wanted to see me. Haneda read me the riot act. "If you want a trip, just ask. You're the senior examiner. You don't have to go behind my back. Jim said that you wanted this trip." I told Haneda what had really happened, but I don't think he believed me. I went on the trip but left knowing that I had probably put another nail in my coffin. Doom had repeated to Falcone my comment about Falcone being jealous of him, and now he had told Haneda that I had asked to take his place on a trip. Neither of these incidents did anything to help my career, and they forever colored my relationship with Doom.

During Haneda's tenure I received my first Exceptional Performance Award. As I mentioned earlier, applicants' admissions of drug use had increased almost fourfold by the time I returned from Vietnam. Two or three applicants a day admitted drug use. Many of the applicants who had admitted minor drug use (the most common drug-related admission) were hired. However, writing up the reports for minor drug use took as much time as writing the reports on major, disqualifying drug use.

It occurred to me that a simple, fill-in-the-blanks form for reporting minor drug use would save examiners a lot of time. I wrote out a sample form, submitted it, and had it approved. Over the next year two or three of those forms were submitted each day, saving secretaries considerable time and effort.

At the end of that first year, I wrote myself up for an award for having suggested the use of the new form. I hadn't known the award for making work-saving suggestions existed until one of my colleagues received it for suggesting that signs be put in Agency busses saying, "Don't discuss classified information." I thought that my suggestion was every bit as good as that one.

Two months later, at an Office of Security staff meeting, Bob Gambino presented me with a $250 Exceptional Performance Award for the suggestion. After taxes, the award amounted to $175, but I was glad to get it. My pleasure was somewhat diminished when an Office of Security officer made it a point to tell me that getting an award for simply doing my job was a prostitution of the awards process.

At the time Haneda took over IRD, the push was on for industrial contractor testing. The damage assessment done after the Boyce-- Lee case showed how easy it was for foreign agents to access the CIA's high-tech people and set off alarms. Five days a week in any of a hundred bars in and around Redondo Beach, California, anyone who wanted to could rub elbows with people working on the CIA's most sensitive projects. It was estimated that between fifteen thousand and twenty thousand contractors needed to be tested.

In 1980 IRD, which was soon to become Polygraph Division (PD), did not have the resources to adequately support an industrial polygraph program, and the decision was made to send two-man teams of examiners to TRW in California and E-Systems in Texas to get the programs started. Another examiner and I went out to TRW on one of the first trips. Introducing polygraph tests into an environment where there has been no previous experience with polygraph is difficult, but I found it less so than I had anticipated. Most of the derogatory information we obtained involved the mishandling of classified information and none of it was significant. Only one test I did was significant in that it pointed out a lapse in the CIA's security-screening process.

On my second day of testing the man I was to test that morning appeared to be extremely nervous. My pretests can vary in length depending on my initial impression of a subject; if I see that the subject is more nervous than usual, I take a little more time trying to settle him or her down. I had talked with the subject for about half an hour in an attempt to calm him down when he held up his hand and said, "I came in here, intending to lie to you, but I just can't do it. I'm gay." The man further advised that when he and his wife acknowledged that he was living a lie, they agreed to separate. He and his partner had been living together for almost a year. When I asked how his wife and children were adjusting, he said that he and his wife still got along very well but that they hadn't told their children about his homosexuality. He also said that there was no way he could ever be blackmailed because of his homosexuality.

This man's BI had been completed less than three weeks before our interview. He had been living apart from his family in an open relationship with another male for almost a year. He was described in the BI as an "outstanding family man," and there was no mention of his current living arrangement. This is another incident in which a polygraph test uncovered derogatory information that the background investigator had missed. I never learned whether or not this man had his clearances rescinded, but I hoped that he didn't.

Before Haneda retired, I worked on two of my more interesting cases. One involved a Soviet illegal who had written a letter to DCI Turner stating that he wanted to turn himself in. Arrangements were made to set up a contact with the letter writer, and the FBI was brought in on the case. The illegal's bona fides were established, and I was asked to test him. At the time I tested him, the illegal was in the FBI's custody. When I met with the FBI agent who was handling the illegal, one of the first things the agent said was that he had never done anything like this and didn't have a clue as to how to handle agents. I used an alias with the illegal, and when I introduced myself, he said, "You have to do something. That guy [the FBI agent] doesn't know what he is doing, and he is going to get me killed." The illegal passed his test, but I have no idea what happened to him.

Stan Levchenko, a Soviet KGB defector, was the subject of the other memorable test I did during Haneda's reign. Levchenko had defected in Tokyo and was proving to be a goldmine, but to ensure that his information was credible he had to be tested. My test of Levchenko took two days, and I was pleased with the results. But more significant was the impression Levchenko made on me.

I began my interview with him in Russian, and we had been speaking for about five minutes when he said, "You learned your Russian in Germany, but you are Irish." I don't know how many CIA case officers would have been able to make that kind of assessment in so short a time. My thought was, "If this is the kind of case officer the KGB has working for them, we have a formidable enemy."

During Haneda's tenure our newly trained Reid examiners started conducting tests. Before the new examiners were allowed to begin testing, they were assigned to conduct the pretests for the other line examiners, after which they would turn the subject over to the line examiner who conducted the actual test.

"Wayne Teller" was one of the new examiners whose pretest I monitored. After the pretest, Teller said that he thought the subject was the original All-American boy. "This kid looks like a black Adonis. He is a member of USMC Eighth and I Ceremonial Drill Team and is applying for a job as a guard."

I had read the subject's file. He was six feet two inches tall, weighed 190 pounds, and could serve as a model for a U.S. Marine Corps recruiting poster. The only item in his application that struck me as odd was that he had not mentioned being a member of any kind of athletic team. During testing the subject had no problem with the counterintelligence questions, but when I ran the first chart of the lifestyle questions, he had a very strong reaction to the question about homosexual activity. When I saw the reaction, I did something I cannot recall ever having done before; I stopped the test and confronted the subject.

"You're clearly having a problem with this question. What is it?" I asked.

"I thought I could beat this test, but I guess I can't," the subject immediately replied. He continued, "I'm gay, and I guess I have to forget about this job."

I felt bad knowing that this young man was not going to be hired, but occasionally, subjects who had been honest and forthright during their polygraph tests were penalized for their candor, and dealing with such situations was part of the job.

The only admission of murder I ever obtained from an applicant occurred during a pretest. In response to the question about having committed a serious crime, the subject said, "Well, yeah, I killed somebody once." When I asked for details, the man said that he had stabbed a man in a fight and was pretty sure he had killed him.

Occasionally, subjects volunteered information before I even asked a question. One such incident occurred when the wife of an employee came in for her RIP test. I had no sooner taken her coat and asked her to sit down when she said, "Before we go any further, I want to tell you right now that I am cheating on my husband."

I was getting admissions, traveling, and for the most part, enjoying life while working for Haneda. I didn't see a promotion over the horizon, but I really didn't care. At home, Lee and I had two sons with whom we were enthralled. Life was good and about to get a little more interesting.

The agents I had tested in Vietnam were much different than those I dealt with in the United States. In Vietnam, many of my subjects were unsophisticated, sometimes almost illiterate, peasants. In the United States, I worked with diplomats, academicians, scientists, and international businessmen. There were also the Mata Haris or Mata Hari wannabes. During Haneda's tenure I tested a woman whom I will forever remember as Mata Hari.

One of the residual effects of my Vietnam experience was that on occasion DO officers I had worked with in Vietnam would contact me directly and ask me to do cases. "Stan Konec" was one of these officers. Konec called one day and said, "I have a favor to ask." He said that one of his subordinates was running an agent with great access to Russian and Red Chinese diplomats.

"John, this lady is East European, an absolute knockout, and she has given us some good stuff. I want you to find out if she is a 'dangle' or just selling information to the highest bidder," Konec said.

The day before I left to do the test, Konec asked me to come up to his office. "Could you do me another favor?" he asked. "Find out if 'Chuck Hary' [the agent's case officer] is sleeping with her." This is not that uncommon a request, but complying with such requests jeopardized my rapport with case officers. Because I knew Hary from his bad reputation for incompetence and drinking, I told Konec that I would find out for him.

When I met with him before the test, he was quite affable. He gave me a rundown on his agent. "John, she is beautiful, bright, but a little naive," he said.

"This is one very good looking lady. Are you involved with her?" I asked. To make his point as to how beautiful the lady was, he showed me a picture of her. The lady was indeed beautiful. "Wait 'til you see her. She just doesn't give off any sexual vibes," he answered —not a righteously indignant "no" but an evasive answer.

Hary then gave me the key to the hotel room where I would conduct the test and told me to go up to the room and wait for the subject. Just as advertised, the agent was a very beautiful lady. She spoke fluent English and neither voiced any objection to taking the test nor seemed nervous. She was well dressed, coiffed, and made up. As I was talking with her, the word that came to mind was "courtesan."

When I asked her if she were ready to start, she said, "Let's go."

"Please take off your jacket," I said. When she complied, I noticed that she was wearing a see-through blouse and no bra. I was distracted but managed to get through the test, which she passed. Hary's comment that this woman didn't give off any sexual vibes was right up there with "The check's in the mail" and "Read my lips, no new taxes."

I told Konec that Hary denied having sex with the agent but that I had little doubt that he was. Konec replied, "If he isn't, he is one of a rather small minority."

Unfortunately, the agent went back home for a visit, and during a search at the airport, compromising information was found in her belongings. She was arrested for espionage and spent five years in jail. We bought her out of prison, and she relocated to the United States.

In 1980 the issue of whether or not the CIA should conduct polygraph examinations before BIs was still being discussed. In December 1980 an event took place that influenced that decision: A fairly junior examiner was sent to Philadelphia to test twenty-five applicants who hadn't yet been investigated. The polygraph examiner developed disqualifying information on twenty-four of the applicants. The twenty-fifth applicant's test ended with some issues unresolved, and the applicant was invited to Washington for additional testing. During the applicant's polygraph examination at headquarters, disqualifying information was developed. Not having to conduct BIs on twenty-five applicants and/or not having to bring them to the Washington, D.C., area saved the CIA, by a conservative estimate, over $100,000. This was pretty conclusive evidence that doing the polygraph test before the BI was an idea whose time had come.

Haneda's tenure was short, and in looking at the overall history of polygraph in the CIA, it might not stand out as a time of great accomplishments. However, examiners who served in IRD during that period felt it was a good one. Examiners were returning from training at Reid, confident in their abilities as examiners and with more faith in the process, and as a result the overall quality of IRD's product was improving. In addition, IRD was working on a system whereby polygraph charts could be numerically scored in the hope of making chart interpretation more objective. A numerical value was assigned to each reaction for every question on a test, and at the end of the test, each question was scored. Answers to questions with the highest scores were deemed unresolved until additional testing and/or interrogation had been done. Another positive change during Haneda's tenure was the raising of standards for IRD applicants. IRD also received fewer rejects from other offices within the Office of Security during this time. And there was less tension in the office. Compared with Falcone's melodramatic m.o., Haneda was low key in his management style, and in an environment as stressful as PD, this was a big plus.

On a daily basis, polygraph examiners undergo much stress. Confronting subjects, being second-guessed by chart reviewers (and oneself), and conducting two or three tests a day take their toll. Surprisingly, turnover was low during Haneda's tenure, and I can recall only one examiner leaving IRD.

Haneda never said it to me, but I got the impression that he felt like the odd man out in the Office of Security's hierarchy. As parochial as the Office of Security was at that time, I think he was correct, and this was one of the reasons he retired. After Falcone, Haneda was a breath of fresh air, and I knew I would miss him.

On a personal level, I was pleased with some of the tests I had conducted, most of which had been done in the operational arena; this, as I mentioned previously, meant nothing to the Office of Security. Most managers in the Office of Security saw me as a polygraph examiner and not a security officer, and in looking back, I see that as a compliment in the sense that I felt that as a polygraph examiner I did as much to protect the Agency than any security officer did.

Also, several of my subjects wrote letters to the Office of Security expressing appreciation for the way in which I handled their polygraph tests, and several DO managers had commended me for operational tests that I had conducted. One might think that such accolades were a positive, but at that time they weren't, and they were more often than not viewed with skepticism. In my case, these accolades were seen as another indication that I might have been too nice of a guy for the job.

Some skeptics felt that unless examiners received complaints, they weren't doing their job and that a polygraph subject sends a laudatory letter to an examiner for only two reasons: (1) the examiner had been too easy on the subject and (2) the subject was grateful for having lied and gotten away with it. I had obtained enough admissions to reject the latter reason, but I also felt that the former was at the heart of polygraph's very poor image.

I often questioned my own ability as an examiner and wondered how many times I had been beaten. An accurate number of subjects who beat me is probably around eight hundred, but, in truth, I know of only eight.

As Haneda's reign came to an end, I still felt that polygraph was the right place for me. I hadn't lost my enthusiasm for the job and thought the work was important, and although I knew that I had some weaknesses, I felt that I also had some strengths. I obtained my share of admissions, never caused a complaint, was good with recalcitrant and/or nervous subjects, rarely took a day of sick leave, and was a low maintenance employee.

By 1980 I had been in polygraph for twelve years, was a GS-13, and could think of nothing else in the Office of Security that I wanted to do. Other jobs in Security paled in comparison with polygraph, and I saw no reason to leave.

When Katopish announced that "Pat Meager" would succeed Haneda, I wished that Katopish had named someone with polygraph experience and preferably from within IRD. I knew Meager had no polygraph experience and hoped that this would not be a problem. Just before Meager took over, IRD became PD (Polygraph Division). This was an acknowledgment of the polygraph program's recent growth and also resulted in the increase in the number GS-14 and GS-15 positions in the office. Polygraph was no longer a dead-end assignment, and I thought that boded well for PD.

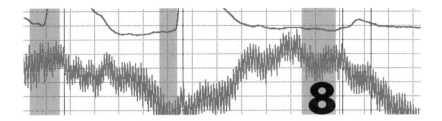

THE NEW BREED

My only contact with Pat Meager prior to his being named chief of the Polygraph Division took place when I was processing to go to Vietnam. Meager was the East Asia Division security officer who gave me a briefing before I left. The contact was very fleeting and left no lasting impression. Between the time I returned from Vietnam and the time Meager was appointed chief of PD, I occasionally ran into him, and I was always surprised when he called me by my first name.

Meager's lack of polygraph experience turned out to be a problem. Bill Osborne had had no previous polygraph experience and had been a disaster. As much as I disliked Falcone, he had been a polygraph examiner and had helped set the stage for significant improvements in the polygraph program. Many of those improvements came into play during Haneda's tenure, and we were concerned that under Meager this trend would not continue. We were told that Meager had been selected to be chief of PD because of a recommendation made by the Church Committee that a nonpolygraph person run the division.

Meager got off to a rather inauspicious start. At his first all-hands meeting, he made it clear that he didn't know much about polygraph and that he didn't think that was particularly important. He also made some disparaging remarks about polygraph that led me to conclude that he was not going to be an advocate for PD. I remember that after that meeting, Milenski said, "I don't know, John. I think he just trashed my life's work."

Had Meager come into PD before we started sending examiners to Reid, I think his impact might have been different in the sense that his lack of knowledge about polygraph would not have been so noticeable. In that first meeting, Meager was addressing a group of Young Turks who believed in polygraph and who for the most part were there because they wanted to be there—not the examiners of the past who were in PD because they had no place else to go. As more Reid-trained examiners came into PD, the way tests were conducted changed significantly, PD's image changed, and Agency polygraph became a whole new ballgame.

One of the first issues Meager addressed was the quality of examiners' reports. He noted a "paucity" of good writing and cited poor spelling, grammar, and syntax in the reports he was reading. This turned out to be one of the issues he and I agreed on. PD examiners who were in place when I entered on duty may have had some deficiencies, but writing was not among them, and I was unpleasantly surprised by how poorly the newer examiners wrote. I can't recall ever being asked to rewrite a report, but on one occasion I did have a run-in with Meager about one of my reports that set off alarms.

During a female applicant's test, I previewed the question on homosexual activity, and her response was not a yes or a no, but, "Why do you want to know?" When I explained to her that the Agency viewed homosexual activity as a vulnerability, the woman advised me that she had been in a homosexual relationship with her current lover for four months. The woman also volunteered that this was her second homosexual relationship and that it had begun after the breakup of a long-term homosexual relationship. She also advised that she and her lover were roommates in a house that they shared.

"Are you and your partner sleeping in the same bed?" I asked.

"Yes," she answered, and I moved on to other issues.

In addition to reportable information on homosexual activity, I developed significant information about thefts from an employer that I felt certain would disqualify her. I wrote up my report and thought nothing about it until Rob Creed brought the report to me. "Pat wants you to include a statement in your report saying that you mistakenly didn't ask this woman if she knew what homosexuality meant," Creed instructed me. I took the report to Meager and asked for an explanation.

"There is a chance that she may not have known what homosexual activity was, and since you didn't ask her to describe the particular activities in which she and her lover engaged, we can't be sure that what they did was homosexual activity," he explained. "Describe the sexual activities!! Are you kidding me? I don't write my reports to titillate the prurient interests of Clearance Division," I said.

I was a bit surprised by Meager's criticism. First, because I couldn't believe that anyone who read my report could conclude that the woman did not know what homosexual activity was and second, because the woman's admissions of theft made the homosexual activity a non-issue.

Meager then made it very clear that I needed to acknowledge my mistake in the report, and that was that. When I left Meager's office, I was furious. I had developed enough information on crime to disqualify

this woman and couldn't understand why Meager was making homosexual activity an issue. His comments about getting the details of the
sexual activities in which the woman and her partner engaged were, in
my opinion, completely out of line, and it concerned me, but as I was to
learn, Meager very much liked prurient details.

Meager reminded me of the type of priest I disliked as a kid—pompous, self-righteous, puritanical, and devoid of a sense of humor. Not long
after his arrival, one of our married examiners began an affair with one
of our secretaries. Meager called the examiner in and told the examiner
that, if he (Meager) had his say, the examiner would be fired. On another
occasion, a recently divorced examiner began dating another examiner.
Meager called both of them into his office and told them that they could
not live together until they were married. In another edict, Meager decreed that anytime a secretary was in an examiner's office, the door had
to be open. Most of us found this insulting. Two concepts that Meager
had difficulty grasping were that polygraph works and that people do lie.
Early on in his tenure I heard him discussing a test with Grant Rollins.
Rollins had engaged in a long interrogation of a subject, and Meager
thought that Rollins had gone after the subject a little too hard. Meager
summed up his comments to Rollins by saying that he thought the subject sounded honest and that Rollins should have let him go. "But Pat,
the kid admitted that he had been using drugs and had been lying to me,"
replied Rollins. Meager hadn't heard the end of Rollins's interrogation.
Meager spun around and walked away without another word.

Meager's arrival in PD preceded by about a month the departure of
DCI Stansfield Turner. President Ronald Reagan named Bill Casey to
replace Turner. In January 1981 William Joseph "Bill" Casey, the former
chairman of the Securities and Exchange Commission, was sworn in as
the fourteenth director of central intelligence. Some defined his tenure
as the most tumultuous years in the CIA's history. On the two occasions
that I saw Casey up close and personal, he impressed me as being one of
those larger-than-life individuals around whom action swirls.

One of Casey's mandates was to repair the damage done to the
Agency by the excesses of the Church and Pike committees' investigations and Turner's reign. Morale, particularly in the DO, had plummeted
during Turner's tenure, and clandestine operations had been relegated
to a backburner. Casey, with his Office of Strategic Services (OSS) background, was partial to covert operations, and initially, some thought his
arrival boded well for the DO. Those views began to change when Casey
named Max Hugel to be the DDO.

Casey, who had been impressed with the way Hugel ran the Reagan
election campaign in New Hampshire, brought Hugel with him to the

Agency where, in February 1981, he named Hugel to be the deputy director of administration (DDA). Less than three months later, in May 1981, Casey appointed Hugel as the deputy director of operations. Hugel had no previous intelligence experience, and his appointment flabbergasted and alarmed the Agency's old guard.

In July 1981, a little over two months after his appointment, Hugel was accused of insider trading, and he resigned. This was the first bump in the road for Casey and, coming as early in his tenure as it had, heralded a stormy future for the Agency. It should be noted that Hugel sued two of his accusers for libel and won his case. When I read about the insider trading allegations, my first thought was, "How did he get through his polygraph?" No one in PD was talking about his test, and that question is still unanswered.

Hugel was the presenter at Falcone's retirement ceremony, and that was the only time I saw him up close. He gave a nice speech and came across as very pro-Agency and pro-polygraph.

Some characterized Casey as a bull in a china shop, but my impression was that Casey always knew exactly what he was doing; his mumbling and stumbling were an act. Casey was one of the most powerful directors in the history of the Agency. To my knowledge, Casey was the only member of President Reagan's cabinet who referred to the president as "Ronnie," and I can't think of any DCI who had the access to a U.S. president that Casey had.

In the DO, Casey was seen as a godsend, but in PD, Meager was perceived as a square dancer in a lindy contest. Morale was not good and was getting worse.

The release of the U.S. hostages in Iran gave the CIA something to smile about, and I was looking forward to seeing Cal Malcomson again. When the hostages arrived at Rhein-Main Air Force Base in Germany, a reporter asked Cal, "Would you like to go back to Iran?"

"Only in the nose of a B-52," he answered.

Cal was a very hard-nosed and resourceful individual who, while in captivity, had managed to recruit one of his captors to send a message to the Agency. The information in the message was valuable in planning the rescue. The fact that the rescue mission ended in disaster didn't vitiate his effort. When Cal got back to headquarters, he immediately asked to be polygraphed. Cal told me that the purpose of his request was "to verify that I didn't sell out when I was a hostage." During our discussion Cal vented about Carter, saying that Carter should not have negotiated with the Iranians. He told me that he had refused to meet with Carter, whom President Reagan had sent to greet the hostages. Cal also told me that he had tried to escape three times. "They beat the shit out of me every time they caught me, and after the third time, they smashed my glasses." Cal was virtually blind without his coke bottle glasses, and his attempts to escape ceased.

Cal invited me to his son's Bar Mitzvah, and we stayed friends until a few years ago, when he was killed by a drunk driver. Cal was another of those larger-than-life people that made the Agency an interesting place to be. He was also one of those people whom I would want on the end of my lifeline or to have with me in any kind of tough spot.

Seeing Cal put me in a good frame of mind, and at least temporarily, Meager didn't concern me. I was convinced that because of Meager's lack of understanding of polygraph, examiners would have to be very successful to gain any kind of support from him. Prior to Reid training, CIA examiners were security officers who, for the most part, had been less than well trained to conduct polygraph tests. After Reid, PD was made up of well-trained examiners who happened also to be security officers. As such, they made some headway in gaining Meager's support.

No group of examiners was more representative of how far PD had come in terms of its recruiting than three examiners PD sent to Reid in November 1980: "Jan Boyle," "Howard Phillips," and "Bruce Gall." Boyle and Phillips are on my list of the top-ten best examiners in PD history, and Gall became our first executive expert examiner. These were the Young Turks.

Gall and Phillips were both very competitive and were always trying to outdo each other in terms of the admissions they obtained. At one point, Milenski had to tell them to ease up, as it was getting out of hand. Both were getting a little aggressive with their subjects and pushing a bit too hard to get minor admissions.

Boyle thought that any woman who wanted to equal a man lacked ambition, and she was a very dynamic examiner. One of her many great tests was a retest on a subject that Phillips had tested. Phillips had obtained admissions of drug use and theft from a young female applicant. When the applicant was denied a clearance, she filed a protest with the Office of Security. During her interview with a senior Office of Security official, the young lady denied making the admissions that Phillips attributed to her, and the official ordered that the young lady be retested.

PD had the woman's applicant interview on tape, and many of us examiners were angry that the Office of Security had taken the applicant's word for what had occurred during the test rather than listen to the tape. It was a slap in the face, especially because Meager could have brought the tape to the official's attention but didn't. During the retest Boyle got the applicant not only to repeat her admissions of drug use and theft but also to admit that she had lied during her posttest interview with the security official who had ordered the retest.

At that year's offsite, I endeared myself to that security officer by asking him why he had declined to listen to the tape of Phillips's interview. He handled it well and said that in retrospect, he probably should have listened to the tape, but at the time, a retest seemed like a good idea.

Good recruits continued to come into PD, including "Frank Cross" in mid-1981. I consider Cross's arrival in PD as a defining event for the division in that he became one of the five best examiners in PD history and was, hands down, the best team leader/mentor any examiner ever had.

"Pete Roberts" also came into PD in 1981. Roberts was a Reid-trained examiner who had practiced in the private sector. He was a recognized authority on polygraph, and I felt that his presence enhanced CIA polygraph's image.

As the number of Reid-trained examiners conducting tests increased, so, too, did the number of complaints being made against examiners. Complaints are to be expected in any polygraph program, but the number of complaints increased exponentially at the outset of Meager's tenure. Many of PD's new examiners were "true believers," meaning when they believed a subject was lying, they went after an admission with a lot of zeal.

There was a grain of truth in many of the complaints made against examiners, but just as many of the complaints were egregious misrepresentations of what had actually happened. Examiners were great targets of opportunity for those who had a complaint to make about polygraph, and I can't count the number of times I have been accosted by CIA employees wanting to vent about polygraph. Two incidents stand out.

While conferring with a case officer and his boss prior to going on an overseas trip, the case officer's boss, whom I had known overseas, asked me to stop by his office before I returned to PD. As requested, I stopped by his office. He began the conversation by asking, "John do you know what happened to 'Ray Brown's wife' when she was polygraphed earlier this week?"

I did know because I had monitored the test, but I said, "No. Tell me."

"She got so pissed off at the asshole testing her that she tore the attachments off and walked out," he answered.

That didn't happen. In actuality Brown's wife declined, and ultimately refused, to answer one of the questions. When initially asked the question, Mrs. Brown's answer was, "I don't think that is any of your business, and I don't think I can answer that question."

"Paul Carlson," the examiner, was new, and I happened to be monitoring the session. When Carlson told Mrs. Brown that all of the questions had to be answered, Mrs. Brown said that if that was the way it was, she would not continue with the test. There was no confrontation or acrimony. Carlson removed the attachments and escorted Mrs. Brown out.

In the second and more irritating incident I was verbally attacked in the cafeteria. I was having lunch with some friends and an older woman whom I didn't know. When one of the guys introduced me as a polygraph examiner, this woman verbally assaulted me.

"You sons of bitches! You just fired a friend of mine because you say he is queer. I have known him for years, and I know that he isn't," she said. After catching her breath, this curmudgeonly lady said that my fellow examiners and I were nothing but a goddamn Gestapo. Her friend may not have been "queer," as she so delicately put it, but I know that he had acknowledged multiple homosexual contacts and had actually acknowledged that he was a homosexual. However I could not reveal this; I had to bite my tongue.

Often Agency colleagues called me to complain that a relative had been poorly treated during a polygraph session. With few exceptions, the relatives had misrepresented their polygraph sessions to my colleagues.

Within a year of Meager's appointment to chief of PD, the Polygraph Division's already poor image had gotten worse. One of the biggest reasons for this was the institution of multiple-session polygraph tests. For applicants, as opposed to staff, this wasn't as big a problem because they lacked a frame of reference for comparing multiple-session tests. For those undergoing RIP and TRIP testing, whose EOD tests had taken only one session, multiple-session tests were a new and unpleasant phenomenon. Examiners were almost as frustrated by the multiple-session tests as the employees they were testing, and morale plummeted.

Many of these multiple-session tests became acrimonious, and subjects often vented their frustration with the examiners in a very loud and profane manner. Examiners began including their subjects' comments in their reports. Clearance Division ultimately enjoined examiners from doing this because it considered profane outbursts an understandable reaction to a stressful situation and reporting such behavior might be prejudicial to the subject. Implicit in Clearance Division's directive was that we examiners might have caused the outbursts.

As noted in chapter 6, in 1979 the first applicant was denied a security clearance based on a deception indicated call without any admissions. Still, Clearance Division was very reluctant to make such a call. As a result, Clearance Division decreed that a DI call without admissions could not be made after one session. Thus, multiple sessions, or as they came to be known, "bring-backs," became a fact of life in PD, and the policy was that a DI call without an admission could not be made until after the *third* session.

DI calls without admissions went from being a rarity to being a new phenomenon, and Clearance Division adjudicators had a real problem dealing with them. Whereas in the past, security disapprovals were based on admissions, now adjudicators had to rely on more subjective criteria. This put an inordinate amount of pressure on the examiners to get admissions. Bring-backs became and still are one of the banes of PD's existence.

For the employees, polygraph tests were no longer just trips to the dentist; they were root canals. Many employees felt stigmatized by being asked to come back for additional testing, but as bring-backs became more common, frustration with and resentment to the process grew.

I remember a second-session RIP done by "Marty Davis," a fine examiner. Davis had been with the subject for over three hours when he brought his charts to Rob Creed for review. "What have you got?" asked Creed.

"Nothing," Davis answered.

"What are you doing out here?" Creed asked.

"Rob, I really don't think we have anything here, and think I should let him go," said Davis.

"Give it another shot, and we'll see," ordered Creed.

After three more hours, Davis again came out and showed his charts to Creed, who said, "Let him go."

This is perhaps a more extreme example of the dynamic between examiners and reviewers, but it was symptomatic of a serious and growing problem. Examiners began to perceive supervisors and chart reviewers as obstacles to be overcome, rather than collaborators.

On another occasion "Burt Causey" monitored one of my tests and reviewed my charts. My subject had some problems with the question on homosexual activity and said that he had recently slept in the same bed with a male friend, but he insisted that no sexual activity had taken place. I believed him and thought I had charts that supported my conclusion. Causey was one of those in PD who thought I was too soft on subjects and disagreed. He said, "I am going in there [the testing room] to get it out of him. Sit here and listen."

For the next two hours I listened and didn't hear any admission. Causey wrote up the report, and when I read his report, I was very surprised to see an admission of homosexual activity. I went to see Causey. "Burt, I listened to your interview with our subject, and I didn't hear the admission you said he made," I said.

"You must have missed it," Causey replied.

I am quite sure that the subject didn't make the admission Causey said he made and felt that Causey was certain that the subject was lying and took it upon himself to make sure that he didn't get hired. Back in those days I used to work out in the gym from 0600 hours to 0800 hours, at least four times a week. One morning while working out, I got a very sharp pain near my right kidney. The pain worsened, I felt a little nauseous as I prepared for my morning test, and I thought that I had better see the medics.

I went to Causey and said, "Burt, I am really hurting and think I have a kidney stone and am going to OMS."

"Could you do your morning test before you go?" asked Causey. I knew that Causey and all team leaders were under a lot of pressure to increase the number of tests PD conducted, but I thought Causey was a bit callous in asking me to do a test under those circumstances, and I declined.

Rob Creed, on another occasion, had me do six RIP tests in one day. Milenski got a little upset about that, and no one was ever asked to do more than four tests in one day again. Doing six tests in one day was extreme, and hearing that I completed so many in such a short time might lead one to believe that PD examiners rushed their tests. That was not the case. If I had needed all day to do any one of the tests I conducted that day, I would have been given the time.

DCI Casey's push to expand the DO meant that PD did much more applicant testing than it had in previous years. Two DO recruitment programs were initiated under Casey's aegis: one in which the DO tried to recruit former New York City policemen and another in which DO case officers went out to American colleges and military posts to find suitable candidates for the DO. Casey's cops had significant problems with their polygraph tests, and that program went bust. The DO recruiters on the campuses attracted some real cowboys. One of those whom I tested told me that he wanted to join the CIA to be an assassin. He volunteered that he was willing to "off" Phillip Agee, the CIA turncoat, or "anyone else you guys feel needs to be killed." We did not hire this young man.

With RIPS, TRIPS, increased applicant testing, and a bring-back rate of over 30 percent, PD examiners were stretched to the limit. It became obvious that the number of examiners PD needed was beyond what Reid training could provide. Milenski pushed for our own school, and by the end of 1981 Casey had approved the establishment of a CIA polygraph training school. With our own American Polygraph Association accredited school, CIA's polygraph examiners were forever out of the Dark Ages and eager to show how effective a good polygraph program could be. In mid-1982 Meager appointed Jim Doom as director of the CIA's

Polygraph School and "Curt Paulson" as his deputy. The first class began in November, and the first graduates began testing in March 1983.

Just before the CIA's school opened its doors, in 1982, "Ken Robey" came on board. Robey was a Reid-trained examiner and turned out to be one of the best five examiners I ever worked with. (Bob Pickell, Mark Verity, Frank Cross, and "Bill Bontiempo" were the other four.) For bring-back tests focusing on questions about criminal activity, Robey became the go-to examiner.

Many of PD's critics complained that the examiners were too young. Robey was one of the youngest examiners in PD, and one of the most effective at getting admissions. I do think some in PD held his youth against him, but regardless, he became my go-to guy for suggestions on how to approach an interrogation. Robey was the one examiner whom I asked to monitor me when I needed a reading on a subject or knew that I was going to have to interrogate. He was generous, right on the money with his advice, and never condescending, and he would always make time for me. Robey's performance, namely his ability to coax admissions from subjects, raised the level of expectations in PD.

Among the other changes DCI Casey's arrival brought about in the Agency was an attempt to incorporate what were considered to be good business practices into the way the Agency did business. To that end, Casey encouraged high-ranking CIA staff to read *In Search of Excellence: Lessons from America's Best-Run Companies* by Thomas J. Peters and Robert H. Waterman, a very popular how-to book for CEOs. Meager read the book and at a staff meeting suggested that PD managers might also do well to read it.

When I discussed the book with Meager, I told him that if he wanted to run McDonald's, this might be a good book but that espionage was generally not cost effective so many of the principles cited in the book didn't apply to the CIA's operations. I think my assessment of the book made Meager decide that I was out of touch and a bit of a reactionary.

Among the hundreds of examiners with whom I worked, none was a better fit with these exciting times than Bill Bontiempo. A former city cop and a high-profile bodyguard, Bontiempo was selected to be a member of the first class in CIA's polygraph school. Bontiempo was to PD what Andy Sipowitz was to *NYPD Blues*, and he was just as effective. He ultimately became chief of the Polygraph Division.

No two personalities could be more disparate than Bontiempo's and Doom's, and Doom thought that Bontiempo didn't fit the ideal CIA polygraph examiner image. To that end, Doom made school difficult for Bontiempo, and according to Paulson, Doom said that he would do everything he could to make sure that Bontiempo didn't become an examiner. Doom's efforts failed, and in early 1983 Bontiempo began testing.

Between running courses at the school, Doom and Paulson returned to PD to monitor the examiners. Not long after Bontiempo began testing, he conducted a difficult interview during which his subject made disqualifying admissions. Subsequently, Doom approached Bontiempo with a complaint from Meager about the test. According to Bontiempo, Doom said that Meager was upset because he (Bontiempo) seemed to "enjoy" interrogating his subject. Without answering Doom, Bontiempo excused himself and went to see Meager. Bontiempo told Meager in short that if he had any complaints about the way he did his job, he should "Tell me, face-to-face."

This was just another example of Meager's lack of understanding of polygraph and interrogation. There is a lot of emotional investment in an interrogation and a concomitant "high" when the interrogation is successful. As dour and cold a person as Meager was, he could never grasp the role that emotions played in the process.

Meager's personality, the volume of work that examiners were doing, and the complaints that were being made against us all combined to cause some burnout among PD examiners. During Meager's "Reign of Terror," twelve examiners left PD. I actually thought about leaving polygraph during this period and told Meager that I was looking for a job outside of the division. Meager said that he didn't want me to leave, making it clear he would do everything he could to keep me from doing so. I think the fact that the high turnover rate of examiners at this time was making him look bad had more to do with his desire to keep me in PD than any affection or respect for me. Meager made one comment that has stayed with me: "John, there are people in this office who love you. You have been here for more than fifteen years, and this is your home. Don't go."

I probably should have gone, but I stayed. As Lee Jensen had predicted, watching incompetent people get promoted ahead of me was unsettling, but still, it was not enough to make me leave.

Up close and personal was not the way Meager did business, and as much as I resented him for his lack of understanding of polygraph and the examiners' work, my most consistent memory of him is of his lack of empathy.

On one occasion one of the younger examiners, "Frank Drissel," had gone for his annual physical, and during the process, the doctor discovered that he had testicular cancer. When Drissel returned to the office, he was understandably upset. Drissel told the chief of the overt desk about his diagnosis and added that he was checking into Arlington Hospital that afternoon. In response to the news, Meager went into Drissel's office and told him that testicular cancer wasn't that big a deal. I am certain that Meager meant well, but when I subsequently talked to Drissel, he was irate. "Pat's telling me that this is no big deal is bullshit. I am scared out of my mind. Are my wife and I going to be able to have kids? How far has the cancer spread? Jesus Christ!" he said.

One of Drissel's testicles was removed, and he did recover. There never had been any love lost between Drissel and Meager, and not long after he recovered, Drissel left the Polygraph Division and later the Agency.

Operational tests were still a refuge and source of satisfaction that kept me hanging on. Two cases in particular recharged my batteries. The first of these was a test I did in New York City of a woman the DO was recruiting for a very sensitive operation. A naturalized U.S. citizen, she was in her mid-twenties and had two master's degrees. She was of Eastern European descent and beautiful.

Initially I was very impressed by her. She was very articulate and poised, and I didn't anticipate any problems with the test. Unfortunately, I was wrong. After three hours I hadn't been able to resolve a problem regarding the question about whether the subject could be blackmailed, and we broke for lunch.

Over lunch, the subject said, "Mr. O'Brian [the name I used with subject], I will do *anything* to pass this test." I had no doubt about what she meant by "*anything*," but I let her comment slide. During the afternoon session, the woman told me what her problem was. "When I was living over there [Eastern Europe] last year, I got pregnant and had an abortion. It would kill my mother to find out about that, and I could never let that happen," she said.

She went on to say that the lady who had arranged the abortion was a member of the country's intelligence service. Other information she provided disqualified this very qualified woman, and I felt bad, but not as bad as the DO recruiter felt. Being able to extract disqualifying information from a subject to whom I was favorably predisposed gave my confidence a boost, and I returned to Meager's sweatshop with a bounce in my step.

My second confidence booster was a test I conducted in Rome. Our examiner in Europe, "Boris Hansen," had requested some help, and I was selected to pick up some of his cases. One of the tests I administered was of the cutout—that is, a go-between whose purpose is to conceal the clandestine relationship between a case officer and an agent—in a sensitive operation. The case officer had never met with his asset face-to-face; all contact was made through the cutout. In recent months the quality of the information provided by the asset had declined, and a polygraph test of the cutout was requested.

After reading the file, I discussed the case with Milenski, who knew and raved about the case officer I would be working with, "Al Todd." "This guy Al is a real pro, John, and you are going to like working with him," Milenski said.

When I met with Todd in Rome, he impressed me as someone who knew what he was doing. He said that he would interpret for me, and that night he picked me up at the hotel and brought me to the safe house. Unfortunately, Todd's language fluency was totally inadequate for the test. During the pretest, he paused in the middle of questions and stumbled over and reiterated words. During the test, his interpreting became a bigger problem. Finally, I said to Todd, "This just isn't working. We're going to need another interpreter." Todd was reluctant to bring anyone else into the operation, but I insisted, and the next night, using another interpreter, I conducted the test.

For the subject and thus for Todd, the test did not turn out well. Todd had given me a copy of a report that the subject handed in, and during the pretest, I asked the subject if the report had been given to him by "Mr. X," the primary source. The subject averred that it had. Initial testing failed to support that claim, and for some reason that I can't recall, I really went after him. Usually, I would dance around to try to elicit an explanation for a reaction. This time I immediately confronted the subject.

"I am absolutely certain that you didn't get this report from Mr. X," I said.

The subject seemed to start to deny my charge but suddenly looked down and said, "You are right. I wrote the report." After some verbal sparring, the subject said that Mr. X had been dead for almost a year. The subject had never told Todd about Mr. X's demise and had been writing the reports.

Todd was clearly disappointed but was gracious enough to thank me for having done a good job. I took a lot of satisfaction from that test. When I briefed Hansen on the test, he seemed surprised that I had obtained an admission, but he also complimented me.

Back in headquarters, it was more of the same. As PD grew to meet the increasing demand for examiners, so, too, did the PD bureaucracy. Branches were set up within PD for each testing venue: applicant, RIP, TRIP, Industrial, and Operational. One examiner was made to be a full-time scheduler, and as is the case in any bureaucracy, numbers became the god to which PD management paid obeisance.

When I took the Reid Advanced Polygraph course, commercial examiners in the class told me that they had only one hour to conduct a test; otherwise, they couldn't make money. In PD, time is not the factor that it is in commercial testing. A further difference between PD and commercial tests is the fact that CIA examiners work with and sometimes for subjects they have tested and the opportunities for coincidental contact are always present. If the tests went well, this is no problem, but posttest contact with a subject who had a difficult time with his or her test has the potential to negatively impact the contact or professional relationship. For me, this was rarely a problem. But the possibility was always there.

More important, working with case officers who had problems with their tests or even those who know that they "beat" the examiner during their test, can make for a difficult working relationship. What kind of confidence can case officers have in an examiner whom they beat on a test?

For that reason, whenever I tested an applicant who was applying for a position as an ops officer, I made it a point to tell them, "If I have any reservations at all about any of the questions on this test, I am going to do what it takes to resolve them. In the future, I may have to test one of your agents, and I can't afford to have you go out of here knowing that you beat me."

Posttest contact between examiners and subjects can be a bigger problem when a disgruntled subject wants a little payback. A young woman I tested did not do well in her TRIP polygraph test. The test and her behavior led me to conclude that she had used illegal drugs since entering on duty. My ensuing interrogation failed, and the young woman was not a happy camper when she left my room. The examiner who did the bring-back told me, "I know she lied about her drug use, but I couldn't get her to admit it." No action was taken against the young woman.

Each time I processed for an overseas trip, I had to go through this young woman's office. On two consecutive trips after I had tested her and while I was overseas, Lee received telephone calls from a woman asking for me and refusing to leave her name. During the second call, the woman mentioned to Lee that she had met me in the country where I was supposed to be testing. I am sure the woman was trying to create in Lee's mind the idea that I might be cheating on her. While en route, my plans had been changed, and I wasn't in the country the woman claimed to have met me in. The young woman whom I had tested had known where I was going but was not aware that my plans had been changed. She also had my file with my home phone number. I had no doubt that she had either made or was behind the calls. I mentioned this to Meager, but he didn't seem to see it as a problem and ignored the complaint.

Meager was aloof, taciturn, and humorless. I could not warm up to him, and it came as a great surprise to me when he complimented me for a test that I had conducted. An applicant whom I was testing reacted very strongly to the question about homosexual activity. When I so advised him, he became more than a little indignant, and to prove to me that he was "all man" and not a "queer," my subject admitted to committing three rapes. Looks can be deceiving. My initial impression of this applicant was that he was a real Li'l Abner country boy.

In describing one of the rapes, he said that after the rape, he went out to a Dunkin' Donuts. When he came back, his victim was lying on the floor, naked, and crying. "I said, 'What's the matter? You hungry?' I took a jelly donut out of the box, squatted down and said, 'Here, this will make you feel better.'"

I found the callousness and lack of empathy for his victim as scary as the sexual assault. Knowing that without a polygraph test this cretin would have probably gotten a job with the Agency made his disqualifying admissions especially satisfying.

Meager had apparently monitored the case because he came to my room during lunch hour and told me that I had done a great job. When he read the report of my interview, he complimented me again. Meager passed out compliments very sparingly, and I appreciated his recognition of my efforts.

Within three weeks of that test, I tested another individual who also had a problem with the question on homosexual activity. The man was in his forties, had never been married, and lived with his mother. He exhibited no stereotypical manifestations of homosexuality (effeminate gestures or speech), but I could not clear him on the issue of homosexual activity. I am 100 percent convinced that this man had not engaged in any homosexual activity and was very frustrated with the fact that I couldn't get him through the test. The interview, including a lunch break, lasted over six hours.

This man acknowledged that being over forty and never having been married, as well as living with his mother, could lead people to think that he was a homosexual. However, he followed that comment with, "For religious reasons, I have never had a homosexual experience, but in the future if I become lonely enough, I could see it as a possibility." He added, "The only time I tried heterosexual activity, I got nauseous and threw up." I felt that any man who would tell me that wasn't hiding anything. Charts that I obtained from the interview were erratic, and I called the test inconclusive.

When I asked the man if he would be willing to come back for additional testing, he answered, "Of course, I am willing to come back, but that won't change anything. I have never had a homosexual experience."

We did not hire this man, and I felt bad about it. However, I felt much worse when a Clearance Division adjudicator stopped me in the cafeteria to tell me how uproarious he found it that a man would admit to having thrown up when he tried to have sex with a woman. As I had told Meager, my purpose in PD was not to titillate the prurient imaginations of our customers, and I was offended by the adjudicator's callousness.

Meager also complimented me on how I had handled this man, but I didn't get any satisfaction from the test, especially when I compared this test with Howard Phillips's test of a secretary who had recently returned from overseas and whom I will call "Sara Allen." During the pretest, Allen answered all of the relevant questions with a "no." Subsequent testing failed to support her denial of having provided classified information to an unauthorized person. I was monitoring Phillips during this interview and thought he did a masterful job of eliciting a significant admission from Allen. Allen admitted that she had passed a classified cable to her foreign lover, who was an intelligence officer. Allen also admitted that she had given her lover the name of a nonofficial cover (NOC) officer. (NOC officers are DO officers who work overseas without the benefit of diplomatic status.) After being apprised of the information Allen had provided to her lover, the FBI advised that if the CIA declassified the cable that Allen had passed, the FBI could use it in court as evidence and prosecute her. The CIA declined to declassify the cable, and Allen was allowed to resign. My impression was that the Agency was in a state of denial, unable to acknowledge the traitor in its midst.

Phillips's test of Allen was a milestone in CIA polygraph history. A spy had been caught, and there were probably more to be caught. From that point on, examiners approached employee tests with a healthier skepticism and newfound intensity that made the '80s a very exciting time to be in PD.

Boyle, Gall, and Phillips were the up-and-coming stars in PD, but Gall clearly had the inside track. Gall, a G. Gordon Liddy look-alike, was a former marine whom I had met in Vietnam, and he was a very hard charger. Early on Milenski singled out Gall as a future great. At the end of Gall's first year in PD, Milenski gave Gall all 7s, the highest rating, on his performance appraisal review (PAR).

One of the better tests Gall conducted was on a foreign asset in Latin America. During the test Gall coaxed the asset to admit that he was a double agent working for the Cubans. This was a big deal and helped Gall's career.

During that same trip, on the stop after he caught the double agent, Gall had a run-in with a chief of station (COS). Gall had just finished a test in a hotel, and according to a conversation I had with the COS, Gall called him to "demand" that a car be sent to pick him up. The COS told

Gall to hail a taxi and get back to the office. Gall was a prima donna, and although he conducted some good cases in terms of public relations, I felt that he was a liability.

Less than a month after his test of the Latin American asset, Gall conducted a very high-profile test of a subject who was the station's number-one asset and who, he concluded, was another double agent. Gall didn't get an admission from the subject and had apparently rubbed the case officer and station management the wrong way. The chief of station, "Al West," came to headquarters, complained about the way the test was conducted, and asked that another examiner redo the test.

A DO branch chief for whom I had conducted several tests submitted a formal request asking that I retest this subject. I was a little surprised that he requested me because of previous interactions I had had with one of the station's case officers. A few months before I was asked to do the retest, I had tested an asset at the station and had concluded that he was a DGI double agent. I had confronted the agent in front of the case officer, "Jerry Clay," and said, "You are working for the DGI and are a double agent!"

"No, sir, you are wrong," the agent replied mildly.

Whereupon the case officer commented to the agent, "It's not the worse thing in the world to fail a polygraph test."

Earlier in the week I had conducted another test for Clay, at Clay's home, a location that surprised me. During the pretest, I asked the agent, "Did Mr. Jerry tell you that you were coming here today for a lie detector test?"

"Oh, yes, Mr. Jerry told me. I am not worried about it," he answered.

Fortunately the test went well, but after the test I asked Clay, "Jerry, why did you tell him that he was coming here for a polygraph test?"

Clay was defensive. "I didn't see any harm in it," he initially answered.

"Jerry, let's assume the worst," I began. "Your guy is working for the local service. He could have either had them break in and arrest the both of us or he could have had your house surveilled, and I could have been identified. I don't just work here; I work all over the world," I said. I followed up with, "Just as important, the locals could follow me, and I could lead them to every asset I test. There are good reasons why examiners don't like the subjects to know when and where they are going to be tested."

Clay then became more defensive. "I guess that makes me a terrible case officer," he commented sarcastically.

"No, but what I told you is something you should think about," I said. Clay had been a DO case officer for twenty years, and I thought his disregard for the most basic operational security was appalling. This is what came to mind when I was asked to go back to the station to read-minister Gall's test.

Readministering another examiner's test is a tricky situation at best. I spoke with Gall about the test and reviewed his charts. I had no doubt that Gall had made the right call and that the subject he tested had been deceptive. I also felt that with charts as good as the ones Gall showed me, selling a DI call should not have been a problem.

After reviewing all the headquarters files on the subject and meeting with one of his previous handlers, I flew out to the station. I spent my first day in country discussing the case with the asset's case officer, "Art Ramirez." Ramirez accepted the possibility that his asset could be bad but saw it as very remote. Station management envisioned a disaster if this asset were bad and impressed me as being totally unprepared for such an eventuality.

"Stan Johnson," the deputy chief of station (DCOS), was going to interpret for the test, and we spent a lot of time preparing the questions.

Although I never mentioned it to anyone in the station, I felt very confident that the asset was bad. I didn't care for the way Gall conducted business, but he was right on the money with his DI call on this asset. With that in mind, I did something I hadn't done before in an ops test. I knew that if the asset were "bad" and likely under hostile control, he would have told his foreign handler about his last and upcoming polygraph tests. With that in mind, I composed a test with the question: "Did you tell anyone about your last test? Did you tell anyone you were coming here today for a test?" I thought these questions would elicit answers that were as close as I could get to known lies. If the asset didn't react in his responses to these questions, I would call the test invalid. If he did, I could confront him and let him know that, at least on that day, the polygraph was working.

Johnson and I were waiting in the safe house when the asset arrived. No one had told me how big this guy was, and I was a little taken aback by his appearance. He was over six feet tall and weighed about 250 pounds. He was also stoic, taciturn, and mean-looking. I would not have wanted him to interrogate me.

During initial testing the subject showed strong reactions to the questions about telling anyone about his tests. I confronted him by telling him that I was certain he had told someone about his last test, as well as the test he was now taking. The man just shrugged his shoulders and said, "No, señor, I have told no one." At that point I didn't interrogate him. I just wanted him to know that I had caught him in a lie.

One of the issues I tested the subject on was a very sensitive operation in which he had been a prime player and which had gone badly. Essentially, I asked the subject if he had compromised the operation in any way. Testing strongly indicated that he had. Subsequently more specific testing also strongly indicated that he, the station's number-one asset, was working for the Russians and/or the Cubans.

Johnson, who had been interpreting for me, was behind the subject, parallel to me, and when the test was over, I made a thumbs-down gesture. Johnson reacted with a very displeased look and pointed to the door. We went into a hallway where I told Johnson, "Stan, this guy is bad."

"That goddamn box! I don't believe it," Johnson immediately replied.

He said it loud enough for the subject to have heard, and I didn't think that was a good thing. Johnson didn't want me to interrogate the subject, and we just let him go. The test results cast a pall over the station office. After we delivered the news, Johnson sent Ramirez out to talk to the subject to see if Ramirez could find out "what was on the subject's mind."

On the following day I had to brief the station on my test. Prior to the briefing, Ramirez told me that the subject had admitted that he had told his wife about his two tests. At the outset of my briefing, COS West asked me, "John, how sure are you of your call?" In response, I showed the attendees the charts I had run during testing on the issue of telling anyone about his polygraph tests. I pointed out the reactions to the relevant questions.

"These are reactions to what we now know are lies," I pointed out. I then held up the charts of the other tests that I ran and showed the attendees the even stronger reactions to the relevant questions. "Ladies and gentlemen, polygraphically speaking, this is as good as it gets. I wish this guy were a good guy, but he isn't," I said, ending my briefing. I returned to headquarters without the best wishes of the station.

In this test, I was particularly pleased at how effective my testing of the subject on the issue of telling anyone about his previous test had been. To my knowledge, this was not an issue that had previously been covered in operational tests, and based on my experience with this asset, I decided that in future tests of assets who had been polygraphed at least once before, I would always address the issue of whether or not they had told anyone about a previous polygraph test. I also thought that I should pass word of the effectiveness of this question on to the other examiners.

At the first PD staff meeting after I returned, Meager asked, "Does anyone have anything else?" I said that during my last trip I had come up with a new question that had proved effective. As I started to go into the details, Meager cut me off, saying, "I don't think anyone here is really interested." He followed with, "If that's all there is, the meeting is over." This was pure Meager. In this instance, as much as I resented his rudeness, I was more concerned by his lack of understanding about polygraph. Meager may have thought that what I had to say was of no interest, but I can think of five examinations that I conducted in which asking a subject if he or she had told anyone about a previous test contributed to the success of the test.

In an interesting followup, when KGB defector Col. Vitaly Yurchenko was being debriefed, he was specifically asked about Soviet operations against the station at which I had conducted the test of Ramirez's agent. Yurchenko did not identify the subject by name, but he did say, "We have it very well covered."

Subsequent to that debriefing, I ran into COS West in headquarters, and he asked me, "John, do you think Yurchenko was referring to our guy?"

"There isn't much doubt in my mind," I answered.

The fact that DCOS Johnson had refused to let me interrogate the subject was a disappointment, but in the operations world case officers and chiefs of station often discouraged examiners from interrogating subjects. Probably the most important reason for this was that no contingency plan was in place to deal with an agent who failed a polygraph test. Some felt it easier to avoid the truth than to deal with the reality of a bad agent.

A less important but more common reason for case officers to refuse to allow examiners to interrogate agents was that without an admission a case officer can argue that the polygraph test results are wrong. Being unable to interrogate a subject whom I thought was lying left me feeling as though my job were only half done, and I didn't like it, but at times I understood that it was necessary.

On one occasion I tested a senior intelligence officer in a country where anti-American sentiment was on the rise and diplomatic relations with the United States were strained. The chief of station suspected that the agent was a double and wanted a polygraph test to verify his suspicions. My test supported the COS's suspicions, but to have confronted and interrogated this agent would have served no useful purpose and could have had serious consequences for the station.

The test was conducted late at night so that as soon as the test was over a case officer could take me to the airport to catch my flight. The subject would be kept in the COS's house after the test for training that, we hoped, would last until the plane took off. The COS told me they didn't want me arrested at the airport.

Back in PD, the Reid examiners were certainly proving their worth, and I found myself learning a lot from them. However, I felt that some aspects of the Reid training were not applicable to CIA testing. For example, in the Reid technique the examiner must "take control" of the test from the beginning of contact with subject. An examiner could take control by using subjects' first names and getting them used to following directions by directing them to "Hang up your coat" or "Take a seat." In a professional interview, I feel it is inappropriate to use first names. Even when subjects asked me to use their first names, I was always reluctant to do so. My impression was that many of our subjects resented the fact that examiners called them by their first names, and their resentment contributed to the negative image we projected.

On a very memorable occasion, I had as my subject a female septuagenarian who was a renowned scholar. She was being considered for a consultant position and had to undergo applicant testing. During her polygraph test, she had difficulty with the question about homosexual activity. Questioning this lady (I would certainly not interrogate her) about homosexual activity was a bit awkward, but I did tell her that she reacted to that question more than any other question on the test, and I wondered why. I got nowhere. When I took my charts to Doom, he told me that they were clearly DI, which they were.

"Jim, there is no way that lady is ever going to admit having engaged in homosexual activity, and I don't see it as being relevant," I commented.

Doom picked up her file and said, "Let me talk to her."

"Brenda, I'm your examiner's supervisor, and you seem to be having some problems with your test," said Doom as he entered the room.

"Young man, *you* are not old enough to call me by my first name," my subject heatedly replied. I think many of our subjects felt this way but were reluctant to make their feelings known. Calling a sixty-seven-year-old, ethnic Chinese grandmother by her first name, as I heard one of the younger examiners do, may have been consistent with the Reid approach, but I found it not only rude but also indicative of the examiner's lack of cultural awareness.

One maxim I imparted on younger examiners was, "Your subjects don't have to like you, but they can't *dislike* you." A corollary to that was, "Don't unnecessarily aggravate your subjects." Rudeness and insensitivity fall into the category of behaviors that aggravate subjects. While I meditated on ways to address this problem, an event occurred that shocked and enraged me.

On April 18, 1983, a Hezbollah terrorist drove a truck loaded with four hundred pounds of explosives into the American embassy in Beirut. Sixty-three Americans were killed and 120 were wounded in this attack. Several of those killed were CIA employees. The Islamic jihad that, I felt, had begun with the taking of the embassy in Tehran took a significant turn for the worse with this bombing.

A few of the CIA people killed had served with me in Vietnam, and I considered them to be friends. I had tested one of them when he entered on duty. Another, Bob Ames, was as fine an operations officer as I ever met. During my four years in Vietnam, I can recall only one CIA officer being killed as a result of hostile action,[1] but in this one terrible day, we lost several. My sadness over the loss of three friends almost equaled my anger at those who were responsible for the attack. Each of those who died was missed, but Bob Ames's loss cast a pall over the entire Agency. A few days after the attack I went down to the passport office to pick up my passport. The man I usually dealt with was almost in tears as he told me that if he had not expedited Ames's processing for his trip to Beirut, Ames would probably still be alive.

We in the CIA had little time to grieve the loss of those killed in the embassy bombing because the day after the bombing U.S. forces invaded Grenada. The following week I was in Grenada busily conducting tests.

During this time I also tested my last Cuban asset. The case officer with whom I worked was "Frank Diehl." He had a Cuban asset who was giving him some pretty good information, and he wanted the asset tested. We did the test in a safe house at night, and it went well. The asset spoke excellent English, and I didn't need an interpreter. The charts that I obtained from the asset were not very reactive, and so I had some reservations about passing him. To assuage my doubts, I told Diehl that what I would like to do is tell the asset he passed, let him go, and then surprise him with a test at the next meeting. I also told Diehl that I had done this before and found it to be a very effective technique.

"Frank, if this guy is bad and is working for the DGI, I am quite sure that within the next couple of days he will report to his DGI handler about his polygraph test. When he shows up for your next meeting, I will test him on whether or not he has told anyone about his polygraph test." Diehl thought that this was a good idea, and we ended the session.

The next morning, when we briefed Chief of Station "Dudley Tubbs" and told him what we wanted to do next, Tubbs vetoed the second test idea. "It will insult him, and we don't want to risk offending him," Tubbs reasoned. When I wrote my report, I cited the test as NDI, but I made mention of my reservations and Tubbs's refusal to let me do another test. To my knowledge, this is the only Cuban asset who beat me.

Back in headquarters, PD examiners were obtaining disqualifying information from applicants at a very high rate. I remember conducting an informal study over a two-week period during which at least three

---

1. In June 1971 Paul Davis, an Agency paramilitary officer whom I had tested when he entered on duty, stepped on a land mine and was killed.

subjects a day admitted to having committed felonies. During that same period, the chief of OMS wrote a letter in support of polygraph, in which he cited the fact that PD examiners had obtained admissions of recent drug use from sixteen applicants whose physical examinations had not uncovered any signs of illegal drug use.

PD was still on the lookout for another Sara Allen, although some did not consider her to be a "real" spy because her transgressions were motivated by love and not money or ideology. Then one day Bontiempo caught a "real" spy by anyone's definition.

As the result of a telephone tap, the FBI heard a Soviet bloc intelligence officer ask a man on the other end of the phone, "How did you beat the CIA lie detector?" The FBI subsequently identified the bloc intelligence officer's interlocutor as "Oleg Kurtz," an Agency officer, and notified Bill Katopish.

Kurtz had undergone EOD testing earlier that year and had already entered on duty. I reviewed his EOD polygraph charts three days after his test and recommended that he be brought back for additional testing, as I was not satisfied with the NDI call. In particular, I saw homosexual activity as an issue that needed to be resolved. The branch chief to whom I made the recommendation said that since homosexual activity was the only issue that really stood out, he would let the NDI call stand.

After receiving the FBI information Katopish ordered that Kurtz be given a specific issue polygraph test, and Bontiempo was selected to conduct it. In the eight days it took to get a confession out of Kurtz, Bontiempo did some of the best interrogating I have ever heard. I was monitoring Bontiempo on the eighth day, when I heard Kurtz admit that he had been recruited by the Communists as the result of being blackmailed by his bloc case officer, who had videotaped him engaging in homosexual activity.

It was unfortunate that I had signed off on Kurtz's charts and taken the file to the branch chief without making a written comment that Kurtz should be brought back for more testing. In the subsequent damage assessment, it was noted that I had signed off on the charts.

Specific issue polygraph tests were not that frequently conducted and were usually deemed necessary only in response to a specific complaint or allegation against an employee. I had conducted one SIP after a Bureau of Narcotics and Dangerous Drugs (BNDD) agent accused a CIA officer of involvement in drug trafficking. I resolved that case in favor of the CIA employee.

On another occasion a U.S. citizen was caught smuggling drugs during a customs search. The man had concealed the drugs in a large doll made of straw. In addition to the drugs, the man had a check made out to him by an Agency contract employee assigned to an overseas station. I was asked to travel to the station that the woman was assigned to, to get to the bottom of the case. No one, except the COS and the communications officer who had handled all the cable traffic dealing with the incident, was to know that I was in country for the test, and I could not go into the office.

At the outset of the test, I told the subject about the man who had been arrested and said that upon arrest he had had a check in his wallet made out to him by her. I also told her that the drugs had been found in a straw doll. The woman was flabbergasted. To explain why the man had a check made out by her, the woman said that the straw doll had been made by a friend of hers. "My friend doesn't speak English very well, and I interpreted for her when she was negotiating the sale of the doll. The man seemed very nice, and I asked him if he would pick up some things for my kids in the States. He said he would, and I gave him a check," the woman said. Subsequent testing absolved the lady, and I felt very good about the outcome.

Another SIP, this one conducted by Ken Robey, involved a CIA employee accused of embezzlement. In a very emotional session, the accused admitted to Robey that he had embezzled $50,000. The Agency prosecuted the man, and he was convicted. The day before he was to begin serving his sentence, he committed suicide. Lee had worked with this man in Vietnam, and we knew him and his wife. Suicide following a polygraph test was, thank God, extremely rare, but this incident did serve as a reminder to PD examiners that what we did had serious consequences.

The year before I entered on duty, an Agency employee was caught in a homosexual sting by a local police department. The employee denied the charge and was given an SIP. Upon leaving the polygraph session, the man drove to a Potomac River overlook just off the George Washington Parkway and shot himself. Every time I began an interrogation of an employee, this incident was on my mind.

Terrorism was also always on my mind. After Beirut, we received many requests to test CIA station walk-ins who reported on what they claimed were imminent terrorist attacks. Of the twenty-two of these tests that I did, twenty of the subjects turned out to be fabricators. The next example illustrates the type of walk-in we tested at the time.

On a Monday morning a desk officer in Africa Division (AF) called PD to advise us that a man had gone into an African station claiming to have heard three men discussing plans to blow up a Pan American Airlines plane, and the Africa Division wanted an examiner to test him. I told Meager that I would like to do the test, and Meager told me, "Keep in touch with AF but don't start processing. Maybe they can resolve this without a test." For once I agreed with Meager and checked in with Africa Division every day to see if there was any news. By the close of business on Friday, there was still no news, and I went home.

At about 8:00 p.m., when I returned from my son's Little League practice, I saw Lee standing in the doorway of our house. As I walked to the house, Lee was saying, "You have to call Boris Hansen [the chief of ops] right away. You have to leave tomorrow." I immediately called Hansen. "John, the threat against the Pan Am flight just got a little more real. A lot of dynamite was stolen from a factory, and AF wants you in country tomorrow," he said. Hansen then told me that he had made plane reservations for me and that the next morning I was to go to headquarters, where a finance officer would give me $2,000 for the plane ticket and expenses. Because I hadn't applied for a visa, I would have to be declared to the local service and an officer would meet my plane and get me through immigration and customs. This trip turned out to be interesting and tiring.

By 7:00 Saturday evening, I was in country. A station officer, "Mike Diggs," and a local intelligence service (IS) officer met my plane and took me to a less-than-third-class hotel. Diggs told me that the locals had the walk-in in custody and that they were rounding up suspects in the dynamite theft.

"Can you be ready to do your thing on Monday?" Diggs asked.

"Sure, I have read all the cable traffic, and I can do it tomorrow, if you want," I answered.

I spent Sunday basking in the glory of the third world, and on Monday morning Diggs picked me up and took me to the local prison where the walk-in and three suspects in the dynamite theft were in custody. I had been in a couple of prisons in Vietnam and found them to be primitive at best. This one was slightly better.

First on my agenda was the walk-in. He was in his early twenties and was a street hustler. His English was good, and he worked very hard at conning me. He had not been fed for two days, and after the first test I had some food brought to him. After he had eaten, I continued my interrogation, and by 6:00 that evening he told me that he had been stoned on ganja, a kind of marijuana, when he came up with the story about blowing up the Pan American flight. When he saw how excited the Americans were about what he had told them, he couldn't back out of it. There was no plot to blow up the Pan Am flight.

Frankly, I was hoping that I could forego the pleasure of testing the suspects in the dynamite theft and get home, but Diggs told me that it could really help his rapport with the local service if I continued with the tests. All three suspects were employees of the construction company that the dynamite had been stolen from.

Over the next two days I tested the three suspects. Resolving a theft of this nature is the type of case for which the polygraph was supposedly invented. In the three tests I conducted, it certainly fulfilled its purpose.

The first subject was a jolly, rotund man who did not seem at all fazed by the polygraph. He ran NDI charts, and I was confident that he had not been involved in the dynamite theft. I asked that he be kept isolated from the other two suspects until I completed my tests.

Number two on the suspect list did as well as the first suspect, and again, I was confident that he had had nothing to do with the dynamite theft. I was beginning to think that the locals had picked the suspects at random.

Suspect number three was huge. He reminded me of the Houston Rocket center Olijawon, and he completely dwarfed me. He was well over six feet tall, weighed over 250 pounds, and did not appear to have an ounce of fat on him. As sure as I was that the first two suspects had had no involvement in the theft, I was more certain that suspect number three had been involved. He ran some of the best DI charts I had ever seen. "There is not a doubt in my mind that you were involved in the theft of the dynamite," I said to him, after I had run two charts.

"No, sir, not me," he initially answered.

As it turned out, suspect number three had stolen the dynamite so that he could sell it to local fishermen. The fishermen would detonate the dynamite under water and then gather in the fish killed by the concussion.

After writing up the reports for my tests, I left on the Pan American flight that was the target of the fabricated plot. I was pleased with the work I had done, but for the first time, I felt a loss of enthusiasm for operations work and the travel that went along with it. These feelings were in part a product of fatigue. The interrogation of the walk-in exhausted me, and at forty-six, battling wits with a sleazy con man wasn't as exciting as it had been. Time away from the family was also a factor. Over the years I had learned that time away is lost time and can't be recouped. My sons were getting older, and as much as I felt they needed me to be around, I needed to be around them more. The one positive aspect of the trip was that, because I had been declared to the local service, I could never again return to the city where I had conducted the tests.

The station and AF commended me for the work I had done, and I felt that I had earned my pay for that month. Two days after returning I was back in PD, conducting two tests a day.

That fall, on October 23, a U.S. Marine barracks in Beirut was blown up and 241 marines were killed. Col. Tim Geraghty, the commanding officer of those marines, had been detailed to the CIA prior to his assignment in Beirut, and I had gotten to know him then. He was the finest military officer I had ever met, and I have met many military officers. I grieved for the marines and for the end of Colonel Geraghty's career. In the DO, I noticed shock, tension, and a touch of panic. In the field, the CIA was trying to hunt down those responsible, and PD was receiving many requests to test people claiming to have leads on the perpetrators. I took no pleasure in the fact that tragic events resulted in good business for polygraph examiners.

Less than six months later, Bill Buckley was kidnapped in Beirut, and DCI Casey went ballistic. Less than a month before the bombing, Bill Buckley had gone to Beirut to take over the station. The previous Christmas, Lee, our two sons, and I were waiting in line outside the White House to take a tour when Buckley, a good friend of mine, saw us. "John, what are you doing here?" he asked. When I told him, he said, "Come with me." He then took us to a Secret Service agent and asked the agent to take us on a tour. Casey's furor over the kidnapping translated into a lot of work for PD. Examiners went to Beirut and many other places to follow leads on the whereabouts of Buckley. Buckley's kidnapping also gave impetus to what was to become the Iran-Contra Affair in the sense that it motivated Casey, the Agency, and possibly even President Reagan to seek revenge on the Iranians.

The Contras were the armed opponents of the Sandanistas, who overthrew the Somoza regime in Nicaragua in the summer of 1979. The Reagan administration secretly supported the Contras, and the Agency was heavily involved in providing that support, in part via polygraph testing. Because of my near-fluency in Spanish, I made some trips to Central America in support of the Contra-support operations. On my first trip I was sitting with some case officers in the station office when another case officer came in and said, "We just had a guy come in and say he wants to defect. He says he is a lieutenant in the Nicaraguan army. John, can you test him?"

"Sure," I said, "let's go."

We went to an army post where the defector was being held. My first impression of him was, "This kid is no soldier." He was chubby, clean-cut, and obviously hadn't spent much time outdoors. His teeth looked as though he had spent a lot of money on dentists. By Latino standards, he was pale, and when I shook his hand I found his grip weak and his hands soft, without calluses.

Before testing the defector, I debriefed him about his experiences in the Nicaraguan army. He claimed to be an infantry officer but had no knowledge of military terminology or infantry weapons. When he told me that he had been trained to shoot the M-16 rifle, I excused myself, found an M-16, and asked him to field strip it. The "lieutenant" didn't have a clue; he wasn't a lieutenant or any kind of soldier. He was the son of wealthy Nicaraguans who didn't want him drafted into the army.

Asking a subject to field strip a weapon was a technique I had picked up in Vietnam. The South Vietnamese offered rewards to Viet Cong (VC) who turned themselves in or "rallied" to the South Vietnamese government, and to get the reward, many men who weren't Viet Cong would turn themselves in, claiming to be Viet Cong. On one occasion while debriefing one of these VC, I happened to notice an AK-47 hanging on the wall. I took it down and asked the self-claimed VC to field strip it. It would not have been proof positive of his claim if he had been able to do it, but that he couldn't do it was a pretty good indication that he wasn't who he said he was. My Nicaraguan "lieutenant" was the first person I had used the ploy on since Vietnam, but he was not the last.

Less than a month after testing the Nicaraguan, I was in South America to test a walk-in who had showed up at a U.S. embassy, claiming to be a member of a terrorist group and offering to sell us information. "Bob Miles," the case officer who interviewed the walk-in, became enthralled with him and thought he had another Oleg Penkovsky, the lieutenant colonel in the Soviet Strategic Rocket Forces who volunteered to spy for the West in the late 1950s. With the concurrence of his COS, Miles cabled headquarters for polygraph support.

The station didn't have a polygraph instrument, but there was one in a neighboring country. Because Miles had diplomatic privileges, he could pick up the instrument and bring it back to the station without having his bags searched. It was arranged to have Miles pick up the instrument, meet me in a hotel, and brief me on the walk-in before we traveled back to the station.

Over dinner Miles launched into a PR blitz about his walk-in that would put a Madison Avenue flack to shame. "You are going to be amazed by this guy. He told me that he knows so much about the terrorists in Latin America that I am going to have trouble thinking up enough questions to ask him," was Miles's opening salvo. "He is clearly wired and has $25,000 for the drug dealers. I think that he is a potential gold mine," he continued.

"Bob, I am always prepared to be amazed, and hope you're right, but did you actually see the $25K?" I replied.

"No, but when we get back tomorrow night, I can call him and make sure he still has it," Miles answered. Miles's enthusiasm was understandable but also disconcerting. Miles was comparatively new to the field, and I was afraid his expectations were unrealistically high.

One of the more disturbing aspects of the walk-in's story was that he had no identification documents, no passport, no cedula (ID card), nothing. My experience with walk-ins had been that they claim that they don't have documents to conceal their identities. Either they have tried to peddle their information to one or more other embassies and have had their names put on a "burn list" (list of known fabricators), or they are wanted for criminal activity and can't risk a name trace. Miles told me that the walk-in claimed that he had lost his documents, and he didn't seem to think that this was unusual. Miles had lived for years in Latin America, and I thought he should have known better.

As soon as we arrived the next evening, Miles called the walk-in and arranged for a meeting the next day. Before hanging up Miles asked, "Do you still have the $25,000?" There was a pause, then, Miles said, "OK. I'll see you tomorrow." Miles then turned to me and said, "He met with the drug dealers this morning and passed them the money."

Miles and I were in the luxury suite of a local hotel the next morning when the walk-in showed up. My first impression of the walk-in was, "This guy is a dirtbag." He was short, thin, fairly well groomed, and intelligent looking. "This is not the sort of guy who loses his ID documents," was my second thought.

My first comment was, "Mr. Bob tells me that you have had a lot of training. Have you had any surveillance training?"

"Of course," he said.

"Did you notice anyone following you here this morning?" I asked.

"No. Mr. Bob told me I would be safe here, and I didn't think I had to worry," he answered.

"We had three people follow you here. One of them was a very attractive woman, and you didn't notice," I said. Miles's superspy seemed disconcerted; this reaction had been my intention. There had been no surveillance.

My next gambit was to ask him what kind of weapons training he had had.

"All kinds, the Colt pistol, the Browning 9mm, the M-1, the AK-47," he answered.

"How many bullets does the Browning 9mm hold when it is fully loaded?" I asked.

"Seven, I think," he said.

I then handed him a Browning 9mm and told him to take it apart. As I had expected, he couldn't do it. From that point on, it went downhill. As it turned out Miles's walk-in was an absolute fraud. I took a certain amount of satisfaction from ferreting out this fabricator but also felt that Miles should have been able to find holes in his story, just as I had, without using the polygraph.

There was a nice letter from the COS waiting when I returned from that trip. The next day I conducted two RIPs—business as usual.

As much as I hated being away from Lee and our kids, doing TDYs really helped me to maintain my equilibrium.

Later that year Al Tremayne took Jan Boyle on her training trip. Tremayne was the chief of ops, and while he was gone, Meager named me acting chief of ops. For a little over six weeks I scheduled ops tests and reviewed ops charts and reports. When no examiners were available to run ops tests, I conducted them. During those six weeks I enjoyed my work more than I had at any time since Meager's arrival.

Meager allowed me to travel while I was acting chief and asked me to take two of the newer examiners, "Ron Lisle" and "Naomi Jewell," on their training trips. I hadn't taken an examiner on a training trip since I took Bob Fester on his training trip in 1978. The trip with Lisle went very well. Lisle was a Vietnam veteran, a former Baltimore City detective, and a very street-wise guy. He was also cultured and a lot of fun to be around. During the trip, Lisle conducted some good tests, but he also made a good impression on the DO officers he worked with by volunteering to do some personal protection/bodyguard work.

Jewell's trip went differently. She was a former police officer, and I had tested her before she entered on duty. As much as I liked her, I thought she was a little rough around the edges. I remember reading her BI before I tested her and finding out that she had been written up for "not waiting for backup" in a "man with a gun" situation. Jewell had disarmed the man and thrown him off a motel balcony.

As Jewell's training officer on this trip, I was to work with her for a week at our first stop and then let her go on by herself to complete the trip. I monitored her first test and thought she did fine. I let her do her second test on her own. When she finished she came to me and said, "John, this guy is bad, and he may be a spy." I looked at her charts and thought, "Naomi may have something here," and wished that I had sat in on the test. Jewell told me that she had really gone after the subject but couldn't get anything out of him. We had other tests to do, so I arranged to retest the subject after completing the other tests.

Two days later Jewell claimed that she was sick and couldn't continue the trip. She left for headquarters the next day, and I conducted the rest of the tests that had been scheduled. Because I didn't have visas for the other countries on Jewell's itinerary, I had to cancel the remainder of the trip.

When I retested Jewell's "possible spy," I got him to admit that a Russian diplomat had recently tried to recruit him and that he had concealed the pitch because he thought that if he told us we would fire him. After he made that admission, I tested him, and he came out well. Dealing with this man in Spanish certainly helped, but there was another factor in play: Before I let the subject go, he volunteered to me, "Señor, that woman who tested me was not a nice lady. She was rude and talked down to me, and there is no way I would ever tell her anything."

When I returned to headquarters, I found out that on her return trip, Jewell had stopped in her hometown, where she interviewed for and accepted a job. I am convinced that Jewell undertook the training trip with no intention of completing it and, in essence, used the Agency to pay for a trip to do an interview for another job.

Shortly after these training trips, Meager did something for which I was very grateful. On my next-to-the-last day as A/COPS a request came in for a test in Ireland. When I told Meager that I had been waiting for many years to return to Ireland, he said, "Go ahead, John, take the trip."

The subject of the test was an academician from a denied area whom the CIA had recruited several years previously and with whom the Agency had lost contact. He had recently resurfaced and contacted his case officer. "Lee Chang" was the case officer I worked with in Ireland. I reviewed the agent's file and discussed the case with Chang. We made arrangements to meet in the lobby of the Gresham Hotel in Dublin.

When I reviewed the charts of the agent's previous polygraph test, I became concerned because I thought that they indicated deception by the subject. During my brief tenure as A/COPS I had overturned nine calls made by the examiner who had conducted the previous test of this agent. I took the examiner's charts to Milenski, and he agreed with my assessment.

The examiner who had conducted the original test had come into PD during Falcone's tenure and had seemed to be destined for greatness. At the end of his training he had been selected for a plum overseas assignment. Two senior examiners, believing that he was not ready for an overseas assignment, went to Falcone and told him that if he sent the examiner overseas, they would go to Gambino to try to have the assignment rescinded. The examiner was given some token additional training and was then sent overseas.

During this examiner's overseas assignment, to my knowledge, he never obtained a significant admission, and in a conversation with me, he said, "The Iranians beat me like a drum." Regardless, he was given an outstanding fitness report and promoted to GS-14. He had requested a return to PD and was turned down because, as Milenski told me, "He is an incompetent examiner." When I asked Milenski how he could have gotten an outstanding fitness report and been promoted based on such a poor performance, Milenski just shrugged his shoulders.

Knowing that an incompetent examiner had tested and most likely been beaten by the agent I was about to test added a little spice to the job that lay ahead. If the subject did badly on his test, I wanted very much to get a confession, but knowing the cultural and ethnic background of the agent left me less than optimistic. I had only tested two subjects of this agent's ethnicity, had passed one of them, concluded the other was lying, and was unable to get an admission during my interrogation.

Traveling to Ireland in February as a tourist can be a tough story to sell, but I was willing to give it a try. I flew to London and met with a case officer with whom I had worked in Germany. He gave the name and number of someone I was to contact if I ran into any problems, and I was off to Dublin.

A British immigration officer gave me a bit of a hard time as I was leaving London. "And why would you be going to Ireland at this time of the year?" he asked.

I told him that I was between jobs and that this was a good time for me to go.

"Do you have any relatives in Ireland," he asked.

"None whom I have met," I answered. When I told him that I didn't have a hotel reservation, he seemed to get more suspicious, and I became convinced that he thought I was an American IRA sympathizer. I don't know why he finally cleared me, but he suddenly said, "Well, now, have a good trip."

Dublin, the city of my mother's birth, didn't hold much attraction for me. On a trip there that I had taken while in the army, I had found it to be a dirty, rundown city. This time, it had undergone a minor facelift, and it looked much better than I remembered.

Chang and I met as arranged, and he drove me to an old farmhouse about twenty miles outside of Dublin. The farmhouse was rustic and had not been well maintained, but it was comfortable. The only heat was a fireplace, but I thought that for one or two days I could manage. I had worked in places that were much worse.

"John, this is where we will have the meeting and do the test. I will drive back into Dublin, meet our guy tomorrow morning, and bring him out here," Chang said. Chang also told me that there was a pub about half a mile down the road where I could eat. Then, with a "see you tomorrow," he was off.

My dinner at the pub that night was an interesting experience. This pub was definitely not for tourists. It was smoke-filled, dimly lit, and borderline seedy. About twenty men were there when I arrived, and the youngest of them appeared to be over sixty. When I walked through the door conversation came to a standstill. Each and every man there sized me up, but no one said a word. I spotted an empty table, sat down, and waited. A waiter approached and handed me a menu without saying a word. The singing and political debate I had witnessed in pubs in Dublin during my previous visit was absent from this one, and it was almost eerie. I felt like a Freedom Rider in a Ku Klux Klan bar. My meal was simple, inexpensive, and poorly cooked. It seemed to me that the other patrons were waiting for me to leave so that they could back to doing whatever they were doing before I arrived. I am a fast eater, and that night, I ate faster than usual and was out of there in less than an hour.

At about 10:00 the next morning, Chang showed up with the agent. Once again I tested the subject on the issue of whether or not he had told anyone about his test. I conducted two tests. The first did not support his denial of having told anyone about his previous test; the second test did not support his denial of working for his country's intelligence service. I confronted him. Based on the results of the two tests and my interrogation, I concluded that from the very beginning of the operation, this agent had reported his contacts with us to his superiors. Although I couldn't get him to admit that he was a double agent, he did blurt out something that I considered very telling: "I am so glad it is over. I never wanted to do this." This convinced me that the agent's government had coerced him to maintain contact with us. Failing his polygraph test was the agent's way out.

Chang didn't seem disappointed, and I think he agreed with the test results. He drove the subject back to Dublin, then came back, and took me into Dublin. I spent one night in a hotel and left for home the next day.

Back in headquarters, changes were afoot in Security. Later that year Casey named Dr. James Lynch to replace Katopish as director of the Office of Security. Doctor Lynch's CIA career had been in the Directorate of Intelligence, and he had a PhD in biology. Lynch made a good impression on me in his first appearance in PD. Meager kept referring to him as Doctor Lynch, but every time he met one of us, he said, "Call me Jim." He was very informal, and I liked that. I also liked the fact that Lynch did not seem to have any negative feelings about polygraph. He praised the work we examiners were doing, and after his first appearance in PD I had the feeling that in Lynch PD had a real friend in a high place.

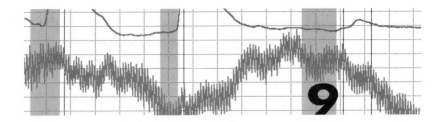

THE ERA OF GOOD FEELINGS

In his first act as director of OS, James Lynch replaced Meager as chief of PD. Meager's tenure had seen a mass exodus of examiners, and morale was very bad. I don't know why Lynch replaced Meager, but I was pleased that he did and I was almost ecstatic when I learned who Meager's replacement would be: "Jack Parnell." Parnell was one of the most respected men in the Office of Security. My contacts with Parnell had been very positive, and I was a fan of his. Parnell had no previous polygraph experience, but if Lynch wanted to change PD's image, naming Parnell as chief was a giant step in the right direction.

Lynch's predecessors' benign neglect of polygraph ended on day one of his directorship. From the very beginning of his tenure, Lynch made it clear that he was not only interested in polygraph but also very proactive in his efforts to improve PD. Early on Lynch realized that polygraph was much more cost effective than background investigations were. Lynch gave Parnell and PD a blank check to do whatever it took to make PD better. Demands for polygraph support continued to increase, and Lynch authorized PD to double its examiner cadre. We never reached that goal, but the authorization of the expansion alone sent a clear message that PD was no longer Security's bastard child. For those of us who had suffered through Meager's Reign of Terror, these were heady times. Lynch and Parnell launched what, on reflection, I consider to be an Era of Good Feelings in PD.

Parnell's arrival on the scene coincided with another event that had far-reaching implications for CIA's polygraph program: the arrest and conviction of Sharon M. Scranage for espionage. In 1984 a Security inspection team surveyed the CIA's office in Accra, Ghana. A member of the inspection team, while visiting Scranage's apartment, noticed a picture of Scranage with a local male, and upon his return to headquarters, he wrote a memorandum to the Special Activities Division expressing concern that Scranage was dating a foreign national.

My overseas travels, in conjunction with hundreds of polygraph tests I conducted on Agency people who had served overseas, led me to the conclusion that an overwhelming majority of CIA's unmarried (and some married) employees who are assigned overseas dated foreign nationals, and normally, this was not a concern. Office of Security lore has it that the only reason Scranage was reported was because she had refused to go on a date with the man who wrote the report.

The Office of Security's Special Activities Division was the entity responsible for looking into case officers' relationships with foreign nationals. A SAD investigator, who was a former polygraph examiner, read the report and recommended that Scranage be brought home, short of tour, to be given a specific issue polygraph test regarding her relationship with her Ghanaian boyfriend. This recommendation was overruled as none of the managers in SAD felt that dating a foreign national was out of the ordinary.

When Scranage finished her tour in Accra, she was to make a lateral transfer to another overseas post. Because Scranage would be overseas when her reinvestigation polygraph examination would come due, SAD requested that she be given her RIP during her home leave, prior to her departure for her next assignment. Initially, PD had a difficult time scheduling her because we were overbooked. Two investigators from SAD asked Frank Cross, the chief of PD's Employee Branch, to juggle the schedule to make room for Scranage. The investigators, according to Cross, assured him that Scranage's test would be routine, and they did not mention any suspicions SAD had regarding Scranage, nor was any special coverage requested. My sense is that SAD had no suspicions that Scranage was a spy.

"Ted Terrell" conducted the test. During the first session Scranage showed indications of deception in her response to the question about providing classified information to an unauthorized person, and the session ended with the issue unresolved. Over the next four days Terrell coaxed Scranage to admit that she had become involved with a man named Michael Soussoudis, a Ghanaian citizen who had permanent resident alien status in the United States and who was living in Accra. Scranage also admitted that she had supplied classified information regarding Ghanaian agents to Soussoudis.

Terrell did a masterful job with Scranage. On the occasions when I monitored the interviews, I never heard him raise his voice or be in any way aggressive. My impression was that Terrell bonded so well with Scranage that she wanted to tell him what she had done.

Before Scranage's test was complete, the CIA told the FBI that an Agency employee had admitted to committing espionage. When Terrell completed his interview, Security called Parnell and told him to have

Terrell report to an office on the fourth floor. Parnell went with Terrell, and when they arrived, they were confronted with a room full of FBI agents and Office of Security managers. The FBI agents immediately began grilling Terrell as to exactly what Scranage had told him and how he had cajoled her into making the admissions. Terrell fielded their questions flawlessly.

Scranage was arrested and agreed to cooperate with the FBI. At the FBI's direction she contacted Soussoudis and lured him to the United States to meet with her. During their meeting, Soussoudis was arrested.

Initially, Scranage was charged with eighteen counts of espionage. All but one of the counts was dismissed, and she was sentenced to five years in prison. That sentence was eventually reduced to two years. Soussoudis was sentenced to twenty years in prison. His sentence was waived on the condition that he leave the United States within twenty-four hours.

Admissions of espionage had been obtained from Agency employees previously, but Scranage was the first to be convicted and sent to prison. In PD, obtaining the confession from Scranage was a very big deal, and Parnell put Terrell in for a $10,000 award, which he not only received but deserved. Everyone in PD was pleased for Terrell. However, when "Bruno Gerard," the chief of SAD, was also given a $10,000 award because, according to the award citation, SAD investigators had actually broken the case, PD's euphoria was diminished.

Gerard had written up a memorandum on the case and essentially took credit for its success. At a subsequent interagency polygraph conference hosted by the FBI in Quantico, Virginia, the moderator commented that no spy had ever been caught through the use of polygraph. Pete Roberts, who was PD's representative at the conference, challenged the moderator, citing the Scranage case. The moderator defended his statement by citing Gerard's memorandum and claiming that investigators had given the polygraph examiner the information that led to Scranage's confession. Nothing could have been further from the truth. I knew that the SAD investigators had told Frank Cross that Scranage would not be a problem and had not mentioned any suspicions they had regarding Scranage. Gerard's memorandum was a lie. In fact, by disregarding the recommendation to have Scranage brought back to headquarters for a SIP, SAD may have allowed a spy to remain in place for over a year. Gerard's memorandum was a preemptive strike to head off any criticism.

There was another factor in play in this case. When employees are suspected of espionage, examiners are not given a heads up regarding those suspicions. When Ames was polygraphed in 1991, for example, the examiners were not advised that Ames was on the list of mole suspects. When Harold James "Jim" Nicholson, a CIA staffer who began spying for the Russians after Ames's arrest, failed three polygraph tests on the issue of concealing contact with a foreign intelligence service, some claimed that the examiners who tested Nicholson were told prior to his being tested that he was suspected of espionage. That is categorically not true. Had Scranage, Ames, or Nicholson been confronted and interrogated by the Counterintelligence Staff or SAD and not made admissions, in all probability, a SIP would have been requested.

To add insult to injury, in the study of the Scranage case published by the Directorate of Intelligence, the role of Terrell's polygraph test was ignored. During their five days together, Terrell and Scranage bonded, and I believe that he had more insight on what made Scranage tick than anyone else in the Agency. Scranage bared her soul to Terrell, and the statements she made as well as the rationales she offered could have enhanced the DI study. The DI's failure to acknowledge the role of polygraph in the Scranage case and the Office of Security's award to Gerard were symptomatic of the disdain that many in the DI and Security had for polygraph. That disdain notwithstanding, PD did gain some status as a result of Terrell's efforts.

Shortly after Scranage's arrest, Vitaly S. Yurchenko, a KGB colonel, walked into the U.S. embassy in Rome and claimed that he wanted to defect. If his defection were legitimate, he could effect an intelligence coup of tremendous significance. Yurchenko was polygraphed, and when he passed, the euphoria in DO went up a notch. Four months later Yurchenko "undefected," prompting many questions. Was Yurchenko a plant directed by the Russians? Many thought so, but as I reflect on what I have learned since the Yurchenko affair, I am about 99 percent sure that he was legitimate at the time he defected. One of my colleagues in Security told me that at the time Yurchenko walked away from his keeper, Casey was waiting for him, to host a dinner in his honor. Casey had been euphoric over Yurchenko's defection and, as was his way, blew the Agency's horn loud and long over this coup. This was the last thing Yurchenko wanted, and it may well have contributed to his decision to undefect.

As if Scranage's arrest and Yurchenko's undefection were not enough, news of CIA involvement with the Contras was coming to light, and again this did not bode well for the Agency. In 1984 the Agency had launched an operation to mine the harbors in Nicaragua, an act of war, without notifying Congress. Charges that the Agency was a "rogue elephant," which had been bruited about during the Church and Pike committee hearings, were once again heard.

I was traveling quite a bit within the United States at this time, and some of that travel involved conducting tests for the FBI, including one of the more interesting cases I was involved in.

MI6, the British foreign intelligence service, had contacted the FBI and asked it to detain and then send back to England an individual who had been involved in a kidnapping in which a $6 million ransom had been paid. The individual, whom I will call "Ibrahim," was on a flight to New York's JFK Airport when the FBI received the call. The FBI met the plane and detained Ibrahim. Ibrahim immediately asked the FBI to contact the CIA. He gave the name of a CIA officer who he claimed would vouch for him. The FBI did as Ibrahim requested, setting off alarms at headquarters. A meeting between Ibrahim and an Agency case officer Ibrahim had worked with was subsequently arranged.

During that meeting Ibrahim acknowledged his role as a go-between in the kidnapping and said he would be willing to serve a prison sentence, but only if he could serve it in the United States. Ibrahim then went on to say that if he were deported, he would make public the CIA operation he had been involved in. At that time the Agency could not afford to have that happen, and Ibrahim was told that if he passed a polygraph test regarding his involvement in the kidnapping, the Agency would intercede to block his deportation. I was asked to conduct the test.

Ibrahim's FBI watchdog, "Joe Farrell," was a big, physically imposing Irishman, who was also one of the more profane men I have ever encountered. "John, I hate this fucking low-life," said Farrell as he introduced me to Ibrahim, and his language only got worse.

I spent about an hour debriefing Ibrahim on the details of the kidnapping, and although I noticed some minor inconsistencies between what I had read about the kidnapping and what Ibrahim told me, there were no major discrepancies. Just before I hooked Ibrahim up for the test, Farrell approached Ibrahim and said, "Asshole, you come up lying, and I will make you wish you had never been born." These comments were not at all helpful.

During my first test of Ibrahim, I concluded that the details he gave me about the kidnapping were false. I told Farrell, and Farrell went off on Ibrahim raging and swearing. I then interrogated Ibrahim. During the interrogation, I became convinced that the kidnapping had been more a collusion between Ibrahim and the alleged victim than an actual kidnapping. I confronted Ibrahim but could not get a confession out of him. A final test supported my suspicion that the kidnapping had been a scam.

Farrell's treatment of Ibrahim was disturbing, and I couldn't help but think that had Farrell been more civilized, I might have gotten something out of Ibrahim. I had worked with FBI agents before, and although I liked many of them on a personal level, I found that some of them did not handle their sources professionally. Several of my DO contacts who have worked on joint operations with the FBI have told me, "The Bureau coerces its assets. We charm ours." Farrell's behavior was consistent with that comment.

Back in headquarters I waited to see an article in the newspapers about Ibrahim's arrest or about the sensitive CIA operation he had been involved in, but that article never appeared. When I ran into the two headquarters officers I had worked with on this case, neither of them volunteered any information about Ibrahim, and I didn't ask. To this day I have no idea as to what happened to Ibrahim.

The year 1985 came to be known as the "Year of the Spy" as more than a dozen Americans were arrested as a result of espionage related activities. In addition to Scranage, nine other Americans were arrested for espionage in 1985. The most infamous among them was John Anthony Walker, a retired U.S. Navy chief warrant officer, who sold classified information to the Soviets for eighteen years, from 1968 to 1985. Walker, his son Michael, his brother Arthur, and a Navy buddy, Jerry Whitworth, were in the Walker net and were all arrested and convicted of espionage. The fact that Walker had never been polygraphed during his career suggested to some that if he had been he might have been caught earlier. This played well with those in government who were advocating an expansion of polygraph programs. Certainly, this helped Doctor Lynch in his efforts to expand the Agency's polygraph program.

One slight bump in the road to expansion was the case of Larry Wu-Tai Chin, a retired CIA employee who was arrested in 1985 for spying for the People's Republic of China. Chin was sentenced in February 1986, and two weeks later he committed suicide in his cell. He had beaten his polygraph test many years before, a fact that was not lost on polygraph detractors.

Ronald Pelton, an NSA employee, was also arrested for espionage in 1985, and in 1986 he was sentenced to three life terms in prison. Pelton, I believe, had been polygraphed before he began working with NSA but not after he began spying. Pelton gave up the Ivy Bells Project, in which U.S. intelligence had tapped into a Soviet undersea communications cable. Yurchenko had identified Pelton.

Scranage was the only active CIA employee among the spies who were caught in 1985, and PD's image had been boosted by Terrell's success in that case. The division's improved image helped recruitment, and not only more but also more highly qualified security officers began applying for positions with PD. At about this time Parnell decided that PD needed a full-time recruiter, and he asked me to take the job saying I would have a better chance of getting promoted to GS-14 in the new position. I took it.

When I became PD's full-time recruiter, PD examiners were being recruited either from within Security or from the ranks of commercial and military examiners. As good as many of the commercial and military

examiners were, most of their previous testing experience had been focused on resolving crimes and lent credence to one of the many criticisms leveled at PD: that PD examiners had a cop or security officer mentality and were too parochial in their thinking. Examiners were often
accused of being unable to relate to members of the other directorates
and of being out of touch with the Agency population. From my perspective, these perceptions had more than a grain of truth, and I felt that to
change those perceptions we needed a more diverse group of examiners.

Since my first day in polygraph, I had had difficulty understanding
the Office of Security's policy of accepting only security officers for polygraph training. A few former DP officers were in PD when I entered on
duty, but they had been brought in primarily for their language ability
and were treated as outsiders. In addition to denying PD access to the
rather large talent pool within the CIA, this policy also promoted an us-
against-them mindset among the examiners, exacerbating PD's isolation
from the rest of the Agency. When I suggested to Parnell that PD try and
recruit from the entire Agency population, he agreed it was a good idea
but wasn't confident that the Office of Security's management would go
along with it. However, Doctor Lynch's expansion plans for PD trumped
any naysayers in Security.

With the growth of the RIP and TRIP programs, PD was testing
more staff employees than ever before. For the most part, the examiners
had little experience working with Agency staffers outside of the DO.
Lack of contact with the other directorates was a deficiency that inhibited examiners' relationships with their RIP/TRIP subjects and was a
problem that had to be addressed. I thought that, until we had tested a
sufficient number of staffers from the other directorates to reach an understanding about how they functioned, it would be in PD's best interest
to try to recruit examiners from the other directorates.

With the less-than-enthusiastic approval of Security, I put out
Agency-wide announcements that PD was looking for examiners and
was inviting those interested to attend a recruitment presentation in one
of the Agency auditoriums. The turnout was much better than I had
expected, but as I suspected, many of those who showed up were employees who were dissatisfied with their current jobs and looking for a way
out. Of the eighty-plus employees who showed up for the presentation,
eleven actually applied for examiner positions. All eleven were interviewed
by a panel made up of senior PD officers, and of the eleven, five became
examiners.

One result of my recruitment campaign that I had not expected
was complaints to Security from personnel officers from other directorates that I was stealing their employees. That ended my broad-brush

recruitment presentations, and from that point on, I recruited one examiner at a time.

Recruiting took up much of my time, and I couldn't travel abroad at all, which was the only downside of the recruiter's job. In the fall of 1986 an officer in Latin America Division (LA), "Andy James," with whom I had worked in Laos and South America, asked if I would be willing to take a trip to South America and work on a case for them. "One of your guys tested a walk-in last summer and called him 'good.' We are having some doubts and would like to have him done again," he said. I got the details of the case and told James that I would get back to him.

What intrigued me about this case was that the walk-in had given almost the same story as another walk-in I had tested before; specifically, both claimed to have been in the same prison at the same time. Initially, I thought they were the same individual, but after seeing a picture of this latest walk-in, I knew that he wasn't the walk-in I had previously tested. In any event I suspected that the walk-in James was asking me to test was as phony as the one I had tested previously. I asked PD to let me conduct the test.

The examiner who had conducted the first test was a PD supervisor who had been on a training trip with a new examiner when he administered the test. I reviewed the charts and read the examiner's report. It was clear to me that the examiner had been beaten, and when I discussed the case with him, I told him so. He didn't disagree, but said, "John, if you knock this guy in, I am going to look bad." It was clear to me that what he was trying to say was, "I hope you call this guy good," and I resented it as I saw it as an attempt to influence my call. I wanted to say, "Wouldn't that be a shame," but just said, "I guess we will have to see how it goes."

It went poorly. When I arrived in the station and found out that the case officer who was handling the walk-in was "Pete Proll," I became even more sure that this was a bad operation. I had worked with Proll in Latin America and in Vietnam, and I found him to be a real James Bond wannabe. He was not a case officer I enjoyed working with.

Proll gave me his take on the walk-in, "Jose Rodriguez," and expressed absolute certainty that he was pure gold. "John, this guy has information about the terrorist movement down here that is outstanding, and he is the real deal." Proll also told me that when Rodriguez had walked in, he had given Proll his ID card but had asked Proll not to show it to the police. Proll didn't show the ID card to the police, but he did do a name check on Rodriguez. The registration number on the ID card did not match the name on the card (which Rodriguez was using with Proll), making it obvious that Rodriguez was concealing his real name from Proll.

COS "Gene Harkins" told me that the station had invested a lot of time and money in the operation and was hoping for the best. The reports officer "Mireille Spellman," whose husband I knew, took me aside and said, "Pete may think this guy is great and Gene may want him to be, but take it to the bank, he is a fraud." Spellman was right.

That night Proll, another officer, named "Ben Carson," and I went to the safe house to conduct the test. I had brought a picture of the walk-in I had previously tested, planning to show it to Rodriguez to see if he would admit to knowing him, since both had claimed to have been incarcerated in the same prison at the same time. When I showed Rodriguez the picture, he appeared startled and said, "Yes, I know him." He refused to tell us his name. At that point, I think Rodriguez knew I had him. Rodriguez failed the subsequent test. I told Proll that his agent had failed and also said that I wanted very much to interrogate Rodriguez. "John, let me talk to Jose," Proll said. Proll and Rodriguez then went into an adjoining bedroom to confer. While Proll and Rodriguez were conferring, DCOS "Ivan Nadler" showed up.

"How's it going, John?" he asked.

"Ivan, this guy is a complete phony," I answered.

"Where is Jose?" Nadler then asked.

"Pete is talking to him in the bedroom," I said.

"Look, John, I don't care what you have to do, but I want this thing resolved," Nadler said as he went out the door.

When Proll came out of the bedroom, he said that he had talked with Rodriguez and was convinced that Rodriguez had been telling the truth. I then told Proll that Nadler had just been there and had directed me to do whatever I had to do to resolve the test. "Pete, I want to interrogate Jose," I said.

"I won't allow it," answered Proll. "If you do that, you will alienate him, and we will never get anything out of him," I added.

"At least let me test Jose on his ID card. We know it's not his, and maybe we can use that to get him talking," I said.

"No way! This guy trusts me," Proll said.

"Pete, this guy is a fraud, and you should at least let me try to get at the truth," I responded. I also repeated what Nadler had said.

"I don't care. This is my agent, and the test is over," were Proll's final words on the test. Proll didn't say a word to me on the way back to the office and was obviously bent out of shape.

The next day Proll didn't say a word when I saw him in the office. Later that morning Harkins convened a meeting of the entire station. He asked me for the results of my test. I told him that Rodriguez was a fabricator. Proll took exception, but Harkins interrupted him and said, "Ben, I want you and Pete to take Jose's ID card down to Colonel 'Rivera' at the

National Police and see what they have on him." Proll and Carson left for
the National Police headquarters.

Approximately two hours later I saw Proll slowly walking down
the hall, mumbling to himself, "I've been lied to again."

Carson later told me, "When Colonel Rivera saw Jose's ID card, he
burst out laughing. 'That guy is the biggest paper mill [fabricator] in the
country. The police in San Marcos are looking for him because he
scammed them out of some money,' Rivera told us." Carson also enumerated other scams that Rivera attributed to Jose Rodriguez.

COS Harkins thanked me for my efforts. Mireille Spellman said,
"I've been trying to tell Gene that for six weeks." Proll wasn't speaking
to me. I was very pleased that I hadn't been beaten but a little disappointed that Proll wouldn't let me interrogate Rodriguez. As it turned
out, this was my last overseas operational case.

I was very much enjoying recruiting and was hoping I could find
more examiners like "Rorie Schiff." Schiff was one of the best of the
thirty-one examiners I recruited. A former teacher and Agency personnel officer, Schiff was very attractive, articulate, intelligent, poised, and
compassionate. Schiff had applied for PD years before when PD was accepting only candidates from within Security, and she had maintained
her interest even after her application was declined. When the Office of
Security's policy changed, she reapplied. Schiff conducted herself as a
consummate professional and was the best example of a steel fist in a
velvet glove that I have ever seen. I recall a specific issue polygraph test
Schiff conducted on an Agency employee suspected of stealing money.
The subject had agreed to take a polygraph test to clear himself.

During the session the subject was a bit rude with Schiff. When
Schiff responded, the anger in her voice turned the subject's rudeness
into docile compliance. Bob Fester and I were monitoring this test, and
Fester commented, "I hope to God she never comes after me." Schiff obtained a confession from the subject.

Although PD was now looking outside Security for recruits, Security was not being ignored. I made a pitch for polygraph to every Security
Officer Recruit Training class. My two main selling points were that as
professional security officers it was incumbent upon them to know as
much about polygraph as possible and that as polygraph examiners they
would gain more insight as to how the Agency functioned than was possible in any other job in Security. I also pointed out that the elicitation
and interrogation skills they learned as polygraph examiners would serve
them well in any future job in the Agency.

In addition to recruiting from within the Agency, I traveled around the country, attending APA conferences and visiting polygraph schools. The students at the polygraph schools I visited had a lot of interest in becoming Agency examiners, but the college degree requirement eliminated many potential candidates. When I spoke to the Texas Polygraph Association, a few of the attendees became a bit hostile when I mentioned the college degree requirement. Once a police examiner confronted me: "I'll outtest any of you CIA examiners any day of the week. You CIA people are nothing but a bunch of goddamn thugs and assassins, anyway."

A third source of candidates was the CIA applicant pool. Although I was a full-time recruiter, I continued to conduct at least three tests a week and was always on the lookout for applicants who I thought had the potential to be good examiners. I also solicited the other examiners for leads on applicants who they thought had the potential to be good examiners.

Examiner candidates were required to have at least a BA or BS degree and to pass the Agency's Professional Aptitude Test Battery (PATB). On several occasions the PATB requirement was waived for minority candidates, and on one occasion Rump had me allow a candidate to retake the PATB. When the candidate failed it the second time, Rump waived the requirement. I thought the Office of Security used failure of the PATB as an excuse to reject some security officer candidates but, in the name of political correctness, occasionally waived the requirement. Diversity had come to the fore with the arrival of Doctor Lynch, and so I had to live with a few waived PATBs . I understood why the Agency did this, but in the short term I believe it hurt PD and represented a lowering of standards.

"Ben Harmon," an examiner for whom the PATB requirement had been waived, came into PD during Pat Meager's tenure. He was a weak examiner, and on a couple of occasions while I was acting chief of ops, I had to overturn his calls. His reports were poorly written, and at one point I gave up asking him to revise them and rewrote them myself. In terms of communications skills, Harmon was the Yogi Berra of PD. Stickler for good writing that Meager was, he and Harmon did not get along. Meager made it clear that Harmon had no future in PD, and Harmon eventually left.

At the time Parnell came into PD, demands for tests were surging and PD didn't have enough examiners to meet the requests. Several examiners who had left during Meager's Reign of Terror were shanghaied into coming back. Among those was Harmon.

When I heard that Harmon was coming back, I went to Milenski and asked him, "Greg, how can we bring Ben back? He is one of the weakest examiners we have ever had in here."

"We are scraping the bottom of the barrel," said Milenski.

Not willing to let it go, I went to Parnell. I tried to make the case that bringing Harmon back was a mistake, but my words fell on deaf ears. Parnell told me that the PD panel had recommended bringing Harmon back. Frank Cross, who had been on that panel, subsequently told me that the panel had been reluctant to bring Harmon back.

Shortly after his return, Harmon was given a team leader position under Bob Fester. When Harmon wrote PARs for his subordinates and passed them on to Fester for review, Fester brought all of them to me. "John, these are god-awful. Would you see if you can fix them?" I don't think a single line of those PARs went untouched.

Harmon eventually became a GS-15, although not in PD, and his promotion did not particularly bother me. What did disturb me was the fact that, according to a Security personnel officer, in the Office of Security GS-14s were promoted to GS-15 because they were good writers.

A lack of communications skills was not the only problem with PD examiners who had their PATB requirement waived. One of these examiners came to me one day and said, "I know there are two Germanys. One is good and one is bad. Which one is the bad one?" I was also asked, "Is Italy a Communist country?" and "What part of Africa is Quito in?" These questions illustrated the lack of historical and geographical knowledge that some of the newer examiners brought to PD. Some would say this knowledge is not important. I disagree.

After a test by one of the aforementioned examiners, a staff employee I had worked with overseas called to tell me about his son's applicant test. "Jesus, John, the examiner told my kid that it was 'No problem if he belonged to the Birch Bayh Society,'" he laughingly said. "My kid almost broke out laughing."

Some examiners occasionally shortened the questions. For example, I heard one ask, "Are you hiding any foreign nationals?" instead of "Have you had contact with a foreign national that you want to hide from the CIA?"

I almost broke out laughing myself when, while monitoring an examiner who was conducting an interrogation, I heard him say, "If you could make up something, what would it be?"

Other amusing solecisms:

"We consider the polygraph session not only classified but very confidential."

"Didn't you do anything you wouldn't be arrested for?"

"Have you significantly *overestimated* your drug use?"

"Do you understand the Agency's drug problem [meaning policy]?"

In some offices, such malapropisms might be overlooked, but in an environment that requires daily interaction with a fairly sophisticated clientele and, more important, with a clientele who is looking for reasons to criticize polygraph, such verbal gaffes cannot be ignored. On some occasions coming across as inarticulate and intellectually slow, a la Peter Falk's bumbling Colombo, can be used as an interrogation ploy, but in a polygraph session, an examiner's verbal ineptitude is, more often than not, perceived as a weakness by a subject. Just as I objected to professional broadcasters who used poor grammar, I also had a problem with examiners whose spoken English was deficient. The examples I cited above became in-house jokes, but when subjects commented on and laughed about poorly worded questions, PD's already negative image was tarnished even more. My philosophy has always been that Agency examiners should speak, dress, and comport themselves at least as well as, but preferably better than, their subjects.

Bringing back poor examiners was not PD's only problem at this time. Several of the examiners PD wanted to bring back were doing well in their new jobs and did not want to return. At a meeting between PD and Security management, I commented that I thought it had been wrong to shanghai examiners, adding that the last person I wanted to conduct a polygraph test was someone who didn't want to be there. Bill Katopish, who chaired the meeting, responded, "I can't imagine anyone not wanting to do what's best for the Office of Security." Katopish had always treated me cordially, and I was a little taken aback by his reaction to my comment. After the meeting a couple of my colleagues told me that although they agreed with me, they thought I had made a big mistake in challenging a Katopish decision.

Not long after the meeting, and in response to the criticism of polygraph generated for the most part by the high bring-back rate, Katopish held a forum in the "Bubble," the Agency's largest auditorium. The purpose of the forum was to give Agency employees an opportunity to ask Katopish questions about the reinvestigation process in general, and polygraph in particular. I thought the forum was a good idea, until I heard what Katopish had said in response to the question, "What happens if an employee fails his polygraph test but doesn't make an admission?" According to an examiner who attended the forum, Katopish's answered, "Probably nothing."

My colleagues in PD and I felt that this was the wrong answer. Katopish had essentially told the Agency populace, "Whatever you do, don't make an admission." The job was tough enough without having the D/OS making it any more so. Katopish could have said, "We address each case individually," or "It depends on the issue. If a subject does not pass a test on the counterintelligence issues, we proceed differently than we would if he or she were having problems with the drug question." Almost anything would have been better than what he said.

The increased demand for polygraph tests also focused much attention on PD's physical plant. PD had occupied the same suite of offices for over twenty years, and it was no longer adequate. In the two years prior to Parnell's arrival, more than $900,000 had been spent in modernizing the headquarter's PD facility. Testing rooms were added, an audio monitoring system was installed, and two-way mirrors were put in some of the rooms. The modernization notwithstanding, the increased demands on PD rendered the new, improved IRD facilities inadequate.

The mirrored rooms installed during the modernization were a great addition to PD, and being able to monitor tests both aurally and visually improved the polygraph process. Many subjects assumed that their tests were videotaped, but that was not the case.

On one occasion, I was testing a U.S. Army general. He pointed to the sprinkler apparatus in the ceiling and asked, "Is that where the video camera is?"

"We don't videotape our interviews," I said.

"You're a goddamn liar, but if that's what you want to tell me, go ahead," the general said.

In my thirty-one years with PD, I know of only two interviews that were videotaped. Both of those were of specific-issue polygraph tests and the tapes were used as exemplars in PD's school.

In his grand plan to expand PD, Doctor Lynch proposed a table of organization for PD that called for more examiners than the current facility could handle. An external site had to be found since there was no room for more examiners in headquarters. After a short search, a newly completed, four-story building was selected. PD was assigned three floors of the new building, and the fourth floor was leased to a civilian corporation. From the day the new building was leased until PD moved in, every effort was made to create the best polygraph testing facility possible. The remodel took almost a year, but by the time PD moved in, in the summer of 1986, we had what I felt was the finest polygraph facility anywhere.

More significant than the new facility was the increase in the number of supervisory positions that went along with PD's expansion. Historically, candidates lost interest in PD when they realized the lack of potential for promotion in the division. When I entered on duty, the chief of PD was a GS-17, his deputy was a GS-15, and there were three GS-14 supervisors. All of the examiners were GS-13s and below. As PD grew, separate branches were established for each testing venue: the Applicant Branch, the Industrial Branch, the Employee Branch, and the Covert Ops Branch. Within each branch were teams of examiners, each with a team leader. Branch chiefs were GS-15s and team leaders were GS-14s. There was also a Training Branch and a Research Branch.

Examiners were assigned to the various branches based on experience. The least experienced examiners were assigned to the Applicant

Branch, not because applicants were the easiest of the subjects PD tested but because their examinations resulted in the most reportable information. Applicant tests provided the more junior examiners with opportunities to develop their elicitation and interrogation skills. Applicant Branch examiners did eight or nine tests a week and would develop reportable information in at least six of the tests. Two-thirds of the examinations required interrogations. In the Applicant Branch examiners not only developed their skills but also learned whether or not they were cut out to be examiners. Simply put, if an examiner in the Applicant Branch went more than ten tests without developing disqualifying information on an applicant, he or she should have started looking for another line of work.

As candidates completed the PD examiner course, they started to conduct tests for the Applicant Branch, replacing examiners who had done well in the Applicant Branch and had been moved into the Industrial or Employee branches.

When testing branches were formed in PD, getting assigned to the Ops Branch became the goal of every nascent examiner, and there was a perception that only the best examiners were assigned to Ops. Positions in Ops were limited, and most examiners who were assigned to Ops had tested in one or more of the other branches for at least two years. Foreign travel was the big draw of the Ops Branch, but the opportunity for a break from testing was also a factor. Conducting two tests a day, week in and week out, was mentally and physically exhausting. Becoming Ops-qualified was a status symbol and allowed examiners a reprieve from the routine of daily testing.

In 1975, when a formal reinvestigation program was begun, lifestyle questions (drugs, crime, homosexual activity) were not covered in the RIP tests; only counterintelligence issues (foreign national contacts, mishandling of classified material, foreign intelligence service contacts) were covered. However, after the Kampiles case in 1978, trial period (TRIP) testing was initiated and lifestyle questions covering the period since entering on duty were added to the reinvestigation tests. Compared with applicant and industrial testing, reinvestigation tests were less demanding. There were fewer reports to write, and interrogations were far less frequent. Unfortunately, this provided some examiners the chance to become complacent and to lose their edge. Interrogation and elicitation are skills that have to be constantly honed. Examiners in the Employee Branch could conduct many tests without having to do an interrogation, and as a result their skills could wane and they could fail to gain or could lose the confidence that came with obtaining admissions and that was so essential if one was to be an effective interrogator.

I remember an occasion during my tenure as a team leader in the Reinvestigations Branch, when the Applicant Branch became overwhelmed and asked for help. Two of my team members had not been doing very well in terms of developing information, and I sent them to the Applicant Branch for two weeks. One of the examiners developed disqualifying information in eleven of the seventeen examinations he conducted; the other obtained disqualifying information in eight of the fifteen examinations he conducted. Both came back to the Employee Branch with a renewed sense of confidence.

Concomitant with the increase in the number of examiners in PD was the growth of a bureaucracy to support them. Each branch chief had a secretary, and additional clerks were brought in to handle reports.

More tests also meant more complaints. No chief I worked with in PD was more proactive about complaints than Parnell. Shortly after PD relocated to the new facility, Parnell brought three senior Office of Security retirees in to review the tapes of every test that had resulted in a formal complaint being made. During Parnell's tenure, only one examiner was removed from PD because of a complaint, but reprimands were handed out and several examiners were counseled.

PD had always had someone to maintain the instruments, but as the division grew, the task became too much for one person and a Tech Branch was created. Three persons were assigned to the new branch, and their responsibilities were to maintain the instruments, pack instruments for overseas shipment, and service the monitoring equipment. The tech staff also trained new examiners in routine first echelon maintenance and basic trouble shooting to identify the source of problems with an instrument.

To keep current with polygraph research and to improve the profile of PD, Doctor Lynch pushed for a Research Branch within PD. In theory, this was a good idea, but in practice, it didn't work well. No one in PD was remotely qualified to do genuine research, and the chief of the Research Branch position became a sinecure. From the day of its creation until the day I retired, PD's Research Branch was a waste of manpower and money.

With the increase in the numbers of examinations that PD conducted, scheduling became very complex. Initially, each branch scheduled its own tests, but when that became unworkable, an examiner was taken offline to schedule all tests, except for operational cases. Being PD's scheduler turned out to be one of the more difficult and thankless jobs in the division.

On an almost daily basis, at least one examiner would either not show up for work or for some other reason be unavailable to test. Usually, that examiner had been scheduled to conduct two tests and replacement examiners would have to be found or the tests would have to be rescheduled. On occasions when a subject failed to show up for a test, the scheduler was often directed to call staff employees to see if one would come in on short notice to take the place of the subject who had not shown up. More and more, polygraph became a numbers game.

One of the more positive aspects of Agency testing was that the examiners generally were not impeded by time constraints. If an examiner felt that he needed another session to resolve an issue or that he wanted to bring a morning subject back that afternoon, it usually wasn't a problem—for anyone but the scheduler. On some occasions examiners in each branch asked their morning subjects to return for an afternoon session. That meant that the scheduler, on very short notice, might have to find three examiners to conduct tests.

Examiners live for cancelled sessions. When a subject didn't show up for a test, examiners would usually rejoice in the break the cancellation afforded them. That euphoria was usually, however, short lived because the scheduler would ask the examiner to fill in for a coworker who hadn't shown up or who was otherwise unavailable to do a test. Examiners could wax profane on these occasions.

As busy and hectic as it sometimes was, Parnell's management style kept things on an even keel, and morale was high. This was in part because the examiners were doing some very good work. I could fill a hundred pages describing some of the tests and the information developed, but for now, I will cite just two examples.

"Janet Banes" was the first female PD sent to the Reid school for training. She was intelligent, attractive, and effective at establishing rapport with her subjects. Although she was an experienced examiner who had been working in one of the other branches, on the occasion I will describe, she was asked to test an applicant who was being processed for the Agency's Career Trainee (CT) Program. CT candidates were a step above the usual staff applicant and were perceived by many as an elite group. Many had master's degrees, had attained success in a profession, and were looking for a new challenge.

From monitoring the test, my impression was that Banes's subject seemed a bit pompous and conformed to my vision of what a yuppie was supposed to look and sound like. During initial testing, the subject clearly and consistently reacted to the question, "In the last ten years have you committed a serious crime?" After a comparatively short interrogation, the subject admitted to Banes that he had been sodomizing his one-year-old niece. His followup comment that "she's too young to ever tell anyone" enraged me. Almost twenty years after that test, I still find it hard to believe that this subject made the admission that he did.

Every CIA examiner has done tests about which they get emotional.

For me, a man who was molesting his six-year-old nephew was such a case. As is true with most child molesters, he blamed the victim. In describing what had occurred with his nephew, this man said, "He (the nephew) would rub up against me and get me aroused. Even if he was only six, he knew what he was doing."

Critics of polygraph often comment, "If investigators do their jobs properly, there is no need for polygraph." I dare any background investigator to show me a BI in which he or she has found evidence of child molestation or has even come up with an allegation of molestation that was investigated further and substantiated. Most people engaging in criminal activity don't advertise it. References interviewed during a BI are often reluctant to provide derogatory information about the BI subject because they may like the subject, they may have participated in the activity with the subject, or they may be afraid that the subject will find out.

Banes was given no more recognition than a verbal "nice job" for her efforts. No one outside of PD and Clearance Division was aware of what she had done. This was another missed opportunity for PD to get some good PR.

When I suggested that each week PD could make known the number of tests conducted, the number of subjects who were disapproved for security clearances based on polygraph-derived information, and the reasons for which they were disapproved, I was told that this couldn't be done because of "privacy issues." I argued that this could be done without mentioning the names of those disapproved. PD could publish the ten most significant tests conducted each month without mentioning names or dates. That idea didn't fly either.

My sense was that protecting the subjects' privacy was not the issue. The issue was "keeping PD in its place." Some in Security felt the negative image polygraph had was right and just, and they were not about to allow it to change.

Most of the disqualifying information developed during polygraph examinations related to criminal activity and drug use, or as Doctor Lynch put it, "drugs and thugs." However, the parameters examiners had for disqualifying information could be rather subjective, and this was a problem. No clear guidelines established how much drug use was disqualifying. Without such guidelines, examiners felt pressured to get as much information as possible. As a result, sessions lasted longer and were more stressful than they had to be.

I tested a woman who admitted what I thought was enough drug use to get her disapproved for a security clearance. Not wanting to prolong her agony, I closed the session. She was hired. Three years later she was afforded a trial period test during which she admitted to having used marijuana at least five hundred times since she entered on duty. She was given a week's leave without pay and a promotion the week she returned to duty. At an offsite following the woman's trial period test, I mentioned this case to a senior security officer and asked, "How in God's name can you security approve someone who has admitted to five hundred uses of marijuana since entering on duty?" His answer was, "That's a case we don't like to talk about."

The parameters for disqualifying criminal activity were less ambiguous. Any subject who admitted to having committed a previously unreported felony had a good chance of being security disapproved, but even in the case of felonies, there were some cloudy areas. How many incidents of shoplifting were "enough"? William Kampiles had admitted three incidents of shoplifting and that information was not a part of the polygraph report. Was one incident of date rape "enough"? How much theft from a previous employer was allowed?

On many occasions subjects who revealed what examiners' considered disqualifying information were hired. If examiners were not careful, they could get cynical. A running joke in PD was that K-Mart had higher hiring standards than the Agency did.

While some subjects were hired who shouldn't have been, many, many more who did not deserve security clearances were denied them. Steve Andros, one of my early mentors, once told me, "John, keep one asshole a month out of here, and you will earn your pay." During Parnell's tenure, PD examiners obtained disqualifying information at least two or three times every day.

Of the many positive developments in PD during Parnell's tenure, none had a greater impact than his securing premium pay for the examiners. For years people had said that examiners should be getting extra money because of the stress inherent in their jobs. I believed that examiners should be getting extra money, not because of the stress, but because we had a skill that others didn't have. Agency engineers, accountants, doctors, and other specialists were given a boost in pay for their expertise in a given area, and I felt that examiners deserved no less.

Parnell's advocacy and Doctor Lynch's support resulted in a 15 percent addition to each examiner's base salary. This gave an immediate boost to an already strong morale and was also a real plus in terms of recruiting. Although the 15 percent, which was called premium pay, would not be factored into the retirement annuity, with each promotion an examiner's premium pay increased. By the time I retired, that 15 percent amounted to $15,000 a year.

As is the case with many good things, the 15 percent premium pay had its downsides. First, the lure of the 15 percent boost in salary encouraged many people who probably shouldn't have applied to apply for examiner positions. But while the money attracted some would-be examiners, with few exceptions it didn't keep them in PD; the work was just too tough.

Tough job or not, by the summer of 1986 PD was in better shape than it had ever been, and the future was looking rosy. It therefore came as quite a surprise when Parnell announced that he would be moving on. Milenski was Parnell's deputy, and everyone knew that Parnell had been keeping the chief's seat warm for him. Even so, with things going as well as they were, the question, "Why now?" seemed appropriate. I think that Parnell was a bit too popular. PD's image was improving, in large part because of Parnell. I don't think Doctor Lynch saw Parnell as any sort of threat but rather as someone who cramped his style. Therefore, he had to go.

Regardless of why Parnell left, his farewell party was one of the low points in my career. In the short time he headed PD, he had enhanced the the division's prestige and raised the morale of the staff to new heights. I didn't see how it could get any better. Parnell was one of the most gracious and decent men I had ever known, and as much as I would miss him as a boss, I would miss him more as a friend. As expected, Doctor Lynch named Milenski to replace Parnell.

Parnell's departure marked the end of a very good period in PD's history. At the same time another era was coming to an end: the reign of DCI William J. Casey. Casey had been diagnosed with a brain tumor, and his health was failing rapidly. After an extended stay in the hospital, on May 13, 1987, he succumbed.

The Iran-Contra Affair, which had been spawned during Casey's tenure, had given the Agency a black eye and once again raised some serious questions about the role of the CIA in formulating government policy. In an attempt to try and head off additional criticism and attacks on the Agency, President George H. W. Bush named then-director of the FBI, William Hedgcock Webster, to replace Casey. Webster had been a federal judge prior to his being named director of the FBI in 1978. Prior to nominating Webster as DCI, Bush had nominated Robert M. Gates for the position. Gates had been with the Agency since 1966, and when Casey's brain tumor incapacitated him in December 1986, Gates assumed the position of acting director, CIA. Gates's nomination seemed logical, but in the furor over Iran-Contra, he was seen as being tainted by his close association with Casey. His nomination ran into problems and this

John Sullivan and his wife, Lee,
at their wedding reception on August 29, 1970.

The author (center) poses with friends from his unit, the 513th
Military Intelligence Group, following his promotion to sergeant E-5,
in Bremerhaven, Germany, in October 1965.

Lee with her first son, John, in the garden of the Duc Hotel, Saigon, Vietnam, May 1974. John was born in Saigon on December 4, 1973, at the start of the Sullivans' second two-year tour in Vietnam.

The author with his son John at their first home in Reston, Virginia, September 20, 1975.

The author with his son Jimmy at his Commencement ceremony at Virginia Commonwealth University, May 2004.

The author, running a Stoelting Diplomat polygraph instrument, the predecessor to the computerized instruments that are used today.

Sheriff Bob Pickell, a former CIA polygraph examiner and the best interrogator the author ever worked with. In one of his major cases, Pickell obtained an admission from a former New York state police officer who had planted evidence in an arson case.

John Sullivan (far right) on November 11, 1998, at the Heroes and Heritage award ceremony, during which Felix Rodriguez (center) was presented the Heritage Award. Rodriguez was a provincial reconnaissance unit (PRU) advisor whom the author worked with in Vietnam.

would jeopardize his nomination. There were members of Congress who felt that under Casey the Agency had gone awry and needed to be reined in, and that in confirming Gates they would be telling the American people that they (Congress) were unwilling or unable to do this. Whether President Bush asked or Gates volunteered to do so, I don't know, but Gates withdrew his name from consideration.

Bush could not have picked anyone with a cleaner public image than Webster's, but we in IRD were concerned. Whenever a new DCI is appointed, the first question on examiners' minds is, "What are his feelings about polygraph?" We knew the FBI didn't use polygraph the way we did and we were concerned that Webster might be anti-polygraph. Webster had declined to take a polygraph examination prior to being sworn in as DCI but did take one after he came onboard. PD's fears proved to be groundless. Webster was neither pro- nor anti-polygraph, and pretty much left us alone.

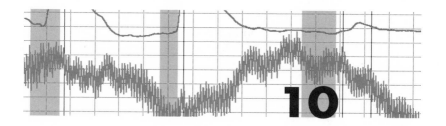

COMING OF AGE

$\mathbf{N}$o one in PD was surprised that Milenski had been selected to replace Parnell—only that it happened when it did. The old adage, "If it ain't broke, don't fix it," was very applicable to the situation in PD. Morale was high, and I couldn't remember a time when things had been better. This begged the question, "Why change?"

Milenski's entire professional life had been spent in polygraph, and his only job with the Agency had been with PD. At the time that Parnell moved on, Milenski was considered to be the Agency's expert on polygraph. With PD expanding as it was, I think Lynch might have felt that the time was right for a change and that Milenski's background, as well as his good working relationship with Lynch, made him the right person to oversee PD's expansion.

Some in the Office of Security's Old Guard had resented Milenski's promotion to GS-14 back in 1976. The perception at the time was that Milenski's promotion to GS-14 might be his last, and that assuaged some of Security's polygraph critics. None of those holding such views foresaw PD's tremendous growth. More startling and even threatening to many of the Office of Security's reactionaries was Lynch's lack of anti-polygraph bias. Under Lynch, polygraph began to acquire status.

Milenski's appointment to chief of PD was not only a personal milestone for Milenski but for PD as well. With the appointment, Lynch made it known that specialists had their place in Security and that a polygraph examiner could spend his entire career in PD without foregoing opportunities for promotion. This made my job as a recruiter easier and improved PD's retention rate.

For Milenski, being named chief of PD was a dream come true. A Ukrainian immigrant who fled the Soviet Union with his parents during World War II, Milenski was an unabashed anti-Communist and flag waver. Milenski joined the U.S. Marine Corps after high school and, upon completion of his enlistment, enrolled at Michigan State University, where he earned a degree in criminal justice. After Michigan State, Milenski took a job with John Reid and Associates and rose to the position of chief training officer by the time he applied for a position as a polygraph examiner with the Agency. He applied to PD during Chet Crawford's reign as chief, and I think Milenski's Russian language capability was at least as big a factor in his being offered a position as was his polygraph expertise.

Milenski had been in PD for four years when I arrived on the scene. From day one, it was apparent to me that he knew more about polygraph than anyone in the office and was PD's guru on all matters relating to polygraph. My first impression of Milenski was that he was the kind of Agency officer I wanted to be. In the vernacular of the '60s, he was the "coolest" guy in the office: poised, professional, bilingual, competent, confident without being arrogant, and an overall good guy. As I noted in chapter 4, when Milenski obtained a confession of child molestation from a staff employee, his already good reputation spread beyond PD. Had that case come after PD's Reid-trained examiners began testing, it probably wouldn't have drawn much attention, but in 1969, Milenski was more than likely the only examiner in PD who could have obtained that confession.

In the summer of 1971 Milenski was assigned overseas, where he did very well. When he returned in 1975, he was made chief of the Applicant Branch. Once in management Milenski became a prime mover in changing the face of PD. He was instrumental in expanding the training of the CIA's examiners, first with outside training at Reid and then with the opening of the PD school.

The professional relationship between Lynch and Milenski was the closest I had ever seen between a director of OS and a chief of PD. As much as Lynch recognized Milenski's abilities and contributions to PD, he was also very cognizant of the fact that polygraph was more cost effective for the Office of Security than were all other personnel security procedures. With those thoughts in mind, Lynch cared not a wit if some noses in Security were out of joint over Milenski's appointment.

Lynch was much less conservative than any of his D/OS predecessors and rubbed many in the Old Guard the wrong way, but he served PD and its examiners very well. Of the OS directors I encountered during my career, Bob Gambino was the one I most admired and Lynch was the one I most liked to socialize with.

One of Milenski's first acts upon becoming chief of PD was to create an expert examiner, GS-15 position in PD. Milenski was very DO oriented, and one of the criteria he established for expert examiners was that they be able to test and interrogate in at least two languages. At that time, only one examiner in PD met that criterion, and everyone knew that Milenski had created the expert examiner position with one person in mind: Boris Hansen, who spoke German and French. Hansen was a former nonofficial cover officer with whom Milenski had worked overseas and whom he had encouraged to come into PD.

The selection of experts was very subjective. Milenski had the first and last word on who was chosen to be an expert examiner, and eventually, this became a sore point with many of PD's examiners. A part of the problem was the term "expert." At the time Hansen was made an expert examiner, at least ten examiners in PD had much more expertise than Hansen. Hansen was much more comfortable in the operational arena than he was testing applicants and employees, and he had conducted a very significant test on a Soviet asset, getting the asset to admit that he had stolen thousands of dollars from his superiors. He had also conducted a test in which he had coaxed an employee to confess that he had sabotaged an elevator in headquarters. Those cases were significant, but in comparison with the other examiners, Hansen's track record for obtaining significant admissions did not measure up.

On one occasion Ken Haneda, the then-chief of the Covert Branch, came to me with a tape recording of an examination Hansen had conducted on an East German asset. The test had been conducted in German, and Haneda came to me and said, "John, the desk officer wants someone to listen to this tape to see if the questions were translated correctly." Hansen had called the subject "good" (NDI), and apparently, the desk officer had reservations about the test results. This was a first for me: I could not remember the DO ever questioning a favorable call.

I reviewed the tape and concluded that the questions had been translated correctly, but I also concluded that Hansen had run the test contrary to PD procedures and that the results should have been called inconclusive at best. Hansen had run three charts during the test, one chart to make sure the instrument was functioning properly and two test charts. While running the second chart just after the subject answered question #4, the paper jammed, causing an almost forty-second delay between questions #4 and #5. Question #5 was, "Are you cooperating with any other intelligence service besides the CIA?" The subject answered, "No." The forty-second delay between questions #4 and #5 invalidated the chart. Hansen then ran a third chart and made his call. Hansen should have rerun the second chart from the beginning.

Two years later I was asked to test this subject. I did my, "Have you told anyone about your last test?" question, and as before, it was effective. When I tested on the more substantive issues, the subject had clear and consistent reactions to the relevant questions. When I informed the case officer of the test results, he was at a loss for words but was able to articulate "Don't interrogate him."

This man turned out to be one of the East German assets who "beat" us. What I remember most about this agent was how well he came across as a nice guy. He was witty, urbane, and impressive. When I reflected on the test, I concluded that he had followed to a T Doctor Dufek's guidelines for getting through a polygraph test, i.e., "Be nice, cooperate, and don't antagonize the examiner."[1] An aspect of this operation which I found odd was his refusal to take any pay. In my experience, most agents were motivated by money, and I couldn't understand why he wouldn't take any pay. In lieu of any financial remuneration, he accepted American jazz records.

More so than usual, I wanted to interrogate this man, mainly because I thought I might be able to get an admission out of him. His refusal to take any money led me to conclude that he was being coerced to participate in a double-agent operation. The difference between this agent and the agent I tested in Ireland was that this agent enjoyed what he was doing.

For another case Hansen traveled nine thousand miles to test a Soviet bloc asset. Hansen called the asset "good" and was in the air returning to headquarters when the case officer coaxed the asset to admit that he was a double agent. That case officer was a friend of mine and never failed to bring this up whenever we saw each other.

As fine a person as Hansen was, among his colleagues in PD, he was not seen as a strong examiner, and his selection as PD's first expert examiner raised some questions. In Milenski's vision, among the expert examiner's primary roles would be serving as a mentor for the junior examiners.

In addition to being a mentor, the expert examiner would be the examiner of choice for the more difficult or high-profile tests. This vision of the examiner never came to fruition. The high-profile cases were given to the examiners who had the best track record and who had Milenski's confidence to get the job done.

Milenski also deigned that the expert examiner be a spokesman, or public face, for PD. Milenski, a reserved person, did not seem at all comfortable speaking in public, and he decided that the expert examiner would be his surrogate. In the ensuing years Milenski's choices for expert examiners and the roles they played in PD were the sources of some contentiousness among the examiners.

---

1. Dr. Miroslav Dufek was a Czechoslovakian psychologist who trained Czech intelligence service agents in polygraph countermeasures. I first heard of Dufek while I was in the army. During Falcone's tenure I tested and caught a Czech agent who had been trained by Dufek.

Computers were another fact of Agency life that Milenski had to learn to deal with. In the mid-1960s PD was involved in a study to determine the feasibility of computerizing polygraph. The study demonstrated that given the same data, one of our examiners, Steve Andros, outperformed a computer. By 1986 the Agency was caught up in the computer revolution but made no move to revisit the question of a computerized polygraph instrument. That changed with the appointment of Lynch as the director of OS. PD adopted two computerized polygraph instruments, the Axiton and the Lafayette. Luddite that I am, I resisted switching to a computerized instrument for years, but ultimately, in 1996, succumbed.

I found the computerized polygraph instruments we were using to have more psychological than practical value in the polygraph process. Most Americans are geared to accept computerized results, as opposed to results arrived at through subjective analysis, and I found that telling a subject, "The computer results indicate that there is at least a 92 percent chance that you have not been truthful," was an effective way to obtain an admission. At least in theory, the subjectivity, or much of the guesswork, was removed from chart analysis, and I saw this as a positive.

The Agency's move to computers also resulted in the expansion of the questions covered during testing. Computer misuse and abuse became areas of concern for the Agency that PD had to address. At that time few examiners in PD had sufficient knowledge of computers to adequately question or interrogate an individual on the misuse or abuse of computers.

It is critical that an examiner have sufficient knowledge of the issues being addressed in an interrogation. If a subject being interrogated realizes that the interrogator doesn't know what he or she is talking about, the chances of obtaining an admission are considerably diminished. With this in mind, I made a concerted effort to recruit some computer-literate examiners. I was fortunate enough to find a couple of examiners who met that criterion, and when an examiner ran into a problem with a subject regarding computer misuse, the subject was rescheduled so that one of our more computer-oriented examiners could conduct the test.

In terms of the process, switching to computerized instruments was a step in the right direction, but to improve PD's image more had to be done. Milenski had not been in place for more than a month when I suggested to him and his deputy, "Mike Larrabee," that we should undertake a public relations effort that would make us seem more approachable to our Agency clientele. My specific suggestion was that we afford all those scheduled for trial period or reinvestigation polygraph tests a pretest briefing during which we could answer questions and try to allay concerns. Initially, Larrabee was a little concerned about the idea; he seemed to think that such sessions could get very acrimonious and be used by employees as a vehicle to attack polygraph. I argued that if after twenty years in PD I couldn't handle a disgruntled former subject or adequately defend polygraph, I should probably look for another job. I also told Larrabee that I was very confident that I could make the briefings work.

I managed to convince Larrabee and Milenski that it was worth a shot and proposed that on each Thursday before a payday another PD representative or I schedule a briefing in one of the auditoriums in headquarters. Those scheduled for RIP/TRIP tests would be told about their briefing when they received their appointments.

Milenski ran my idea by the Office of Security management. Will Rump and some of the other managers in OS decided that the idea wasn't necessarily a bad one but that letting PD fly solo was. To make sure that Security was allowed to share in any positives that accrued from the briefings, the prepolygraph briefings I proposed degenerated into generalized security briefings run by Clearance Division. Instead of addressing only polygraph questions and concerns, the briefings would cover the entire clearance process: background investigations, polygraph tests, and adjudications. The fact that few, if any, of those attending the briefings were interested in anything except polygraph was lost on Security management, but half a loaf being better than none at all, the pretest briefings became a part of the polygraph process.

For nine years (minus about five absences) I delivered every briefing. Larrabee's concern about the briefings turning ugly never materialized. Given the antipathy toward polygraph extant in the Agency, I have to admit that I was surprised. In approximately 220 briefings, I encountered only one slightly hostile person.

During one such briefing I had an encounter with an individual who tried to embarrass me and PD. The young man raised his hand and asked me, "Why do all you people in polygraph think that just because we come from the District [Washington, D.C.] we use drugs?" In response, I asked him to explain. He said that when he was polygraphed he told his examiner that he had never used drugs. According to this young man, his examiner's response was, "Who are you kidding? All of you guys in the District use drugs." Based on my experience, I knew with absolute certitude that none of PD's examiners would have said something like that, but I also knew that the briefing wasn't the place to accuse this man of lying. Instead, I requested that the young man see me after the briefing and give me the details of the incident. During my subsequent conversation with the young man I reminded him that his interview had been taped and assured him that, if what he said were true, punitive action would be taken against the examiner. I took down the young man's name and a telephone number where he could be reached and assured him that I would be in touch.

As soon as I returned to PD, I pulled the young man's PD file and noted that he had undergone two polygraph sessions as part of his TRIP processing. Rather than listen to both tapes of the interviews, I called the young man to ask during which of the two sessions the alleged incident had occurred.

"Well, maybe it wasn't during a polygraph test that it happened. Maybe it was after the tests when some security guy talked to me," he answered. The subject had been deemed deception indicated on the issue of using illegal drugs since entering on duty after two sessions. As a result, he was afforded an interview with a security officer from Clearance Division.

"I don't care whether it was during a polygraph test or other interview. If a security officer said that to you, I want to know who it was," I said.

"Maybe that wasn't exactly what was said, but I know that guy didn't believe me," said the young man. It was clear to me that the incident this young man brought up during the briefing had never taken place and that he had mentioned it only to embarrass me.

Sharing these briefings with Clearance Division diluted their effectiveness and discouraged attendance. With one notable exception, the CD presenters selected had no desire to participate in the presentations, and it showed. During the very first briefing, the Clearance Division representative introduced me and my presentation on polygraph by saying, "We all know that polygraph admissions aren't allowed in court." The fact that this statement was inaccurate is almost irrelevant when compared with the reason he said it. When I confronted him after the interview, he explained that in the interest of "openness," he thought his comment was appropriate. I suggested that he leave comments regarding polygraph to me. I also pointed out that I thought his comment was unprofessional, once again disaffecting myself to an OS careerist.

When a presenter for CD literally read her presentation, nearly putting the attendees to sleep, I was embarrassed for the Office of Security and complained to Larrabee. "John, it's their show, and you will just have to live with it," Larrabee said.

I had been conducting the briefings for a few years when the security officer assigned to the DI called me. "Our people are up in arms about polygraph and the bring-backs. Would you mind coming over here and addressing their complaints?" he asked.

"I'd be delighted to do it, but I have to run it by my boss before I can," I said.

PD was willing to let me do it, but the Office of Security, once again, insisted that someone from Personnel Security go with me. The person they selected to go with me was "Darwin Lark," a rising star in OS. Lark actually ran the briefing and was about fifteen minutes into his explanation of the clearance procedure when the most senior DI attendee stopped him and said, "This really isn't what we are here for. All we want to do is discuss polygraph." Lark seemed embarrassed, and I know I was embarrassed for him.

Over the next forty-five minutes, I fielded many questions, mollified some dissatisfied subjects, and dealt with one very unhappy camper. The unhappy camper said that during his two TRIP sessions he had been repeatedly accused of mishandling classified information. "I just don't understand it," he lamented. I felt that this young man wasn't being honest. The source of my feeling is difficult to pin down, but I thought his smile was insincere and the tone of his voice belied the righteous indignation he was trying to project. As he went on, it became clear that several of the attendees weren't buying this young man's story, and I closed the discussion by saying: "Without seeing the charts of your tests, I can't make a judgment. There are such things as false positives, and you may be the victim of a false positive. They are the bane of our existence. That being said, I know, as surely as I am standing here, that during your tests you reacted strongly and consistently to the question to which you were deemed deceptive. I can't offer any other explanation."

After the briefing, the senior DI attendee thanked me, as did many of the other attendees. I was satisfied that I had given a good briefing and had done some pretty good PR for PD.

In the midst of switching to computerized instruments and trying to improve the division's image, PD examiners still had time for some very good polygraph work. PD examiners were developing more disqualifying information from applicants at a higher rate than ever before and significant reportable information from staff employees during their TRIP and RIP sessions. But there was also a rise in the number of false positives. One examination that may have resulted in a false positive led to a mini-crisis.

"Frank Brennan," one of PD's younger examiners, was a real hard charger and a good examiner. During one of his sessions he went a bit over the top during an interrogation. Milenski ended up apologizing to the subject, and during a subsequent briefing regarding that session, Milenski told PD, "After listening to the tape of that session, I was almost ashamed of being in PD, and I don't ever want to hear another interrogation like that one." His underlying message: "If you go after someone like that, you damn well better come away with an admission."

In defense of Brennan, I can say only that no one, except the test subject, knows if the test was a false positive. I do know that, for a test I conducted later, my favorable call was overturned, and the subject was brought back for another session. Brennan did the retest, turned the subject into a basket case, and obtained significant admissions of recent criminal activity.

As I have mentioned, when Parnell had named me PD's recruiter, he told me that the new position might help me earn a promotion. After two-and-a-half years as the recruiter, I realized that, at least in my case, Parnell had been wrong. Milenski, reaching the same conclusion I had, asked me to become a team leader. Team leaders were GS-14 positions, and Milenski thought that if I were in a GS-14 position, it would be only a matter of time before I would be promoted.

During my tenure as recruiter, I brought thirty-one examiners into Polygraph Division, and I enjoyed the job. I continued to conduct many tests, gave many briefings, and felt that I was making a significant contribution to PD. As a team leader, I thought that I would have to cut back on my testing and briefings, and I really didn't want to make the change.

I had noticed that when PD line examiners moved into management, most lost all desire to go back into the rooms and test primarily because each and every time an examiner tests he or she puts his or her reputation on the line. "If I don't test, I can't get beat," seemed to be the philosophy of former examiners who became managers.

Bill Bontiempo was a notable exception to this rule. On a couple of occasions he was asked to conduct retests on subjects who needed "attitude adjustments," and he was very effective. On one of these occasions, I was asked to assist two Department of Justice agents review the tape of Bontiempo's tests. Bontiempo had obtained significant admissions of fraud and malfeasance from a staff employee, and the two agents were checking the accuracy of Bontiempo's report. The two agents were awed by Bontiempo's performance. At the conclusion of the tape review, one of them said to me, "Tell that guy, if he ever wants a job, give us a call." During my career I had conducted some good tests, and I was not ready to hang up my gun. Had I caught an employee engaging in espionage as Bill Bontiempo and Howard Phillips had, I may have felt differently, but I hadn't. Many of my colleagues transitioned from examiner positions to supervisory positions with the attitude, "I have gotten this far without a significant miss, and rather than push my luck, I will rest on my laurels, such as they are." Perhaps I didn't have enough laurels to rest on but I knew that I was not ready to join the coterie of nontesting supervisors and managers. More important, as a team leader, I knew I would occasionally have to take over a test for one of my subordinates, and I wanted to be prepared. It is hard to explain the challenge of interrogating; unless one has interrogated a subject, it is hard to appreciate how very difficult it is. As previously stated, interrogation and testing skills must be constantly honed. If I stopped testing for a prolonged period, I would not only allow my skills to diminish but I would also lose my feel for the process. To maintain their ability to identify with and relate to not only examiners but also subjects, supervisors should have been required to test regularly.

Lip service was paid by PD management to the belief that managers and supervisors should test. On three occasions proposals to have managers and supervisors test were made. The first proposal recommended that supervisors conduct fifty examinations each year. Unfortunately, each time the scheduler tried to assign one of them a test, he or she would beg off.

Bruce Gall, who succeeded Boris Hansen as PD's expert examiner, became notorious for avoiding tests. On one occasion I heard Gall tell the scheduler, "If you have to assign me a case, make sure it is an easy secretary." By avoiding tests, Gall not only wasn't setting a good example for junior examiners. Also, Gall was probably making about $15,000 a year in premium pay, and as far as I was concerned, he was taking that money under false pretenses.

Gall not only wouldn't conduct tests, he also wouldn't monitor tests. On an occasion when I was asked to conduct a bring-back test of an employee who had been deemed deception indicated on the issue of concealing contact with a foreign intelligence service, I asked Gall to monitor my test and give me some feedback. He declined, saying he was "too busy." When Gall refused, I went to Frank Brennan and asked him to monitor my test. Brennan did and gave me some great feedback.

As noted previously, being able to conduct a test in two languages was one of Milenski's criteria for being an expert examiner. Milenski had sent Gall to Berlitz to study Spanish so that he could meet the requirement. When, after completing the Berlitz program, Gall still couldn't pass the Agency's Spanish proficiency test, he was sent to the Agency's language school where he was trained one on one for several months. When this didn't resolve the problem, Milenski changed the requirement: experts needed only to be studying a foreign language. I never thought that the language requirement was legitimate, but I did think Gall's refusal to test and his inability to learn a foreign language negated other expert qualifications that he might have had.

Gall took great pride in being selected, along with Flynn Jones, to debrief Aldrich Ames. When I saw the videotape of the debriefing, my impression was that Gall and Jones had not done a good job. Subsequent to the debriefing, Gall put the young man who had videotaped the debriefing in for a $1,000 cash award. I was on the panel that voted on the award. The panel recommended that Gall's request be turned down on the grounds that the man was just doing his job. (I knew the young man and liked him very much but felt that Gall was prostituting the award system. Another factor in my decision, which I didn't bring up at the panel meeting, was that the young man was the son of a senior Office of Security officer, and I saw Gall's recommendation as a blatant attempt to curry favor with someone who could do him some good.)

Gall's recommendation was ultimately rejected, and he wasn't pleased. He pleaded his case to Larrabee, who overturned the panel's rejection and approved the $1,000 award. As much as that infuriated me, Gall's and other PD managers' refusal to test bothered me more.

Bob Fester was the only manager/supervisor who opted not to test and passed up the premium pay. Fester was not a strong examiner, and because as a manager he rarely did it, he was uncomfortable testing. His team leader and ultimately branch chief positions were true sinecures. Fester had been a manager for more than five years, probably hadn't conducted ten polygraph tests since going off-line, and his skills had diminished. To me, his reluctance to test was understandable. Understandable or not, Fester and PD management seemed not to realize that by not testing, managers further isolated themselves from their subordinates and diminished their ability to relate to or mentor them.

By the time I became a team leader, I was one of only two team leaders willing to test. Other PD managers were recalcitrant when asked to test but were not at all reluctant about taking the premium pay. At one point I told Larrabee that having supervisors who had never done an interrogation or a truly significant case tell other examiners how to conduct a test didn't make sense.

"You can't say that," Larrabee answered.

"Yes, I can," I said. I named two supervisors and asked Larrabee to cite an interrogation or good test that either of them had done. "Mike, I know every good and every bad case that has ever been done in here, and I don't know of one good case that either of those guys has done. Prove me wrong," I said.

Larrabee chose not to cite any examples.

Another factor that played into my reluctance to become a team leader was self-doubt about my qualifications to be a supervisor. I was the only examiner left in PD who had not undergone the full Reid course or completed PD's training course, and I felt awkward instructing examiners who were better trained than I was. It wasn't only my lack of confidence. My comparatively low-key approach to testing was not the modus operandi recommended by PD management, and I couldn't see myself encouraging examiners to get tough with subjects.

Of course, I didn't bring this up with Milenski and agreed to accept a team leader position in the Employee Branch (EB). My boss was Flynn Jones, and I had some of the more experienced examiners on my team. As a team leader, I monitored my team members as they conducted their tests, reviewed their charts, and offered guidance as to how to proceed with an examination. If an examiner concluded that all reactions on a test had not been addressed and resolved, and I agreed, I signed off on the charts and told the examiner to release the subject. However, if I felt that some reactions had not been addressed or that some issues still needed to be resolved, I sent the examiner back to resume the test. With few exceptions, I didn't enjoy interrogating people and could easily identify with examiners similarly disposed.

On three occasions that I recall, I gave examiners verbatim instructions on how to confront subjects whom I believed were being deceptive. "I want you to go back in the room and tell your subject, 'There is not a doubt in my mind that you are withholding information from me.'" Not one of them followed my instructions. When I subsequently confronted the examiners, they told me that they just weren't sure enough of themselves to do what I had asked. The subjects of each of these examiners' tests were brought back for additional testing. I conducted one of the bring-backs, and I obtained an admission of mishandling classified information. The other two acknowledged lying during their initial sessions and made admissions: one admitted marijuana use since entering on duty and the other admitted computer misuse.

Being a team leader was much more stressful than being an examiner. If one of my examiners was beaten, so was I. Instead of having to worry about one subject beating me, I had to worry about five. Telling an examiner that he had more work to do with a subject occasionally created tension between team leaders and examiners, and for me, this was particularly stressful. In as much as I viewed polygraph as much more art than science, my rule of thumb in reviewing my team's charts was: "Don't miss the obvious." A reaction had to be strong, consistent, and timely before I directed an examiner to address it, had he or she not already done so.

Milenski once told me, "Reading another examiner's charts is very difficult and involves a lot of guesswork." This is a bit of a simplification, but it holds more than a grain of truth. The dynamic between an examiner and a subject has to be factored into chart analysis. If I had aurally and visually monitored one of my team member's tests, I felt much more confident in analyzing the charts of the interview. Without the monitoring, I had a tendency to accept the examiner's assessment of the subject's behavior and sent an examiner back to do more work only if I saw a reaction that had been obviously missed.

After signing off on one of my examiner's charts, I then waited for the examiner to write up a report, proofread the report, and forwarded it to the branch chief. In theory, the branch chief would review the charts and report, and if he concurred with my call, he would forward the report to the Clearance Division for adjudication. The branch chief had the option of disagreeing with a team leader's call, but I cannot recall one instance when Jones overturned one of my calls.

My days as a supervisor were much longer than those of an examiner. When I was an examiner, I usually had some free time after I finished a test. As a line supervisor, my free time began only when all of my team members finished their tests. When all of my team was testing, I was constantly tuning in on their sessions. If I sent an examiner back into the room to do more work, I had to focus on monitoring that session so that I was prepared if I had to become more directly involved in the test. I spent many lunch hours waiting for an examiner to finish a session.

When subjects had problems with their tests and asked to see a supervisor, an examiner's team leader was the first person to respond. This was one part of the job that I enjoyed, and I was fairly successful in allaying subjects' concerns.

When I became a team leader in the Employee Branch, the sections had two other team leaders. Invariably, whenever we were short an examiner, I either volunteered to conduct the test or Jones asked me to conduct the test. As much as I liked testing, at times when I picked up an extra test my schedule became a bit hectic. During my time as a team leader, I conducted more tests than all of the supervisors, managers, and the expert in PD combined.

Writing PARs was also part of a team leader's job, and for me, it was the part of the job that I liked least. I was very uncomfortable evaluating my team members' abilities. The number of admissions an examiner gets from his subjects is the most significant criterion for evaluating an examiner's performance, and to me, this made sense. The problem was that saying this openly was seen as encouraging examiners to be overzealous.

Also, team member evaluations were made more difficult in the Employee Branch because significant admissions were harder to come by in EB than they were in other branches. In large part, this discrepancy was a product of the clientele whom EB examiners tested and the questions that were asked during these tests. Lifestyle issues were not addressed in RIP tests, and TRIP tests covered lifestyle activity (crime and drug use) only since entering on duty.

In addition to the number of admissions obtained, I based my evaluations on examiners' ability to resolve a case, to produce well-written, timely reports, and to conduct themselves in a professional manner.

My major failing as a team leader was that I didn't have the heart to tell some examiners that polygraph wasn't a good fit for them. On two occasions I recommended that members of my team give up polygraph, and both did so, but I should have offered the same advice to others and I didn't. PD was always in need of examiners, and in general, the division was reluctant to fire examiners. Time and money had been invested in each examiner's training, and with sufficient guidance, even weak examiners could be productive.

Bill Bontiempo was one of the best team leaders in terms of identifying and dealing with weak examiners. I was present when one of his examiners came to him with a set of charts and told Bontiempo, "I think he is OK and want to let him go."

Bontiempo looked at the charts and said, "'Tom,' I have been listening to you, and that kid sounded pretty evasive when you questioned him about his drug use."

"I really don't see it," answered Tom.

"Stay here and listen to me while I talk to him," replied Bontiempo. Within twenty minutes Bontiempo had enough admissions of drug use to get the young man security disapproved. "Tom, I didn't do that to embarrass you but to show you that maybe polygraph isn't for you," Bontiempo said when he returned to his office. Shortly thereafter, Tom left PD.

My team members didn't seem to share my perception of my shortcomings as a supervisor. In what was one of the highlights of my career, my team put me in for an Exceptional Performance Award for my "guidance and mentoring," and I received a $1,500 cash award.

Reservations about being a supervisor aside, I did adapt to my role as a team leader. I continued to test as often as I could, gave briefings, had some opportunities to observe other government agency's polygraph programs, and concluded that the CIA's polygraph program was, hands down, the best in the government. My conclusion was primarily based on the fact that Agency examiners developed derogatory information that resulted in security disapprovals at a rate far above that of other government examiners. In my conversations with examiners and managers from other agencies, I always asked, "How many spies have you caught?" and "How many security disapprovals, based on polygraph information, have you obtained?" The answer to the first question was, "None," and to the second, "Minimal compared to what you guys get."

Under Lynch's aegis and Milenski's leadership, PD came into the mainstream of OS, but the satisfaction the division derived from this accomplishment was short lived.

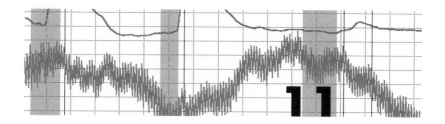

BAD APPLES

I had been a team leader for about three years when an event took place that shook my confidence in and had the potential to destroy the Agency's polygraph program.

Until this time I (and PD management) believed that all of the Agency's examiners conducted honest tests. In chapter 6 I noted that one examiner was caught fabricating a test and was dismissed from PD. I assumed that that incident was an aberration, and since that incident, I had not become aware of any other fabricated tests. Very few in PD were even aware of this incident because Falcone swept it under the rug, and the possibility that it could happen again was never acknowledged or even discussed. In the aftermath of that incident a policy of recording all polygraph tests was put in place, and that may have inhibited some examiners from falsifying their tests.

"Emma Morbid" was a Security employee who initially applied for a position in PD when Pat Meager was chief. The PD panel rejected her primarily because Frank Cross voiced the opinions that Morbid did not have what it took to be an examiner and that she would be a problem. During Parnell's tenure, Morbid reapplied and was accepted. I had not yet, at that time, been appointed PD's recruiter and had had no contact with her before she came into PD. Morbid's mother was a very highly regarded Office of Security employee, and I know that some of the powers that be in OS had interceded on her behalf; this certainly played a part in her being accepted.

Once Morbid came into PD I had a lot of contact with her, and my initial impression of her was that she was one of the more intense people I had ever met. She displayed an infectious enthusiasm for polygraph during training, and once she began testing, her enthusiasm for the job seemed to increase. I liked Morbid but rarely had an opportunity to observe her test. After she completed her training, she was assigned to the Applicant Branch where she developed a reputation for being a very aggressive examiner and strong interrogator. Her reputation allowed her to be selected for an assignment in California, where she would conduct tests on the Agency's industrial contractors.

Before Morbid left for California, I had an opportunity to observe her in action. At that time I was performing quality control reviews on charts for Bob Fester in EB. I overturned the call of one of the EB examiners and scheduled the subject for a retest. Morbid was assigned to conduct the test, which I monitored from start to finish.

Interrogating applicants is entirely different from interrogating employees, and building a reputation as a good interrogator was much easier in the Applicant Branch. That being said, during the three hours in which I monitored Morbid's test, she failed to impress me, and I thought to myself, "If PD managers think Emma Morbid is a good interrogator, they are missing the boat." The subject's charts indicated deception, as did his behavior. Morbid neither confronted nor interrogated him, and the test ended without her having obtained any admissions or having developed new information.

While in California, Morbid conducted a test on a woman who was applying for a position with a CIA contractor. When the woman was turned down, she contacted the expediter in the Clearance Division who had been processing her application and asked for an explanation as to why she had been turned down. "You admitted to recently using drugs," the expediter answered. The woman not only vehemently denied having recently used any drugs but also denied having told the examiner that she had. The expediter contacted PD. Milenski ordered that the tape of the interview be reviewed. When no admissions of drug use were found during the review of the tape, Milenski ordered that Morbid be directed to return to headquarters.

During Milenski's interview with her, Morbid admitted that she had been doctoring her tests, but she insisted that the report she wrote of the contractor's test was the only one in which she had falsely claimed that a subject had made a disqualifying admission. Morbid was fired, and Milenski ordered a review of every test she had ever conducted. In numerous tests Morbid had indicated on her charts that she had asked a relevant question when, in fact, she had asked an innocuous question. For example, Morbid indicated on her chart that she had asked, "In the last five years, have you committed a serious crime?" when in fact, she had asked an innocuous questions such as, "Do you have a high school diploma?"

During the review of Morbid's tests, another test was found in which Morbid had claimed that a subject had made a disqualifying admission that he had not made. To my knowledge, this test and the test that had unmasked Morbid were the only two tests Morbid falsified that resulted in a security clearance denial. In all other cases, Morbid omitted relevant questions, calling the tests NDI. I reviewed the tapes of four of Morbid's tests and found that she had fabricated two of them.

A pall settled over PD, and many of us were in a state of shock. We were just coming to grips with what Morbid had done and were very anxious about the fallout of the discovery when another examiner was caught fabricating a test. "Laura Wilson," the examiner, was comparatively new to PD and was working for Bill Bontiempo.

Wilson had been testing in one of the mirrored rooms, and Bontiempo had been observing her. Bontiempo noted a rather strong reaction to one of the relevant questions, but when Wilson brought him her charts for review, he couldn't find the reaction he had observed on any of the charts. Bontiempo didn't say anything to Wilson, but after work he looked through the trash baskets in every room Wilson would have passed en route to his office. He found the chart.

Bontiempo decided to monitor Wilson more closely. When he saw her artificially produce a reaction to a nonrelevant question during a test, he had had enough. He went to Milenski with his case against Wilson. Milenski notified Lynch. The next day Bontiempo and Lynch visually monitored Wilson while she tested. Wilson lived up to expectations, artificially manufacturing reactions to nonrelevant questions. By the close of business that day Wilson was fired.

I had done a quality control review for only one of Wilson's tests, and I didn't notice that the only reactions to any of the questions I saw on her charts were to three nonrelevant questions. After Bontiempo caught Wilson, I re-reviewed the test I had signed off on for her and realized that the reactions on the test had been artificially manufactured.

With the exposure of Wilson, Milenski's and PD's greatest fear was realized: Morbid's actions were a symptom of a very serious problem in PD. Milenski's immediate response was to start a review of all tests that resulted in admissionsthat disqualified applicants from Agency employment. Milenski wanted to make sure that the admissions cited in the polygraph reports had actually been made as well as reported accurately.

Milenski appointed Marty Davis to oversee a massive review of tests that had been conducted over the previous three years. Davis was a very strong examiner and a rising star in PD. His job was to ferret out "bad apples," and he did an excellent job. His task became known as "Operation Bad Apple." The investigation focused first and foremost on making sure that polygraph files contained all of the charts that had been run during a test. To do this, Davis or one of those he recruited to help him listened to the interview tapes and counted the charts as they were run. If an interview tape indicated that the examiner had run eight charts, eight charts should have been presented in the polygraph file. This was an onerous and very time-consuming project and made for some very long days for Davis.

Second, Davis made sure that the question numbers noted on the charts corresponded with the questions that had been asked. If an examiner noted on chart that he had asked question N4, the tape should have shown that question N4 had been asked.

Third, all reports were reviewed to make sure that every admission made by a subject and cited in the polygraph report was accurate. If a subject admitted to three uses of cocaine, the report should have indicated three uses, not thirty. In the many hundreds of tests that were reviewed, Morbid's two reports, which I have cited, were the only two found in which an examiner claimed that a subject had made an admission that he or she had not made.

With the exception of Morbid, each examiner who fabricated a test seemed to have done so with the intention of either getting a subject through a test or avoiding an interrogation. With as much information as examiners obtained during their tests, many of them were behind in keeping up with their reports. Many weren't getting out of the office until early evening, and it was too easy to rationalize "helping" a subject who "sounded" good get through a test. As an examiner who has conducted tests on and interrogated subjects whom I believed were honest but whose polygraph charts could not support an NDI call, I have experienced the frustration an examiner might feel at times. No examiner was more eager to have an honest person successfully complete a polygraph test than I was, but I never reached the point of fabricating tests.

Interrogation is the most difficult part of the polygraph process, and as technically competent as many examiners were, very few were proficient interrogators. The quality that set the great examiners apart from the rest was their outstanding interrogation skills. With one exception, the bad apples who were caught were weak interrogators, and as it turned out, they were willing to do anything to avoid an interrogation.

"Burt Denton" was the exception to this bad apple rule. On a recruiting trip, a commercial examiner referred Denton to me. I contacted Denton and ultimately recruited him. From his first day of testing, Denton stood out. On three occasions that I can recall, Denton obtained admissions of serious criminal activity from subjects, and as his reputation grew, he was assigned more and more bring-backs who management felt had lied on their tests. Denton's successes in resolving many of these cases led to his being assigned overseas earlier in his career than expected. Denton was overseas when Davis's review uncovered some tests that he had fabricated.

Denton was fired, and before he left, he offered to address PD and tell the examiners why he had done what he did. Milenski declined

Denton's offer, which I thought was a mistake, as I felt Denton's insight as to why he falsified his reports could head off future incidents of fabrication.

Davis identified one other examiner, "Tom Testa," as having fabricated test results. Testa had already left the Agency and was working as a police officer, but he had recently reapplied to PD when his fabricated tests were discovered. In fact his fabricated tests were discovered in the interim between his polygraph test (which was favorable) and the time he was to enter back on duty. When Testa called to check on the status of his processing, he was told that he was being rejected because he had fabricated test results. Testa had been a pretty good examiner, and I was sorry that he had stepped over the line.

Davis's investigation heightened the line supervisors' awareness of potential test fabrication, and as a result one supervisor uncovered another miscreant. One of the examiners had thrown a bunch of charts in the trash, and the supervisor came across them. The supervisor traced the charts back to the examiner, called him into his office, and confronted him. The examiner admitted that he had been so frustrated that his charts didn't support his opinion that many of his subjects were truthful that he had fabricated his test results. To that end, he turned in only charts that supported an NDI call.

The supervisor and I agreed that the examiner had wanted to get caught. He could have destroyed the charts or put them in one of the burn bags used for disposing classified material. Instead, he threw them in a trash basket where it was very likely that they would be seen. The examiner had been eligible to retire, and he was allowed to do so. I liked him and even sympathized with his frustration, but I also knew that he could not be allowed to stay in PD.

Operation Bad Apple continued for an extended period. After Davis had reviewed some of my tests and concluded that I was not a bad apple, he had me review interview tapes to check for other bad apples. During Davis's investigation, five bad apples were identified and fired. In the furor over the bad apples, not much attention was given to the why of the problem. The last example I cited focused on what I felt was the crux of the problem: the most difficult part of my job as an examiner was confronting and interrogating a subject who I believed was honest. But this was part of the job, and an examiner who couldn't adapt to interrogation had no business being a polygraph examiner.

No one knows how long examiners had been cheating on their tests because Davis's reviews went back only three years. During the bad apples investigation, I couldn't help but think, "Five examiners didn't suddenly decide to start fabricating their tests." That led me to surmise that during Meager's reign of terror examiners had been cheating on their tests, and they weren't discovered only because none of the tests in which the questions and charts were manipulated resulted in a DI call or a denial of a security clearance. Complaints were made about the examiners' conduct, but no subjects complained that they had been accused of making admissions that they had not made; this would have precipitated an investigation.

After Meager's departure, during Parnell's and Milenski's tenures, some of the working conditions in PD improved, but the bring-back rate was still climbing, complaints against examiners were on the rise, and the gulf between examiners and supervisors was widening.

Examiners were encouraged to confront subjects forcefully, and there was a perception growing among the examiners that unless they obtained an admission from a subject, they had not done their job. Acrimonious polygraph sessions became more common and disputes over chart interpretation between examiners and supervisors increased. In one year, during Milenski's tenure, subjects made ninety-eight formal complaints of examiner misconduct to D/OS Lynch. Only two of those complaints were found to have merit. In one of those cases, an examiner was given a letter of reprimand; in the other, the examiner was reassigned out of PD.

Another problem was chart review. Supervisors were rejecting favorable calls for charts that I considered textbook examples in support of NDI calls. On far too many occasions I was asked to conduct tests on bring-backs whose charts, in my opinion, clearly did not indicate deception. I remember bringing a set of charts to Milenski and telling him, "Greg, if we are bringing subjects back based on charts like these, we aren't going to get many people through their tests." I was certain that many examiners felt the same way and that the solution for at least five of them had been to fabricate their tests.

Subsequent to Morbid's termination, Will Rump came to PD to pontificate on polygraph. He reminded the division that the CIA had placed us in trust and encouraged us to move forward but not to forget the damage Morbid had done.

Considering the damage Morbid had done, many of us were stunned that after being fired she had been able to take a job with one of the "Beltway bandits," firms in the D.C. area specializing in government contract work. Morbid's new job required a security clearance, and we couldn't believe she had been allowed to retain her clearances. In what might be interpreted as the ultimate irony, one of Morbid's jobs with her new employer was to give prepolygraph briefings to company employees who were scheduled to take Agency polygraph tests.

"Brenda Patrick," one of the team leaders, had the temerity to confront Rump when he came to speak to PD. "How was Morbid allowed to keep her clearances after what she did?" Patrick asked. Rump clearly didn't like the question and could not, or would not, give a satisfactory answer. As it turned out, not only had Morbid not had her clearances revoked, her new employer apparently had not even been told that she had been fired: when the security officer from the firm Morbid now worked for called PD to find out about Emma Morbid, he was told that the Agency had had no problems with her. Within a year of taking her new job Morbid tried to cash a check for approximately $45,000 made out to her company, and she was subsequently fired.

This was not a good time to be in PD, and the Agency's polygraph program did not completely fall apart only because very few people outside of PD knew about the bad apples. Between the time the bad apple investigation was completed and the time I retired, I heard only one person outside of PD even allude to the bad apples.

In the aftermath of the investigation, changes were instituted that PD hoped would prevent a reoccurrence. For example, when an examiner brought his charts to a supervisor and cited the admissions a subject had made during a test, the supervisor instructed the examiner to go over the admissions with the subject before terminating the session. The examiner was also required to tell subjects that the admissions they made would be in the polygraph report that would be forwarded to the Clearance Division. This was meant to help head off any post-test denials by subjects of admissions examiners claimed that they had made. The prerelease review of the subjects' admissions also gave the supervisor an opportunity to hear the admissions, had he not already. If the team leader chose to listen to the examiner review the admissions with a subject, the polygraph report's credibility was enhanced. Examiners were aware that their supervisors would most likely listen in on their admission reviews. Some examiners considered this an indication of PD management's lack of trust, but in view of recent events, nearly everyone agreed that it was a necessary, prophylactic measure.

Milenski and other PD managers also wrote a "PD Code of Ethics" that each examiner was required to sign. I saw this as more of a cosmetic gesture than part of any solution to the problem. If examiners or employees in positions of trust are going to stray, they will. The answer is not writing a code of ethics but ensuring proactive and constant vigilance on the part of management, as well as creating a working environment that makes test fabrication less likely.

Every profession has its bad apples. There are unethical lawyers, incompetent doctors, rogue cops, and disreputable clergymen, and so too

are there bad polygraph examiners. I believe that there is a difference
between what PD's examiners did and what miscreants in other profes-
sions do: PD's examiners were not venal and, except for Morbid, not
malicious. There was no profit motive involved, and with the exception
of Morbid's two tests that resulted in the denial of security clearances,
subjects had not been harmed. This in no way excuses what the bad apples
did, but the difference should be taken into consideration when judging
the examiners.

Had the bad apple investigation been poorly handled, PD could have
been irreparably damaged. The changes in procedures instituted after
Operation Bad Apple made a repeat less likely, but one aspect of the investigation leaves me unsatisfied: the lack of accountability. The only
people held accountable for the fabricated tests were the guilty examiners. After Morbid was caught, Bontiempo and the other supervisor certainly exercised due diligence in ferreting out two more bad apples, but
the original investigation was initiated by a subject's complaint, not by a
supervisor. PD management created the environment that generated the
bad apples, yet I know of no manager who was held accountable for what
had happened. What accountability did the supervisors of the bad apples
have? What accountability did Milenski have? In the military or commercial worlds, the bad apple event would most likely have resulted in
high-level firings. The fact that this didn't happen is a tribute to Milenski's
political acumen.

Just as the bad apple investigation was coming to an end, PD took
another hit. In 1989 Mike Larrabee, Milenski's deputy, was promoted
out of PD. Milenski and Larrabee were a good team, and their different
management styles were very complementary. Milenski was somewhat
reserved and less outgoing than Larrabee, and as big as PD was getting to
be, he had difficultly maintaining as much contact with the examiners as
he would have liked. Larrabee served as the go-between between Milenski
and the examiners and performed the job very well.

Larrabee might not have been missed so much had he not had such
a poor replacement. Bryan Lout was appointed to be Milenski's deputy,
marking a dramatic change in PD, and not a change for the better. Lout
had been, in my opinion, an excellent examiner and the ultimate straight
arrow. However, most people saw him as "Will Rump's man" and thought
that Rump had assigned him to PD as a watchdog or spy. Futhermore,
Lout was not a people person. Larrabee had been great at keeping the
lines of communication between the front office and the examiners open.
Examiners who didn't know Lout or hadn't worked with him in the past
saw him as aloof and unapproachable. This contributed to the widening
of the chasm between examiners and management.

To polygraph's detractors in OS, the bad apples were a sign of loss of managerial control in PD and that the barrel needed to be sorted. Lout was sent to be the sorter.

In fairness, it should be mentioned that on some occasions PD examiners did not project the image that Rump felt was appropriate for a security officer. One of those occasions took place on a fall Friday afternoon. Examiner "Bob Mulligan," a Notre Dame alumnus, had arranged for himself and several other examiners to attend the Navy versus Notre Dame football game in Baltimore that evening. Mulligan had rented an RV to take the entourage to Baltimore immediately after work. The RV, stocked with appropriate libations, was parked in PD's parking lot, and during the lunch hour several of the examiners visited the RV and began to celebrate a little early. The celebration was getting a bit festive when Rump saw the merrymakers in the parking lot and went storming up to Milenski's office. I was talking to Milenski's secretary when Rump stuck his head into the office and said, "Greg, could you come here?" Rump was standing by a huge window overlooking the parking lot. He pointed to two of the examiners standing in the doorway of the RV, beer cans in hand, and to Milenski he said, "Are they your examiners?" Milenski went down and broke up the party, as he should have, but I do think PD lost some ground—not that it had much to begin with—with Rump.

The bad apples, an ever-increasing bring-back rate, a rise in the number of complaints from subjects, and the RV party in the parking lot left PD in dire need of something positive to help it get back on track in the eyes of OS. And then along came Bob.

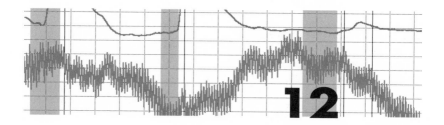

HITS, MISSES, AND
DISTRACTIONS

Following the bad apple investigation, PD went through a rough patch, but some good things were happening. Among these was the arrival of Bob Pickell, who entered on duty just as the Morbid saga began. In *Of Spies and Lies*, I said that Pickell was the best polygraph examiner/ interrogator ever to work in PD. During these hard times, Pickell was a godsend.

Pickell had been a police officer, an investigator for the district attorney, and a polygraph examiner in Flint, Michigan. He brought a lot of experience to PD. As good an examiner as he was, Pickell was also a bit of an iconoclast, very outspoken and one who thought that political correctness was a sign of malaise in those without the courage of their convictions.

On one occasion, Boris Hansen, PD's expert examiner, gave a lecture to Pickell's class of examiners-in-training. When Hansen exceeded his time allotment, Pickell raised his hand and asked, "Boris, how much longer are you going to be? You're taking up our lunch hour." The question didn't go over very well. When I talked with Pickell about that incident, he told me, "Jesus, John, the lecture was boring and bad. If they are going to take up my lunchtime, it is going to have to be for something worthwhile."

In the time he served in PD, Pickell worked more significant cases than any two examiners I can remember, and I don't recall him ever coming out of an interrogation without an admission.

Pickell's arrival on the scene coincided with the departure of Lynch as D/OS. Lynch had shaken OS's Old Guard to its core and had given PD a prestige that no one in PD had ever thought possible. Of the legacies left by Lynch, none was more far-reaching or had more impact than his very progressive attitude toward cultural diversity in the workplace. In the mid-1980s this concept appeared on the Agency's radar screen, bought into it wholeheartedly, his Deputy Chief Rump became Security's cheerleader for diversity, and PD became its poster child.

Proportionately, PD recruited more minorities than any other office in Security. In terms of promotions and assignments to managerial positions, PD became a fast-track career path for minorities.

Diversity was a reality of the workplace that had to be acknowledged and in OS, diversity became a vehicle for promotion for those who went along. Delete "and a politically correct posture for all OS managers to take.

Anyone in Security with the temerity to question the rush to create a diverse workplace did so at personal risk.

Lynch had been very proactive in hiring minorities and he was remembered as the D/OS who brought PD into the mainstream of Security. DCI Webster named Frank Ruocco to replace Lynch. Like Lynch, Ruocco had no previous experience in Security. My only experience with Ruocco prior to his appointment was regarding a test during which an examiner had obtained an admission of theft from a very junior employee assigned to Ruocco's office. The theft was truly petty, and the examiner felt that Ruocco should have taken extenuating circumstances into consideration in meting out punishment for the subject. Ruocco's position was, "A thief is a thief, and I won't have one working for me." The employee was fired. In principle, I can't disagree with Ruocco, but I thought this case called for mercy. With this in mind, I knew the Office of Security was getting a hard nose for a director. I felt it very propitious that his arrival coincided with what was the highest profile admission of criminal activity ever obtained by a PD examiner.

Among the many criticisms of polygraph made in the National Academy of Sciences (NAS) study on polygraph was that, while polygraph might have some effectiveness in addressing specific criminal activity, it was not suited to ferreting out criminal activity in an applicant screening venue. The Harding case is just one of hundreds of examples that I can use to rebut that claim, but its significance makes it the most appropriate example I can choose.

David Harding was a rising star with the New York State Police when he decided he would like to offer his services to the CIA. Mostly because of his extensive police background, Pickell was chosen to give Harding his EOD polygraph test. In what one of the lawyers from the Agency's Office of General Counsel (OGC) described as a "masterful performance," Pickell coaxed Harding to admit that he had planted fingerprints on a gasoline can that resulted in a woman being convicted of arson and murder.

As soon as the OGC received Pickell's report and tape of the interview, the NewYork State Police were notified. Harding was arrested and subsequently sent to prison. The woman he had framed was released from jail, and an internal investigation was launched. Four other state troopers were caught up in the investigation and arrested. One of them, Robert M. Lishansky, admitted to falsifying evidence in twenty-one cases.

I watched Lesley Stahl's interview with Harding on *60 Minutes*, and she noted that Harding had been found out during a polygraph test. In the *New York Times* article I read, I don't recall any mention of polygraph, and I think the article said that Harding had been caught during "security processing."

If ever OS/PD or the Agency had an opportunity to put out some good news about polygraph, this was it. In what to me was a slap in PD's face, the OGC lawyer who handled the case was given a quality step increase, and the security officer who compiled the material that was to be passed to the New York State Police was given an Exceptional Performance Award in the amount of $1,500. Pickell's contribution to the case, except for "well dones" from some of his peers, was not acknowledged. Subsequent to this interview one of the psychologists assigned to PD approached Pickell and said, "Bob, you should really give a seminar to the psychologists in OMS. We could learn a lot from you."

Some examiners in PD never had a "Harding" test, and even if that were the only big test Pickell ever did, he would have earned his salary. But Pickell conducted several such tests, and to conclude my "Paen to Pickell," I will cite two more cases that he handled.

During RIP testing, an employee was deemed deception indicated on the issues of concealing contact with a foreign intelligence service and providing classified information to an unauthorized person. The subject endured three more tests, all resulting in DI calls without any admissions obtained. Desperate measures were called for, and Bruce Gall, PD's expert in residence, was assigned to do the test. Gall tested and interrogated the man over the course of two sessions and came up empty: deception indicated on the counterintelligence issues, with no admissions.

Pickell had listened in on Gall's interrogation, and after the session he went to the Employee Branch chief, Grant Rollins, and told Rollins that he thought he could get something out of the subject and wanted a chance to try. Having nothing to lose, Rollins went along with Pickell's request. Some in PD thought Pickell was being arrogant in thinking that he could succeed where the expert-in-residence had failed, and maybe they were right, but to quote "Dandy Don" Meredith, referring to an NFL player who was perceived as cocky, "If he can do it, it ain't bragging."

At this point, many in the CIA were getting nervous about the test results. The subject was in middle management and on the way up. In addition, he was the son of two retired Agency employees, one of whom had been in upper management. Everyone in PD who had reviewed the charts of his tests and listened to the tapes of his interviews was convinced that the subject was lying. Some, me among them, thought the subject could be a spy.

Pickell had two sessions with the subject. I monitored the sessions and heard the subject make admissions that were egregious enough to get him fired. At no time during either of the sessions did Pickell so much as raise his voice. In closing out the interview, Pickell told the subject, "There is still something you haven't told me."

"I am not ready to tell everything, but when I am, it is you I will tell," were the subject's final words.

Based on my observations of the subject, I was convinced that he was concealing his homosexuality and that he had had a homosexual relationship with a foreign national who worked for the station where the subject had most recently been assigned. During his sessions with Pickell, the subject had acknowledged providing classified information to a local employee who had been hired by the station. That same local employee had been fired because he failed his polygraph test on the issues of contact with another intelligence service and providing classified information to an unauthorized person.

Pickell also conducted a test on a friend of mine, "Whitt Lawrence." I had met and worked closely with Lawrence in Vietnam, and I considered him to be one of the Agency's better case officers. Apparently, his supervisors in the DO shared the same opinion because, by the time Pickell tested him, he had reached the Senior Intelligence Service (SIS), or what we used to call supergrade level. Lawrence had been accused of serious misconduct with the wife of one of his agents, and he denied the charge. Members of Security's Special Activities Division interviewed Lawrence and concluded that he was innocent of the charge. OMS psychiatrists interviewed Lawrence and also concluded that the charge against him had no basis.

Pickell tested Lawrence and developed enough information to force him into retirement. Lawrence actually broke down and cried during one of his sessions with Pickell, but in closing out the last interview, he complimented Pickell for his professionalism and thanked him for helping him to come to grips with some serious personal issues.

Almost a year later, after compiling a file of twenty-two of the outstanding cases Pickell had worked on, I wrote him up for an Exceptional Performance Award. All PD branch chiefs were on the panel I presented my recommendation to. On this occasion, the panel also included two representatives from OS's Office of Personnel. During a discussion of my recommendation, Pat Maxon, who was representing "John Kent," chief of the Covert Branch, spoke out against my recommendation.

"Pat, how can you not approve this request? These are some of the best tests ever done in PD," I said.

One of the personnel officers followed up with, "If these cases don't qualify Bob Pickell for an award, I don't know what does."

"My instructions from John are to vote against the EPA," Maxon replied. The idea that Kent, without having heard or read my recommendation, could order Maxon to vote against the recommendation incensed me.

A vote was taken, and my recommendation was approved. Two weeks later I was present when Pickell was presented his EPA, and I will never forget how Kent, who had ordered Maxon to vote against the EPA, approached Pickell, put his arm around him, and said, "I'm really glad you got it. It is well deserved."

Pickell wasn't the only one conducting great tests in PD. "Lisa Selik," one of my team members, administered a routine RIP test on an employee, "Sam Odell," who had recently returned from TDY in the Soviet bloc. When Selik brought me the initial charts from the first session of the test, I told her that the subject had a clear reaction to the question about concealing contact with a foreign national and I directed her to see what she could get from Odell on this issue.

Reluctantly, Selik confronted Odell. Without pushing very hard, she coaxed him to acknowledge that he had met a Soviet Bloc national female with whom he was maintaining contact and whom he had not reported as was required. Additional testing failed to resolve the issue.

When I reviewed the final charts that Selik had run, I concluded that Odell was at least withholding information, if not actually lying, about his foreign national contacts. I ruminated about the case, and I recall thinking that what Odell told Selik was very similar to what convicted spy U.S. Marine Corps Sergeant Clayton J. Lonetree had told us about how he had been recruited.[1] Odell, like Lonetree, was a loner, with no friends among his peers, and apparently he had no social life. The more I thought about the similarities between the two cases, the more I thought that Odell might be the Agency's Lonetree.

I wasn't confident that Selik would be able to resolve the case but felt she deserved the opportunity to try. The test could be a once-in-a-lifetime chance for Selik, and after I finished reviewing the charts from Selik's test, I said, "Lisa, I am going to have this guy come back tomorrow, and I would like you to do the test."

"John, I really don't want to do the test," Selik replied.

---

1. In 1987, Sergeant Lonetree confessed to committing some serious security violations while assigned to the U.S. embassy in Moscow. Lonetree became involved with a female translator named "Violetta" who introduced him to her uncle "Sasha." Sasha was a Soviet intelligence officer named Alexei Yefimov to whom Lonetree provided classified material. In 1987, Lonetree was convicted and sentenced to 30 years in prison. Ultimately, his sentenced was reduced and he was released from prison in February 1996.

Knowing that if this case turned out to be a big one, Selik might not be the best person to do it, I was a bit relieved but also disappointed. This was the type of case that examiners should be eager to do, and Selik's reluctance spoke volumes about her potential as an examiner. I assigned the case to "Mike Adamczyk." Adamczyk was a Reid-trained examiner, a former Chicago police officer, and a lawyer. He had a very low-key approach to conducting tests, which I felt would be effective with Odell. As it turned out, not only was I right in selecting Adamczyk to do the test, but I was also right about the case being very significant.

Odell told Adamczyk that "Svetlana" had come on to him and that, after meeting him on a few occasions at restaurants, she brought him home to meet her uncle. Odell also claimed that Svetlana told him that she would be traveling to the United States and would like to meet with him. Odell had the name and address of a friend of Svetlana who was living in the United States and with whom Svetlana would be staying during her visit.

The similarities between this case and the Lonetree case and the admissions Odell made were such that the FBI was informed. Svetlana's contact in the United States turned out to be an FBI informant. When Svetlana visited her friend, the FBI met with her and told her what Odell had said about their relationship. Svetlana denied any such relationship and claimed that she didn't even know Odell. When the FBI searched her bags, they found Odell's name, address, and phone number in an address book. An FBI polygraph examiner tested Svetlana and called the test inconclusive but also posited that he felt Svetlana had been truthful in her denials of Odell's allegations. A telephone call between Svetlana and Odell was set up.

"What have you done to me? You have gotten me in trouble," screamed Svetlana.

Odell immediately recanted his admissions. The next day Adamczyk conducted a second test session with him, and Odell took back his recantation. He stated that everything he had said about Svetlana and her uncle was true.

Espionage cases are very difficult to prosecute. Odell had not given the detailed admissions that Lonetree had, and the Office of General Counsel felt that it didn't have enough evidence to prosecute. I thought that because Gorbachev's Perestroika was in full bloom the Agency decided it was not an appropriate time to catch the Russian spies. Odell was allowed to resign.

I put Adamczyk in for an EPA, citing this test as one of the more significant cases in PD's history. The panel agreed and awarded Adamczyk $3,500. Had Odell been prosecuted and convicted, I am sure the award would have been much higher.

PD could have used a boost at this time, and it would have been great to publicize this case, but because Odell had not been charged and prosecuted, PD couldn't publicize the test as it wanted to. Regardless, Adamczyk had done an outstanding job and no amount of criticism of polygraph could change that.

Unfortunately, the euphoria in PD was short-lived. While reveling in Adamczyk's success, PD was advised that most of the Cuban agents had beaten their polygraph tests. In 1989, a high-ranking DGI officer, whom I will call "Field Goal," had defected and provided the CIA with information that the overwhelming majority of the Agency's Cuban assets were double agents. Polygraph Division took a beating over this, and many employees, when they came in for their RIP tests, made it a point to tell us that the Cubans we had missed proved what they had known all along: polygraph doesn't work. Each time I heard this line from an employee, I couldn't help but recall how the COG had once vilified polygraph because none of its agents could pass their polygraph tests.

When "Roy Barry," the deputy chief of the CI Staff came over to PD to brief us on the results of the review of the cases in which Cuban assets had apparently beaten their polygraph tests we were able to match the double agents with the examiners who had administered their polygraph tests. For some of us, this was a moment of truth. I wondered how many of the Cubans I tested had been double agents.

As it turned out, I had tested two of the Cuban double agents, one before he was caught by the Cubans and doubled, the other, was a double agent at the time I tested him, and he beat me. In the latter test, I hadn't been sure of my NDI call and wanted to re-test the agent. The COS refused to allow me to do the re-test, and in his briefing, Barry commented, "John obviously thought there was something wrong with this guy and should have been allowed to test him."

If a lesson could be learned from PD's experiences with the Cubans, it was that examiners should always go with the charts. In almost every one of the tests on which we were beaten, chart quality had been poor, and the examiners were swayed by case officers touting the high quality of the information their Cuban asset had provided.

PD was reeling from the criticisms over the Cuban debacle when, in November 1989, the Berlin Wall was torn down and the move to reunite East and West Germany took on a new life. Ultimately the files of East Germany's intelligence service, the Ministerium fur Staatsicherheit (MfS), were opened and revealed that the MfS had beaten us every bit as badly as the Cubans had. In a discussion I had with a senior DO officer, she was unequivocal in stating that the MfS had controlled all of the CIA's East German assets. I had tested and passed one of those assets. After my discussion with the DO officer, I reviewed the charts from the test and could find nothing that indicated deception.

Critics of polygraph, inside and outside of the Agency, raised the level of the hue and cry to do away with polygraph when they learned of the MfS's success against the CIA's examiners, and as had been the case with the Cuban debacle, polygraph subjects began to take examiners to task during their polygraph tests. In addition, in the operational arena case officers began to voice more skepticism about polygraph, seemingly ignoring the fact that all of the "misses" were tests in which we had called the agents good.

"Missing" the Cuban and East German agents was pretty hard to defend. My colleagues and I had failed many of the East German assets we had tested, but I cannot think of one of those tests in which an admission was obtained.

As PD tried to defend itself against its critics' attacks, an unrelated event at least temporarily distracted us: during a training course focusing on sexual harassment in the workplace run by the Office of Personnel, a female examiner accused a supervisor of sexual harassment. During the course the examiner stood up and asked, "What do you do when a supervisor propositions you?"

Bill Bontiempo attended the class, and when he returned to the office afterward, he told me what the examiner had said. "John, someone better tell Greg [Milenski] about this before he gets blindsided by a call from the IG [Inspector General]." I told Milenski about the examiner's accusation, and his response was, "Why didn't she come to me before going public?"

An IG investigation ensued. One of the investigators called me and asked if I thought the supervisor had propositioned the examiner. I told him that I believed that the incident had taken place but also said that I did not believe that the proposition met the criteria for sexual harassment. The examiner had told me, subsequent to her going public with the allegation, that the supervisor had asked her to go to a motel with him. "I refused, and then he accused me of coming on to him," she said. Recalling that conversation, I pointed out to the IG investigator that there had been no "quid pro quo," in other words, "either do it or suffer the consequences." If any action was taken against the supervisor, I am not aware of it.

By the end of 1990 much of the furor over the Iran-Contra Affair had subsided, Judge Webster had improved the Agency's image, and it was time for him to move on. In May 1991 President Bush appointed Robert M. Gates to replace Judge Webster. After five months of very contentious hearings, on November 6, 1991, Robert M. Gates was sworn in as the fifteenth DCI.

From my perspective as a polygraph examiner, Gates's tenure was essentially a nonevent. What I remember most about that period are the indictments of Joe Fernandez and Alan Fiers for their roles in Iran-Contra. I had known Joe Fernandez even before I entered on duty, had worked with him in South America, and thought very highly of him. I knew him, his wonderful wife, and all of their children. Fernandez was and is an honorable man, and one of the few people I met in the Agency who will be my friend for the rest of my life. I didn't know Fiers as well as I knew Fernandez, but I had conducted tests for him at headquarters and abroad. Fiers was a hard charger, had played football for Woody Hayes at Ohio State, and was on the DO fast track.

Fernandez was indicted in 1989, and to its shame, the Agency hung him out to dry, with no legal assistance. Ultimately, the charges against him were dismissed, but the Agency's failure to stand by Fernandez left a very bad taste in many DO officers' mouths.

Fiers, in my few contacts with him, impressed me as being, for lack of a better term, a real macho guy. I was, therefore, very surprised when he plea bargained his indictment down to a couple of misdemeanors in exchange for blowing the whistle on DDO Clair George and Duane R. ("Duey") Clarridge, one of George's deputies. Both George and Clarridge were indicted.

As I stated previously, during Bush's tenure as DCI, he appeared to have come to love the job and the Agency. In December 1992 President Bush, perhaps in remembering his halcyon days as DCI, pardoned Fiers, George, and Clarridge.

The Iran-Contra indictments no doubt played a part in newly elected president William Jefferson Clinton's decision to replace Gates. On January 21, 1993, Clinton nominated R. James Woolsey to be DCI. Woolsey was quickly confirmed and on February 5, 1993, began his tenure.

Four days after Woolsey was nominated, a gunman killed two Agency employees while they were stopped at a traffic light near the main gate at CIA headquarters. The two men killed were Dr. Lansing Bennett and Frank Darling. I had met Doctor Bennett on a few occasions, and the best way I can describe him is as a very kind and decent man.

We soon learned that a Pakistani named Mir Aimal Kansi was the shooter. The manhunt for Kansi began, and in PD, as was often the case, our workload increased in response to the tragedy. Over the next four years examiners tested many individuals who claimed to know Kansi's whereabouts. When the Fairfax County, Virginia, police polygraphed Kansi's roommate, a PD examiner who had considerable experience in testing Pakistanis was asked to sit in on the test, comment on the subject's behavior, and offer any advice he felt was appropriate.

The long, arduous, and frustrating manhunt for Kansi was the best example of cooperation between the FBI and the Agency that I saw during my Agency career. In June 1997 Kansi was arrested in a small hotel in Pakistan. Extraordinary perseverance and a $2 million reward paid off. A friend who had been involved in the actual arrest told me, "When the FBI agent knocked on Kansi's door, Kansi opened the door, and the first words out of his mouth were, 'Fuck you!' The Kansi shootings provided a dramatic backdrop for the beginning of Woolsey's tenure and left many of us in PD feeling vulnerable. PD was located in a poorly secured area, and if anyone, particularly a disgruntled subject, wanted to exact any kind of revenge, it wouldn't have been that difficult. Kansi's attack upped PD's concern about its employees' security.

Of the DCIs who served during my tenure, Woolsey had the lowest profile and was the least well known, at least in the Agency. No one, at least no one in the lower echelons of the Agency, seemed to have any idea who he was.

In PD, we became concerned when Woolsey refused to take a polygraph examination. We thought his refusal sent a very bad message to the rest of the Agency and foretold the new DCI's lack of support for polygraph.

Woolsey's handling of the Janine Brookner case was also disconcerting. Brookner was a former COS who had filed suit against the Agency for what she alleged was sexual discrimination, claiming that she had been denied a promotion because she was a female. In its defense the Agency claimed that Brookner had a serious drinking problem and had sexually harassed a subordinate. An IG investigation concluded that Brookner's case had no merit. A woman I had worked with in Vietnam who had worked for Brookner told me that Brookner had been coming to work drunk and that she thought that my friend had blown the whistle on her. "John, it was one of the commo guys who blew the whistle on her," she said.

A friend in the IG's office told me that Woolsey wanted the Brookner case taken "off the table" and ordered that it be settled out of court. Brookner settled her claim for $410,000.

At the time it happened, I thought that the Brookner case was just another avoidable public black eye for the Agency, but it also occurred to me that if Brookner did drink on the job and had sexually harassed a subordinate, she was doing only what her male counterparts had been doing for years, and without consequence. I hoped that this was part of Woolsey's reasoning in ordering the settlement.

In PD, some considered this yet another case of someone getting away with running a scam on the Agency and chalked it up to business as usual. Examiners had other problems to worry about. At the top of the list was the bring-back rate. PD didn't have the manpower to properly handle the multiple-session tests that were becoming commonplace, examiners were getting frustrated, and morale was as bad as I had seen it since Meager's reign. As bad as morale was, just over the horizon was an event that had serious and very negative consequences for PD: the Ames case.

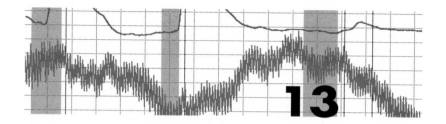

ALDRICH AMES

CIA polygraph examiners have been quite successful at catching deceptive agents. But they have also had some notable failures. Among the latter, none has been bigger than PD's failure to catch Aldrich "Rick" Ames. In 1986, almost a year after Ames began passing classified documents to the Soviets, he beat a polygraph test. In 1991, after spying for the Soviets for six years, Ames beat another test.

On February 21, 1994, Ames and his wife Maria del Rosario Casas were arrested for espionage. The next day I was outside Lout's office when I saw a copy of the *Washington Post* on a desk. A headline on the front page trumpeted the arrest of a CIA officer for espionage. As soon as I saw the name Aldrich Ames, I thought, "I know this guy!" I had worked with him in New York on the best test I ever conducted, and I had also tested one of his agents overseas. Both of the agents I tested for Ames were double agents.

The subject of the test I conducted for Ames in New York, an agent that the FBI had been running for five years, had been scheduled to return to Czechoslovakia. The FBI could not run the agent once he left the United States, so it asked if the Agency had any operational interest in him and offered to set up a meeting between the agent and an Agency case officer. The Agency agreed to meet with and, contingent upon a favorable polygraph test, take control of the agent. Ames would accept the turnover of the FBI agent if the test went well. I met with Ames in Manhattan, and he drove me out to a hotel on Long Island at which I conducted the test. An FBI agent and the agent met us at the test site.

At first I thought that Ames was unkempt. His suit was rumpled, his hair disheveled, and his teeth were tobacco stained. He was an unzipped fly short of being a slob. Ames was friendly but didn't seem very interested in the test, and he seemed more like an absent-minded professor than a case officer.

Ames didn't seem at all upset when I told him and the FBI agent that the agent in question was a double agent. Ames's lack of enthusiasm was disconcerting, and I remember thinking that, if this was the image he projected to agents, he wasn't a very good case officer.

Over the years after this first test I occasionally ran into Ames. He never seemed to recall my name, but he did recognize me. As I read the *Post* article, I remembered that I had last seen him when he came in for his RIP test in 1991. During my lunch break I ran into him by the elevator. I remember thinking at the time, "This is not the unkempt, disheveled guy I remember from New York." He was very well dressed. The tobacco-stained teeth were gone, and he projected a vitality that had been noticeably lacking when I worked with him.

"How's it going, Rick?" I asked.

"They're worried about my money. I have rich in-laws," he answered.

I hadn't known he was in the office for his RIP test, but I assumed that he thought I did know and thus framed his answer in the context of how he was doing on his polygraph test. It didn't occur to me to check with Ames's examiner as to whether or not Ames was having problems with the financial question on his test. I never got involved in tests of people I knew, and so I let Ames's comment go. I still reflect on what might have happened had I sought out his examiner and told him about my conversation with Ames.

In 1991 I was working in the Employee Branch for Bob Fester. On the afternoon of Ames's test Fester brought Ames's charts to me and asked me to look at them.

"Bob, the only thing I see that needs to be resolved is the question about concealing contact with foreign nationals," I said, after looking at the charts.

Fester and the examiner, "Sam Edwards," agreed, and Ames was asked to return for another session. "Don Buonoconte" conducted Ames's second session. Because I had reviewed the charts from the first session, Buonoconte brought the charts to me for a review. I saw no anomalies in the charts, nor did anyone else who looked at them, and the test was deemed no deception indicated. It should be noted that Buonoconte had some reservations about Ames and wanted to go after him. He was overridden.

Within days of Ames's arrest, a nightmare began for PD. An FBI agent was quoted in the *Washington Post* as saying that CIA polygraph examiners had blown Ames's tests, and this comment was only the beginning of the ensuing polygraph criticism. A case like this was what many of CIA's anti-polygraph factions had been waiting for, and they came after PD full bore. In some of the RIP tests I conducted post-Ames, subjects seemed to take a lot of pleasure in reminding me that Ames had beaten PD, and I found this to be depressing as well as infuriating.

Had the efforts to ferret out Ames taken on the same zeal as the efforts to fix blame for the damage he had done, Ames would have been caught much earlier. If Ames had been detected during his 1986 polygraph test, it would have saved the Agency much embarrassment and earned polygraph many kudos, but I doubt it would have saved many agents' lives. Some critics of the Agency's polygraph program have suggested that, because Ames beat the polygraph, agents were killed. From what I know of the Ames case, most, if not all, of the Russian agents who were executed were identified by Ames in 1985 when he turned over his first classified documents to the Russians, and by the time he was tested in 1986, it was too late to save them. Polygraph tests are conducted in an attempt to prove or disprove claims made by subjects, not to uncover their intentions. Polygraph was the easiest and most logical scapegoat. Prior to Ames's arrest, working in counterintelligence in the CIA was a dead-end job, and no better example of the importance DO management attached to counterintelligence (CI) was the fact that Ames had been named the CI officer for Soviet Europe (SE). CI had a very low profile in the Agency and was not a practical target for those looking to assess blame for the Ames disaster.

Implicit in attaching blame to polygraph for the failure to identify Ames as a spy is the presumption that, had Ames failed his 1986 and 1991 polygraph tests, action would have been taken against him. Prior to Ames's arrest, polygraph tests that resulted in DI calls without admissions, for all intents and purposes, were disregarded. A security officer from SAD interviewed subjects of tests deemed DI, and the OMS psychiatrists also occasionally interviewed them, but unless subjects made admissions, their cases would, in all probability, be closed.

In PD, the Ames case provoked a lot of soul-searching. Former examiners called PD to find out if they had conducted any of Ames's polygraph tests and breathed sighs of relief when they found out that they hadn't. I recall that after Ames was arrested, I had occasion to go into Milenski's office while he was reviewing the charts from Ames's 1986 test. "Dammit, John, it was there in 1986, and we missed it," he said.

Some examiners in PD remembered Ames's 1986 test and "Donna Bonwit," the examiner who had tested him. Specifically, they remembered that, as Bonwit escorted Ames down the hall to her room, she asked how Ames's wife, Rosario, was and reminisced with Ames about how Rosario had taken her on a shopping trip during Bonwit's TDY at the station where Ames and Rosario worked at the time. In retrospect, I can't help but think that Ames must have been very relieved when he found out that he might have an "in" with his examiner. Many of the examiners in PD and I were favorably predisposed toward subjects we knew personally. Personalizing polygraph tests is discouraged but difficult not to do. Whether an examiner relates positively or negatively to a subject, personalization usually renders the process less objective.

My supervisors likely saw my tendency to personalize my tests as my biggest weakness as an examiner. Because I hadn't gone through the entire Reid course or PD's training course, I did not believe that polygraph was a science. That being the case, I felt more comfortable dealing with subjects on a personal level. On the plus side, I had little difficulty communicating with my subjects. I obtained many confessions because I could relate to and identify with them. The way I tested was who I was, and I am more than satisfied that, as Frank Sinatra put it, "I did it my way."

Subjects who have already beaten a polygraph test have a better chance of beating a subsequent test because they are more confident and less fearful of the test. According to Ames, that was not the case in his 1991 test.

After his arrest, PD was given a chance to debrief Ames. The interview was videotaped, and everyone in PD was given an opportunity to see the tape. Flynn Jones and Bruce Gall were chosen to conduct the debriefing. During the interview, Ames said that he had been quite nervous about his 1991 test and had actually asked his Soviet handler for some guidance on how to get through the test. Ames said that his handler told him to get a good night's sleep and think peaceful thoughts.

Ames commented that in 1986 had he known that he had a polygraph test coming up he *might* not have initiated his first contact with the Soviets. As near as I can recall, Ames said that at the time he walked out of headquarters with his first bag of classified material he had given polygraph no thought because he assumed he had a much longer time to go before he would be scheduled for a test. Ames had not been informed that a reinvestigation to update his clearances had begun, as was the normal procedure, and he felt safe. Ames's comments led to random testing of employees, which OS hoped would remove the safety net that Ames thought he had had. Put another way, employees could no longer count on four or more years between tests, which OS felt narrowed the window of opportunity for those considering betrayal.

More significant, Ames said that he knew that unless he confessed, nothing would happen to him. "You guys would retest me, have me interviewed by other security officers and the shrinks, but unless I confessed, no action would be taken against me," he said. As noted above, Ames was right. Applicants were denied security clearances based on their admissions, not simply for failing their polygraph tests, and I can't recall an employee who lost his or her clearances unless an admission of serious wrong doing was made.

"I also knew that there was absolutely nothing you could have said that would have made me confess," summed up his comments about his mindset going into his 1991 test. I had my doubts as to whether or not Ames believed this was true. Evidence that he had evaded taxes was out there, and if his examiner had confronted him with it, I think he could have been pressured into making a deal.

When asked about his feelings about polygraph in general, Ames didn't express much faith in the process itself but did comment on the test I did for him in New York. Ames did not cite me by name but did say, "The examiner caught a Czech double agent not because the polygraph was effective, but because he knew a lot about Czech intelligence."

Ames was also asked, "During your last test, did you feel yourself react to any of the questions?"

"Only one. When I heard the question about concealing contacts with foreign nationals, a picture of Val [his Soviet handler] appeared in my head. I thought, 'Oh shit!'" Ames said. In fact this question did evoke the strongest reaction on the test and was the one I had identified to Fester as the question that was clearly unresolved at the end of the first session.

Ames' debriefing set in motion some changes in polygraph procedures that the CIA hoped would diminish the chances that another Ames could beat us. As the investigation and damage assessment continued, I concluded that one thing in particular could have helped PD catch Ames in 1991. Ames's greatest vulnerability was his finances. He had a paper trail indicating extravagant living, and his prepolygraph BI uncovered that he had paid $540,000 cash for his house in Arlington. For reasons unknown, this information was not available to the examiners who conducted Ames's 1991 tests. The BI had been completed in December 1990, and Ames was tested in April 1991. A colleague who had worked on the case told me that a senior officer in the Clearance Division had deleted the information about Ames's paying cash for his house, as well as other information about Ames's finances from Ames's BI on the grounds that this information was none of PD's business. I found this hard to believe, but in Pete Earley's fine book about Ames, *Confessions of a Spy*, he cites the same information.

I am certain that, had PD known about Ames's financial habits before his 1991 test, the test would have gone differently. Specifically, during the pretest, the examiner would have focused on Ames's finances. During testing, any sensitivity at all to the question regarding finances would have resulted in specific testing on Ames's finances. I don't think Ames would have made it through such a test. Given his brief conversation with me, at the time of his first polygraph session in 1991, finances were clearly on Ames's mind.

With 20/20 hindsight, I also posit that during Ames's second 1991 polygraph, he manufactured a reaction to the question on concealing contact with foreign nationals. He reacted so strongly to the question, so much more so than to any other question on the test, that his response had to have been manufactured. Ames would have done this for two reasons: first, to deflect attention away from any reaction he might have had to the finances question and, second, because contact with foreign nationals was part of his job and he could logically rationalize his reactions to that question, i.e., "I meet with foreign nationals and foreign intel types, every day. It's what I do."

Earley also commented on the 1991 test, and on page 282 of his book he writes, "The machine showed that he was being deceptive. The examiner told him not to worry. He had passed." Because I was there, I can categorically state that this did not happen. I mentioned this to a retired Agency lawyer who was a friend of Earley's, and he offered to set up a lunch with the author. When the meeting failed to materialize, I sent a note to Earley via the friend and never heard back.

In the rush to fix blame, the CIA seemed to have overlooked that Ames's did most of his damage between April 1985, when he passed his first package of classified material to the Soviets, and April 1986, when he was polygraphed. Polygraph is designed to catch miscreants who have committed a crime, not someone who intends to commit a crime, and I know of no security procedure or process that might have prevented Ames's first venture into betrayal. I suggest that a flawed personnel system is every bit as much to blame for the Ames disaster as polygraph is. Ames was an incompetent drunk who should have been fired long before he was put in a position from which he could do so much harm.

When Ames was tested in 1991, he was on a short list of suspected moles. Some believe that PD should have been told about Ames's presence on the list before his test. I disagree, as that would have "poisoned the well."

After Ames's arrest, a good friend, "Gordon Corey," asked me to visit him in his office. Corey was a senior DO officer I had worked with overseas and with whom I had a good relationship. When I entered his office, Corey said, "Thanks for coming over, John. Have a seat. I have a favor to ask of you." Corey then closed the door. "John, when I took my last test, were you guys told that I was one of the people they suspected of being a mole?" he asked.

I was caught completely by surprise. I had been asked to conduct Corey's test, but because I knew him, I had declined. I had not been made aware of any suspicions about Corey nor was the examiner who conducted the test. Corey passed the test.

"Gordon, I wasn't made aware that you were under suspicion, and I don't believe that the examiner who did the test was either," I answered.

"Good. These last two years have been a nightmare. I am about to retire and was curious as to whether or not they told you that I was a suspect," Corey said. After I retired, I learned that Corey had been under suspicion along with several others; two of whom I tested. I was not told that they were under suspicion before I administered their tests.

Had the examiner who tested Corey known that Corey was on the short list of suspected moles, I think that he might have treated Corey differently during his polygraph test, and the test might very well have ended with either a DI or an inconclusive call.

Most examiners I worked with were not risk takers. I have never seen myself as a risk taker, but I always believed that my job as an examiner was to make a call. There is much less risk in calling a subject's test results DI or inconclusive than there is in making an NDI call. The former two calls are much less likely to come back and haunt; the latter can and often do.

Few significant changes in the way PD did business were instituted because of the Ames case. Random testing was instituted, and I thought this was a step in the right direction. The Quality Assurance Staff (QAS) was created to review all tests, and a policy of referring to the FBI cases that were deemed DI based on the counterintelligence issues after two sessions with no admissions was instituted.

Of the changes, the decision to add another level of quality control to the process was the worst. Prior to Ames, the examiner, team leader, and branch chief reviewed and checked the quality of charts. After Ames, the QAS that was put in place was merely a redundancy that added to an already swollen bureaucracy in PD and, more important, seriously eroded the confidence of the examiners. QAS reviews sometimes took weeks, and subjects who thought that they had passed their tests were very unpleasantly surprised when they were called back for additional testing. QAS bring-backs were a little more upset about being brought back for more testing than most bring-backs, and the examiners whose calls had been belatedly overturned were almost as frustrated. The fact that the bring-back tests didn't develop any additional information didn't help.

Examiners became tenuous about making calls. Team leaders became more rigid and prone to second-guessing examiners. Branch chiefs pushed team leaders to be more cautious in reviewing charts, and everyone in PD from the chief down became almost paranoid about getting beaten.

Some in PD thought that, were we to get beaten again as we had been by Ames, PD would not survive. Pressure, not necessarily to catch a spy but rather not to get beaten, was extraordinary. Both of the examiners who had tested Ames in 1991 left PD. I don't know whether they were directed to leave or whether they left on their own, but I do know that their departure sent a very clear message: Don't get beaten.

As a result of this paranoia, the number of bring-backs increased dramatically. Examiners and team leaders alike adopted a policy of bringing subjects back for more testing "just to make sure we haven't missed anything." Examiners began to believe that, unless their subjects made admissions, they hadn't done their jobs.

The paranoia also resulted in an increase in the number of inconclusive calls. This drove the Clearance Division crazy, but it was a device that many examiners felt was necessary to ensure they'd covered all bases. No CIA employee's career had ever been hurt by an inconclusive polygraph test, and some examiners were playing it safe. At a PD staff meeting during this period, I pointed out that every time an honest person walked out of a polygraph test with anything less than an NDI call, PD's credibility suffers, and ultimately, we would have to pay a price for our lack of decisiveness. That was a very iconoclastic position to take, and none of PD's managers seemed to agree with me.

After Ames, it became more politically correct in PD to be perceived as a strong, hard-charging examiner. Examiners were much more aggressive. Mild antipathy among employees toward polygraph turned into almost open hostility. Complaints from subjects soared, as did the stress level among the examiners. "We are being treated like criminals" was a frequently heard complaint among the employees. An in-house website was created on which employees aired their complaints about their experiences during their reinvestigation polygraphs.

The Ames case spawned a polygraph policy that seemed to operate on the premise that all subjects were guilty unless they could prove they were innocent. The tests of too many honest people were called deceptive or inconclusive, and the Agency populace was up in arms.

Melissa Boyle Mahle, in her fine book, *Denial and Deception*, commented that examiners were given bounties for obtaining admissions from subjects during tests in the post-Ames period. Initially, I rejected her comment out-of-hand, but on reflection, there was some truth in what she wrote. Examiners weren't given bounties per se, but I know of no examiner who was ever given an Exceptional Performance Award or quality step increase for a test in which no admission was obtained.

In PD parlance, admissions were called "knock-ins," e.g., "I knocked him in on drug use." Shortly after I began testing in 1968, Milenski told me, "Getting people through tests is great, but getting knock-ins is what really counts." After Ames, getting knock-ins became the true measure of an examiner.

One facet of my performance as an examiner that I was very proud of was that, in my thirty-one years as an examiner, I never had a subject make a complaint against me. Knowing that I did more tests than any examiner in the history of the Agency's polygraph program makes this accomplishment more meaningful to me. Many of my colleagues and supervisors saw it as a weakness, and, be that as it may, when a PD manager said, in front of the entire division, "Don't worry about complaints. If you aren't getting complaints, you aren't doing your job," I was personally offended. When I mentioned this to a supervisor, he replied, "This is what we have to do to keep from getting beaten again."

Shortly after the Ames case PD lost its polygraph school. The three examiners who had tested Ames in 1986 and 1991 had all been trained in PD's school. Budgetary factors were part of the decision to do away with the school, but I am certain that missing Ames also played a major role in that decision. Ames beating PD aside, in 1994 Agency examiners as a group were the best polygraphers in the U.S. government. Having had the opportunity to compare other U.S. government polygraph programs with the Agency's, I knew how effective the Agency's program was, as well as how ineffective some of the other programs were. Doing away with PD's school was truly a case of throwing out the baby with the bathwater.

The Ames case also provoked a change in how the division handled DI calls without admissions. Prior to Ames, no mechanism was in place to deal with such calls. As I have mentioned, when a subject was deemed DI on the basis of counterintelligence issues after two sessions and without making any admissions, the case was referred to the FBI. I don't know exactly how many employees' files ended up in FBI hands, but I have heard that it was well over three hundred. Many employees whose files were passed to the Bureau ended up in a state of administrative limbo, with their careers on hold and a cloud over their heads. Of the many cases referred to the FBI, I know of none that resulted in the identification of a spy or the firing or arrest of an employee.

Much to PD's surprise, DCI Woolsey came in for a polygraph test shortly after Ames was arrested. I saw this as an attempt on his part to show some support for polygraph and appreciated the gesture.

The Ames debacle was still haunting PD in mid-1994 when "Marti Kaye" caught a spy. Kaye was a comparative newcomer to PD and conducted a routine test on a subject who reacted very strongly to the question about concealing contact with a foreign intelligence service. Six hours into the session he confessed to Kaye that he had engaged in espionage against the United States. He was subsequently convicted and sent to prison.

If ever there was a time when PD needed a boost, the post-Ames period was it. The spy Kaye caught had not done anywhere near the damage Ames had done, but he was a spy. The fact that OS/PD did not use Kaye's success to generate some favorable press to counter the Ames disaster was unfathomable to me. Kaye's success provided only temporary respite from the Ames case blowback, and Woolsey was under a lot of pressure to fire those deemed culpable for not catching Ames sooner. Woolsey refused to fix blame, and I think that this ultimately led to his resignation in January 1995.

In his book *Nightmover*, author David Wise refers to Woolsey as Ames's eleventh victim, the other ten being the Soviet agents who were executed as a result of Ames's betrayal. Although that case can be made, a more logical person for Wise to have cited as the eleventh victim is Milenski, who retired at the end of 1994. Milenski did more to professionalize the Agency's polygraph program than all of his predecessors combined, and it saddened me to see him retire with the Ames case as part of his legacy.

Many questions about the Ames case are still unanswered, but the question that plagues me most is, "Where is the accountability?" It seems as though the two examiners who tested Ames in 1991 took the brunt of any blame that was passed out. Bonwit, who had tested Ames in 1986, had left polygraph long ago and was out of the line of fire, but how about those who did the reviews of her charts?

Who was it that deleted the information about Ames's finances from his background investigation? Of those involved in the investigation, this is the person I feel should have been reprimanded, if not actually fired.

Another Ames may be walking the halls at CIA, but I doubt that he or she will do as much damage as Ames did. PD has instituted testing procedures that I feel will make it much more difficult for a spy to get through a polygraph test, and these may inhibit some employees from going down the road of a double agent. But others will take the Ames route. I can only hope that procedures now in place will lessen the damage and allow for fair assessment of the blame.

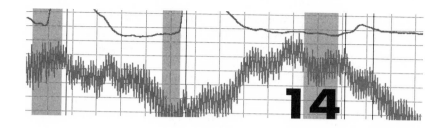

TWILIGHT

Before Milenski's retirement, I was made a senior examiner and assigned to work for Flynn Jones in the Employee Branch. As a senior examiner, I tested some of the more senior employees undergoing RIP testing.

In the fall of 1994 Milenski entered the Agency's transition program for retirees. Robert Iwai, who had replaced Ruocco as D/OS in 1992, named Mike Larrabee to replace Milenski. Larrabee was in London at that time, finishing up a one-year sabbatical, and "Tom Bush" was named acting chief of PD until Larrabee returned in December.

Bush came into PD in 1977, completed a tour overseas, and left PD. My only substantive contact with him while he was acting chief was an occasion when he asked me to tell one of the students in PD's school that he had failed to make the grade as a polygraph examiner. The trainee's father was a very close friend of mine, as was the trainee, and Bush thought the bad news would be best delivered by a friend. Bush asked me to deliver the news on the day before the class's graduation, and I thought that Bush and the school handled the situation poorly.

At the height of the Ames furor, Pickell decided to resign and return to Michigan. To me, PD losing Pickell was comparable to the Boston Red Sox losing Babe Ruth. On a personal level, my best friend in PD was leaving. In the aftermath of Ames, PD desperately needed an examiner of Pickell's caliber to help repair the damage Ames did to PD's reputation. I know that shortly after Pickell announced that he was leaving, Lout asked him, "What can we do to keep you?"

"Bryan, it's too late," Pickell answered.

The Ames case, Pickell's resignation, and PD's failure to publicize Kaye's success at catching a spy all left me less than sanguine. From my perspective, at the time Larrabee took over for Bush in December 1994, PD was in a downward spiral.

Larrabee faced a daunting task. Morale was very low. PD was under a microscope, and the skyrocketing bring-back rate was giving more impetus to an already in-place anti-polygraph sentiment within the Agency. Fortunately for PD, Larrabee was a good manager, politically astute, and well connected in the Agency. As I saw it, Larrabee's mission was to fight a holding action against the anti-polygraph elements. If PD could survive the aftermath of the Ames debacle without any further damage, Larrabee would have accomplished his mission.

One of the best things Larrabee had going for him was his deputy, Grant Rollins. Rollins came into PD during the reign of Pat Meager. He immediately impressed me as being one of the hardest working people I had ever met. Very intelligent and very people oriented, Rollins became an excellent examiner. By 1987 his success had prompted Milenski to recommend him for a promotion to GS-14. With the promotion, Rollins became a branch chief in PD and one of the youngest GS-14s in OS history. At the time Rollins was promoted to GS-14, I was the most senior GS-13 in all of OS, and had Rollins not been as deserving as he was, I might have been envious.

A sidelight to Rollins's promotion that forever endeared me to him was an incident that Milenski related to me. When Milenski told Rollins that he was being promoted, Rollins declined the promotion and asked Milenski to give it to me. Rollins had four young children and clearly needed the money as much as, if not more than, I did. Milenski, confined by the CIA's promotion policies, could not accede to Rollins's request.

Larrabee had a calming effect on the office, but the many different personalities in PD made keeping an even keel a management challenge. Wayne Teller was one of PD's "different personalities." Teller was a strong examiner, and one of the more interesting people I worked with, but he did march to the beat of a different drummer. Teller had been married five times and was one of the more intense people I had ever met. One day he confronted Lout, a senior manager, loudly, passionately, and profanely telling what he thought of him. Had Teller confronted any other manager in PD, it might have hurt his career. The fact that so many people in PD agreed with Teller and felt that he was saying only what they were thinking helped Teller survive his outburst. On another occasion Teller confronted Flynn Jones, literally screaming at him. After this outburst, Teller stormed out of the office, and we didn't see him for a week. Such events spiced up life in PD.

PD was adjusting to the Larrabee/Rollins regime, when along came Deutch. In March 1995 President Bill Clinton appointed John M. Deutch to DCI, filling the vacancy created by Woolsey's resignation. Everyone in the Agency knew that Deutch didn't want the job; Deutch had been the deputy secretary of defense and wanted to be secretary of defense. Clinton had also appointed Woolsey, who had no previous intelligence experience, and with Deutch he did it again. None of the chairmen of the Joint Chiefs of Staff during Clinton's presidency were military academy graduates, and in selecting DCIs, he similarly seemed to eschew career intelligence professionals. Most felt that this was evidence of Clinton's lack of trust in and even disdain for the Agency.

Deutch did take an Agency polygraph test, but he did not make the people he brought with him from Defense take Agency tests. Their tests were conducted by Defense Intelligence Agency (DIA) examiners.

Among those Deutch brought with him was Nora Slatkin. Deutch and Slatkin became the CIA's warlock and witch, and their tenure was the most acrimonious that I can recall. Within a month of his swearing in as DCI, Deutch was confronted with a situation that defined his tenure as DCI.

In April 1995 the Senate Select Committee on Intelligence was informed that a Guatemalan army colonel on the Agency's payroll might have been involved in the killing of two American citizens in 1992. Once again, as during the Church and Pike hearings, the CIA was charged with being a rogue elephant. The IG inspection of the Agency's role in the killings concluded that the Agency had not broken the law but also that senior DO officers "Tom Ware" and "Frank Bagley" had not been as forthcoming in their testimonies as they should have been. In response to the second conclusion, Deutch fired Ware and Bagley and meted out punishment to seven other DO officers. The DO was outraged, and criticism of Deutch was loud, continuous, and dramatic.

In an attempt to pour oil on the waters, Deutch convened a meeting with the DO in the main headquarters auditorium. Officers showed up for the meeting wearing black armbands and actually booed and hissed at Deutch. This was unprecedented and eliminated any possibility for a less-than-adversarial relationship between Deutch and the DO.

I didn't know Bagley and had only met him on one occasion, but I did know and thought very highly of Ware. He had been the COS at three stations I had worked in. He was always very supportive of polygraph, and I remember an occasion when a case officer and I got into a minor argument about a test. I had asked the case officer to prepare a list of the questions for our subject so that he and I could go over them before the test, which was scheduled for the following morning. I had asked the case officer to complete his list before lunch. At about 4:00 that afternoon, I saw him in the hall and asked, "'Jay,' do you have the questions for the test?"

"Don't worry about it, John. We can do it tomorrow morning," Jay said.

"Jay, I don't do it that way. I want to make sure that there are no glitches and no misunderstandings during the test," I answered.

"Well, John, that isn't the way I do it, and you are going to have to wait," Jay jokingly replied.

Suddenly, Ware stepped out of his office and said, "Jay, you will have those questions prepared and go over them with John before you leave today." Jay was more than a little angry, but he brought me the list that evening.

The night before I had obtained an admission from one of Ware's agents that he had been recruited and was being paid by the Soviets. This success may have earned me Ware's support, but regardless of the reason for his help with the Jay situation, it was refreshing and I appreciated it.

On another occasion when Ware was a DO division chief, I administered a RIP polygraph test to a woman assigned to his office and whom I will call "Ms. Jones." Ms. Jones was in her mid-fifties and had been a longtime Agency employee. During the pretest, Ms. Jones almost broke down. She said that she was emotionally worn out and felt overworked and that the pressures in the office were more than she could handle. I managed to settle her down and actually got her through her test. Marty Davis had been monitoring the test, and when I brought the charts to him, he congratulated me on how well I had dealt with this very nice, but emotionally shaky, woman. He also put me in for an award for my efforts.

Although the test had turned out well, I was concerned about Ms. Jones and called her office to make sure she had made it back OK. It had been almost two hours since she had left PD, and from the office window, I had observed her walk across the parking lot and get into her car. After hearing that Ms. Jones had not returned to her office, I looked out the window and saw that her car was still there. With a little trepidation, I ran out to the parking lot, fearing what I might find. I found Ms. Jones, crying in her car.

"Are you OK? Is there anything I can do?" I asked.

"I'm okay. I'm just so glad that my test is over. I had been worried. Now all I have to worry about is how I am going to keep up with my job."

"Ms. Jones, Tom Ware is a friend of mine. Would you like me to talk with him?" I asked.

"Would you, John?" she asked.

That afternoon I spoke with Ware. He assured me that he would make sure that some of the load was taken off Ms. Jones and would get her some counseling. He also effusively thanked me. This was the guy Deutch was firing! I resented Deutch on a personal level because he was firing a friend and on a professional level because he was doing serious damage to the DO.

Deutch didn't have much daily contact with the DO's lower echelons; he left that to Nora Slatkin, whom he named the CIA's executive director. In this position, Slatkin was the most powerful woman in the Agency, and she wielded that power with vigor. Slatkin became the lightning rod for all the bolts directed at Deutch. DO officers certainly disliked Deutch from afar, but up close and personal, they were much more focused in their disdain for Slatkin.

In PD, we had some concerns about Slatkin when we heard that she had said that, if she could, she would do away with polygraph. There was much speculation in PD as to why she was so anti-polygraph, and Milenski, who had come back to PD on contract, said that he thought that Slatkin might have had an unfavorable Agency polygraph. Because she had not taken an Agency polygraph in connection with her current job, we didn't know her maiden name and had no way to check. Regardless of why Slatkin was anti-polygraph, her alleged comments gave impetus to employees to complain about their polygraph tests, rail against the examiners, and appeal the results of their tests to Slatkin. I became directly involved in one of the appeals.

"Mariah DuFarge" was an Agency secretary who had been sent home early from an overseas tour in part because she had been found carrying a loaded gun and also because she had exhibited some erratic behavior. The Office of Medical Services evaluated DuFarge and diagnosed her as slightly paranoid and delusional. When DuFarge was called and advised as to the date of her polygraph test, she was more than a little abrasive toward the scheduler, and she ended up complaining to Lout about her previous TRIP test and about the "bastard of an examiner" who tested her. DuFarge also insisted that she not be tested again by "some young kid." Lout asked me to administer her test.

I arranged to conduct the test in one of PD's mirrored rooms and also asked a psychologist to monitor the interview. When I called for DuFarge in the reception area, she responded with a loud and histrionic, "Here I am. Ready to be tortured!" In an attempt to lighten things up, I introduced myself and said, "Ms. DuFarge, you said you didn't want a young kid to test you. Well, you have the oldest examiner in PD."

"What I want to know is, where is the son of a bitch who did my last test? If I see him, I am going to punch him right in the nose," she responded. DuFarge continued to rant about her previous examiner all the way to the testing room. As soon as DuFarge saw the mirror, she began to vamp and talk to those whom she thought were observing her. She was beginning to get under my skin.

Once she sat down I addressed the issue of her previous test. I told her that I had read her file and saw no complaint in it about her previous test.

"I did too complain. I told the guy who interviewed me after the test that that son of a bitch had accused me of being a lesbian. I will never forget that asshole," she went on. DuFarge might have thought she would never forget him, but her previous examiner had given the pretest briefing before I called her into the testing area; he had stood less than five feet from her in the reception area.

Before going over the test questions with her, I asked her about the gun she had been carrying overseas. "I had a bad divorce and was carrying it to protect myself against my ex," she answered. DuFarge also said that she didn't feel that she could count on anyone else to help her, so she carried a gun with her.

As I reviewed the test questions with her, she balked at each one, obfuscated, and used profanity. It got to the point where I finally told DuFarge, "Ms. Dufarge, this is a professional interview. If you can't conduct yourself like a professional, I will conduct you right out of here. Do we understand each other?" My words proved meaningless to DuFarge. She insisted that she be allowed to take the test while resting her chin in her right hand because she had neck pain. When I denied her request, she complained about the discomfort of the cuff. I tried the cuff on her arm and then leg, and I used a thumb cuff to try and get readable charts— all to no avail.

DuFarge was physically and emotionally unsuitable for polygraph testing, and I wrote the test up as inconclusive. Lout and "Graham Walters," the chief of QAS, had been monitoring the test. Walters told me, "You were much more patient with her than I would have been." PD management had instituted a policy whereby a supervisor could give an examiner an on-the-spot or instant award for what the supervisor saw as a job well done. There were two awards: a Level I, which was a leather portfolio, and a Level II, which was a pen and pencil set. After the Du-Farage test, Lout gave me a Level I award.

A female examiner did a second polygraph test on DuFarge and came up with the same results. In her posttest interviews with the Clearance Division, DuFarge was abusive and noncooperative. Her attitude, more than anything else, resulted in her case being closed with a recommendation that she be given two weeks' leave without pay. DuFarge appealed that decision to Slatkin, who surprised me by denying the appeal.

I subsequently met DuFarge in headquarters. She could not have been nicer, and I was surprised. Her polygraph demeanor was 180 degrees different than her demeanor during our meeting. I concluded that during my interview she was role-playing to the hilt and that the acting out negatively impacted on her test.

What could have been another Ames case occurred on Deutch's watch. In October 1995 CIA operations officer Harold James Nicholson failed the first of three polygraph tests that he took as part of the reinvestigation process. On November 16, 1996, Nicholson was arrested at Dulles Airport for espionage. He was subsequently convicted, making him the highest-ranking CIA employee ever convicted of espionage.

Nicholson admitted that he had been spying for the Russians since 1994 and also advised that the Russians had tried to train him to beat the polygraph. Measures put in place after the Ames case effectively countered Nicholson's attempts to beat his tests. The measures used during Nicholson's polygraph tests are sensitive methods that cannot be discussed here.

DCI Deutch, in a press conference following Nicholson's admissions, declined to attribute Nicholson's undoing to the fact that he failed three polygraph tests, saying that Nicholson was caught through analysis of several factors. I have no idea whether or not Nicholson was under suspicion at the time he was polygraphed, but I suspect that he was. Joseph J. Trento, in his *The Secret History of the CIA*, claims that a Soviet mole identified Nicholson. That might well be the case and the polygraph test might have simply confirmed suspicions rather than giving impetus to launch an investigation.

None of the examiners who tested Nicholson was advised of the CIA's suspicions, and all went into the tests cold. Computerized instruments were used, and the scores of Nicholson's three tests supported a call of deception indicated on the issue of concealing contact with a foreign intelligence service. For reasons unknown to me, Nicholson was never interrogated; this indicates to me that the CIA might have been in the middle of an investigation and that the powers that be did not want to alert Nicholson to their suspicions. Nicholson's case could have been a Waterloo for both Deutch and Larrabee, and both dodged a bullet.

Deutch's antipathy for the DO was probably best manifested in his selection of David Cohen to be the DDO. Cohen was a senior DI officer with little, if any, operational experience, and thus Deutch's choice confounded the DO. One bit of DO lore that amused me was the story that Mike Scheuer, the anonymous author of *Imperial Hubris*, once told Cohen to go fuck himself. From what I knew of Cohen, I hoped that this story was true.

Deutch and Cohen did almost as much harm to the DO as Turner had. Turner might have killed the CIA, but Deutch and Cohen castrated it. During Deutch and Cohen's tenure, they created a bureaucracy that put control of DO operations in the hands of headquarters' pencil pushers and bean counters. Proposed operations were analyzed and backstopped into impotence, and morale plummeted. The edict from on high was, "Take no risks."

In what I saw as Deutch's one attempt to do something positive for the Agency, he blew it. In November 1996, in an article in the *San Jose Mercury News*, a reporter alleged that the CIA had trafficked in illegal drugs to pay for the Iran-Contra war. This, to me, was yellow journalism, but Deutch felt compelled to publicly answer the charge at one of his town meetings, this one held in an auditorium in Los Angeles. The meeting turned into a shouting match and a fiasco. Deutch might have meant well, but responding to the *Mercury News'* charge in this way was stupid and the Los Angeles town meeting turned out to be one of Deutch's last public appearances as DCI.

William Perry was the secretary of defense while Deutch was DCI, and after the 1996 elections Deutch expected to replace Perry. When that didn't happen, Deutch resigned from the CIA.

On December 16, 1996, President Clinton named George John Tenet to be acting director of central intelligence. Tenet had been the deputy director of central intelligence since July 1995. In March 1997 Clinton appointed Tenet DCI, and on July 11, 1997, Tenet was sworn in. Tenet was an instant hit with the Agency populace. The image Tenet projected was youthful, vibrant, dynamic, and positive. He was the second youngest director of central intelligence in the Agency's history (James R. Schlesinger was the youngest), and he was a people person. In terms of what Tenet brought to the job, his years on the Senate Select Committee on Intelligence and his tenure as DDCI to Deutch gave him bona fides that few of his predecessors had.

Image aside, Tenet's early talks with employees emphasized that the Agency had to stop flagellating itself, focus on the future instead of dwelling on the past, and stop apologizing for doing its job. These comments played very well to the Agency and got Tenet off to a great start. Tenet's arrival didn't have much direct impact on PD, but we did see his appointment as a positive. Tenet recognized that PD's image was not what it should be and pledged to work to make it better.

As a senior examiner I was conducting many RIP tests, most of which were bring-backs, during this time. The more of these I did, the more convinced I became that the overwhelming majority of subjects were being brought back without good cause. My criticism of the bring-back policy fell on deaf ears. Regardless of the furor PD's bring-back policy generated, the division was almost paralyzed with the fear of another miss of the magnitude of the Ames case. PD management's position was, if bringing subjects back for additional testing lessened the chances of another Ames, disgruntled employees were a cheap price to pay. I disagreed. Disgruntled subjects have a greater potential to become Ameses. I know of no case in which a disgruntled polygraph subject committed espionage in revenge, but as the furor over the bring-backs increased, I became more concerned.

Not only the subjects were disgruntled; the examiners were too. The team leaders' continual second-guessing and the QAS's overturns continued to erode the examiners' confidence and morale. PD lost some good examiners as a result of post-Ames policies.

Larrabee was very successful in holding the line against any additional attacks on polygraph. Between his appointment and December 1996, when he retired, there were no major flaps. Good tests were conducted and requests for polygraph tests were rising; there were no crises during his watch. The Nicholson arrest had given PD morale a boost, and Larrabee left PD better than he found it. Fortunately, Rollins was named to take his place.

"Jonna Adams" was named Rollins's deputy. Adams was a former examiner, and Lynch had named her as OS's cultural diversity officer. She had also been a branch chief and brought a lot of administrative experience to the job.

Rollins' first couple of months on the job went well, but there were problems on the horizon. One of the problems Rollins would have to face was the increase in anti-polygraph sentiment in the Agency. The Agency website was replete with employees' very harsh criticisms of how their polygraph examinations were conducted and subjects coming in for their trial period and reinvestigations tests were more hostile.

The CIA's anti-polygraph website was replete with horror stories, and on a regular basis a negative story about an employee's polygraph examination appeared.

Other problems on the horizon were racial tension, which had begun to manifest itself in PD, Gall's hubris and arrogance, and IG investigations of two of PD's managers.

PD was heading into some very rough seas when Rollins took over. For a man as young as he was, I thought Rollins showed a remarkable degree of maturity in navigating PD during this tempestuous time. Rollins's appointment to chief of PD was a changing of the guard, and although I didn't realize it at the time, the change did not bode well for me.

On the day that Milenski retired, he was the only officer in PD who had been there longer than I had. I sensed that, rather than being viewed by the New Guard as an eminence grise, I was perceived as a dinosaur who had outlived his usefulness. Nothing did more to solidify the younger examiners' perception than my resistance to the switch from analog instruments to computerized polygraph instruments. Were I to do it all over again, I would be the first to jump on the computerized polygraph bandwagon.

"Cole Garrett," an examiner I had recruited in 1985, had left PD for a while and returned during the Milenski/Larrabee era. Shortly after returning, he conducted a TRIP test in which his subject admitted to participating in an armed robbery after his preemployment polygraph and before he entered on duty. The employee and his accomplice were both arrested. This was one of the very good tests conducted in EB, and Flynn Jones put Garrett in for an EPA, which he received. Not long thereafter, Garrett became a team leader in EB and supervised my tests. He pushed me very hard to switch to the computerized machine, and in January 1997 I began using the Lafayette LX-2000 polygraph instrument.

I had really misjudged the depth of Garrett's displeasure over my reluctance to switch to a computerized instrument. In 1998, while reviewing my personnel file, I found a memorandum that Garrett had written that harshly criticized me for my reluctance to make the switch. I was disappointed that he had written the memorandum but more disappointed that he had not shown it to me before putting it in my file, as was required.

Within two months of the switch, I felt comfortable running the new instrument, but I didn't always agree with the computerized chart analysis. For more than twenty-seven years I had been scoring and evaluating polygraph charts based on a global analysis: visually comparing the reactions on a chart and assigning a numerical score for each reaction. On several occasions I found my global analysis at variance with the computerized analysis. More often than not, the computerized analysis provided a more accurate evaluation of a subject's reaction to a question. That caused me to question my chart-reading skills and made me wonder how many people I had missed.

As much as I liked working with a computerized instrument, on occasion a subject produced erratic and unreadable computerized charts. On three of those occasions I switched back to an analog instrument and was able to obtain readable charts.

Over the course of my last three years in PD, I used the LX-2000 almost exclusively. I doubt that making the switch to a computerized instrument sooner would have made any positive difference in my career, but I know, just as well, that my resistance to the new machine negatively affected my relationship with PD managers. Among those I alienated, I had the greatest philosophical differences with Walters.

Walters had come into PD in the mid-1980s, during Meager's reign. He had been a polygraph examiner with the army's Criminal Investigations Division (CID), and after retiring from the military, he had become a commercial examiner. When Congress enacted laws limiting the use of polygraph examinations, the market for commercial examiners shrank and Walters applied for a position with the Agency. Shortly after he entered on duty, Walters was asked to conduct a very high-profile test because of his language skills. He did an outstanding job, made a most favorable impression on the powers that be, and from that point on was marked for success in PD. Walters, who replaced Jim Doom as director of PD's school, subsequently became a team leader, then a branch chief, and ultimately the first chief of PD's Quality Assurance Staff.

A comment that I often made and that has been cited on an anti-polygraph organization's website (www.anti-polygraph.org.) is "Without an admission, polygraph is just a scientific wild-ass guess [SWAG]." I also believe, and mentioned, that polygraph was about 92 percent art and 8 percent science. Both comments offended Walters. He saw them as direct attacks on his belief that polygraph is a science. Walters and I also disagreed on the appearance of my testing room. Walters believed that testing rooms should be as austere as monks' cells. My room was full of pictures and books. The pictures were of my kids, and I might have over-done it. Had Milenski or any of the other chiefs asked me to remove them, I would have, and I probably should have without being asked. Because no one else bugged me about my decorations, I believe that, until Rollins became chief of PD, PD management's attitude toward me was one of benign neglect. That began to change in the late 1990s, and by the time I retired I was glad my time was up.

On a more personal note I think my advocacy of Bob Pickell rubbed Walters the wrong way. Walters had run the school during Pickell's train-ing and on a couple of occasions had crossed swords with him. Among the younger examiners in the class, Pickell had built up a following, and I think Walters might have felt threatened by him.

Walters may have been a good examiner, but with the exception of the high-profile case I cited, I can't remember any good cases that he worked on or, for that matter, many of his cases at all. More important, when PD needed an examiner to conduct a test, Walters could never be counted on. He was one of a group of prima donnas in PD, who, although they were receiving the 15 percent premium pay for being examiners, refused to test.

In the military, examiners were required to conduct forty tests a year to maintain their proficiency. I doubt very much that any of PD's prima donnas conducted even half that many tests a year, and given the premium pay they received for testing, I posit that they were being not only unprofessional but also dishonest. Many of the examiners and I felt that most of the team leaders and members of QAS had completely lost touch with what it was like to be an examiner or a subject and that they couldn't empathize with either.

Prior to the Ames case, when examiners brought their charts to a team leader, in addition to discussing the charts, examiners would also comment on the verbal and nonverbal behavior of the subject. "I don't see anything on the charts, and the behavior is good," might have been an examiner's quick pre-Ames test summary. After Ames, it seemed to me that team leaders became reluctant to accept an examiner's comment that a subject's behavior was good, particularly if the charts were not of good quality. Examiners who claimed that their subjects exhibited good behavior risked being perceived as "soft" by some team leaders.

Walters was one of those who espoused the hard approach to polygraph testing. He believed, and was correct, that deceitful subjects could fake good behavior, but given PD's clientele, I thought it unlikely that our subjects were acting

Post-Ames, the paranoia of missing another spy combined with the harder approach to polygraph led to a cynicism among examiners that I had not previously seen in PD. Some PD supervisors espoused the idea that "all subjects are bad." In addition, some examiners believed that unless they obtained an admission, they hadn't done their job. It became almost de rigeur to "shake the trees," i.e., hint or imply, if not actually advise, a subject that he or she was showing sensitivity to a question and see what "shakes out." I was never comfortable with this technique.

Walters, it seemed to me, assessed the Agency subjects PD tested by the same standards he applied to the subjects he tested in the CID and commercial arenas. I saw this as the wrong way to go.

During Walters's tenure as a branch chief, I was assigned to test a bring-back who was initially tested by one of Walters's team members. On a previous occasion, I had conducted a bring-back on one of Walters's team members and had complained to the chief of PD that the subject should not have been brought back. Walters took umbrage and requested that in the future, if I had questions about any of his team members' tests, I bring them to him first.

On this occasion, I looked at the charts and was amazed that the examiner, "Harry Prime," had concluded that the subject was being deceptive. Prime was a comparatively new examiner and had recently conducted an outstanding interrogation in which he obtained an admission of criminal activity. He also had the highest bring-back rate and lowest case resolution rate in PD. Mother Theresa would have had a difficult time getting through one of his tests.

After reviewing the file, I conferred with Prime. "Harry, I am doing a bring-back test on a guy you did. Could you take a look at these charts and tell me how you concluded that he was being deceptive? I have looked at the charts and don't see any reactions on which you can base a DI call."

"I think the guy is really bad, whether it's on the charts or not," Prime said after looking at the charts and file.

"Let's go see Graham," I said.

"Graham, would you please take a look at these and tell me what you see," I said. "Harry is calling this guy DI, and I just don't see it. If we are bringing back people based on charts like these, we're never going to get anyone through," I added.

"I don't know if I would call these charts DI, but I also don't know if I would let the subject go," said Walters. Walters was a master of the unequivocal answer.

"Harry says that he doesn't see much, but thinks the guy is lying," I said.

"If that's how Harry feels, then he should be tested again," said Walters.

My impression was that Prime felt the way Walters wanted him to feel. I administered the test and called it inconclusive, a popular call for bring-backs. If subjects were honest during their previous sessions, they are often frustrated when they return for additional testing, often causing them to produce erratic and hard-to-interpret charts. Further, subjects who were dishonest during a previous test knew how the process worked, and their fear often caused them to produce poor-quality charts.

No better example of the hard approach's popularity with managers could be found than Prime's selection to join the Operations Branch, for which he would test DO assets. Selection for the Ops Branch was a plum for examiners, and based on Prime's high bring-back rate, I couldn't believe he had been selected.

Making decisions is a critical part of operational testing. Polygraph examiners, working with DO officers overseas, usually work on their own, and they don't have anyone to review their charts. Decisions have to be made on the spot. Prime cleared one subject in his first fifty ops tests. It is possible that forty-nine of the fifty subjects he tested were deceptive, but I wondered why he hadn't obtained any admissions. When I asked PD's chief of ops how, based on Prime's high bring-back/low case resolution rate, he could have accepted Prime for operational training, he answered, "I didn't know about his low case resolution rate."

Obtaining admissions that resolved cases was a daunting task when testing bring backs. My perception was that most of them should not have been brought back and had no admissions to make. Another factor was that the bring backs, particularly those being asked to return for more testing because of a QAS overturn, were hostile. I was fairly effective in soothing the ruffled feathers of many of these bring backs but much less successful in getting admissions.

PD needs examiners with different strengths. Some examiners, such as Bill Bontiempo, were called on to deal with subjects who had been argumentative during a previous test. An examiner such as Ken Robey, as previously noted, was often called on to deal with a subject who was suspected of involvement in criminal activity. A strength may be no more than a commonality shared by the examiner and a subject. That commonality can be ethnicity, educational background, military experience, or a myriad of other possibilities and will frequently make for a better test when factored into assigning an examiner.

In PD, the examiner and the team leader reviewed a subject's charts prior to releasing him or her. If there was any question about the chart interpretation, the team leader would bring the charts to the branch chief for another opinion. If everyone agreed that the charts did not indicate deception, the subject would be released, but with the following caveat: "Our Quality Assurance Staff will be reviewing the charts from this test. It is possible that they will overturn my call. If that happens, you will be called back."

From its inception, I saw the QAS process as redundant and counterproductive. If three and sometimes four reviewers had agreed on a call, I could not see the need for another review. QAS became an onerous cog in the polygraph process that lowered the examiners' morale and damaged PD's credibility. Between the day QAS began reviewing tests until the day I retired, I cannot recall one occasion when QAS overturned a DI call. My propensity to challenge DI calls earned me the reputation of being the "Pollyanna of Polygraph" and put me clearly at odds with QAS.

One of the team leaders in PD told me that QAS had me in their crosshairs, and although I had suspected that to be the case, it still bothered me very much. I resented the attention but never took it as being personally motivated by Walters. He genuinely believed I was projecting the wrong image of PD. I believed just as strongly that Walters's approach to polygraph in the Agency had the potential to destroy the program.

At the time I retired, I knew of only two QAS bring-backs that resulted in a subject admitting that he or she had lied during a test. I obtained both admissions: one dealt with a serious breach of security and the other with a foreign national contact that the subject had deliberately concealed.

In reviewing the charts and files of bring-backs I was going to test, I noticed a commonality: the previous examiners had written negative comments about their subjects in the notes section of the file. Most of the comments were subjective and addressed the examiner's perception of a subject's attitude. "Very uncooperative." "Hostile!" and "This lady has a chip on her shoulder and hates poly" are examples.

In my conversations with the original examiners about the subjects I was retesting, I heard worse comments:

"That lady is a bitch on wheels. Watch out."

"I wanted to strangle that SOB. He was just jerking my chain all morning."

"He came in here today looking for trouble."

"She needs a real attitude adjustment."

Examiners did not put such comments in their reports because PD management considered them unprofessional and they could call into question the examiner's objectivity. In addition, the Clearance Division enjoined examiners from citing profane, emotional outbursts in their reports—the rationale being that to do so could be prejudicial to the subject, who might have been venting frustration.

In the majority of the tests I conducted on bring-backs, my reaction to these same subjects was quite different and usually positive. It never occurred to me that what I was doing was right or what the examiners were doing was wrong, but clearly, something was amiss.

I had known one woman for more than twenty years who was brought back for additional testing. I had tested both her and her husband and had run into them on numerous occasions while traveling. I knew this friend to be a warm and gracious person. Flynn Jones assigned me to her retest and said, "'Jean tested this woman and says she is a real problem. I think you can handle her." When I looked at the file, I said, "Flynn, I know this woman and her family. I can't test her. I also have a hard time believing that she is any kind of a problem." I didn't conduct the test, but I did speak with the examiner whom Jones assigned to the test. The test went well.

After the test, I spoke with my friend. She vented to me about the first examiner, Jean. Jean was a very good examiner, and my friend's comments reinforced my perception that there was an ongoing failure to communicate between examiners and subjects.

Because I was concerned that the examiners might be causing some of PD's problems, I began monitoring all of the examiners in the Employee Branch (EB), as time would allow, to see if I could come up with any suggestions that might improve the process. Among the things that I noted was that, in many of the tests that resulted in bring-backs, the examiner had come across as aggressive and accusatory. I also noted that some subjects seemed a bit put off by examiners who used their first names. This had been a pet peeve of mine for years. As previously noted, Reid training recommended using a subject's first name as a way to take control of an interview. Anyone I don't know who calls me by my first name, especially if he or she is much younger than I am, is, in my view, being rude.

Some examiners had not read their subject's file. While on occasion a test may be assigned at the last minute allowing examiners little time to prepare, in most cases examiners have time to read a file before a test. On several occasions I heard subjects ask an examiner, "Haven't you read my file?" Instead of asking a subject, "What was your last overseas post?" or "Have you had any overseas assignments?" I thought it better to say, "How did you like your tour in Vietnam?" I felt that this let a subject know that I had done my homework and also created an atmosphere more conducive to obtaining admissions.

On one occasion a female examiner asked her female subject, "What's been going on in your life lately?" The question was a way to start a dialogue and appropriate. However, when the woman answered, "My son just died after a long illness," and the examiner responded with, "People come in here with all kinds of problems, some worse than losing a child," I was surprised. The test resulted in a bring-back, and I conducted the retest. During the retest, the woman complained about her previous examiner: "That insensitive bitch obviously never had a child. How, in God's name, could she ever tell me that there are worse problems than losing a child?" More important, she said, "I wouldn't give her the time of day, let alone admit to her that I had done something wrong."

Fortunately, the woman's test went well and the call was no deception indicated. On the downside, what had occurred between this subject and her first examiner is a good example of what was destroying the Agency's polygraph program.

On another occasion I conducted a bring-back test on a subject who had been originally tested by "Sharon Ellman." Ellman was one of the examiners who had come into PD when I was the recruiter, and I not only liked her, I thought she was a good examiner. Her subject, whom I was testing, was a married woman in her thirties. In discussing the problems with her test by Ellman, she referred to Ellman as "that goddamned bull dyke." Obviously, they hadn't hit it off.

Although these occasions were rare, I sometimes caught an examiner going into a testing room looking somewhat disheveled and unkempt. I recall one examiner who ran a test unshaven and wearing a wool plaid shirt that was not completely tucked in, at a time when coats and ties were required for all examiners when testing. (On days they didn't test, some examiners came into the office sans coat and tie in order to avoid being asked to conduct a test.) The problem wasn't limited to male employees. One Monday morning a female examiner came into the office disheveled, with food stains on her blouse and looking as if she had had a very hard weekend. She should not have been assigned to a test that day.

However, these two examples were not the worst. A young female, who had earned the nickname "Tyra Banks" while at the Department of Defense Polygraph Institute (DODPI), showed up for work wearing a white T-shirt with no bra and with her breasts clearly visible. "Given the political climate around here, there's no way I am going to say anything," her team leader told me. My impression was that the team leader, who was a Southerner, was concerned about a complaint of racial bias.

After about two months I went to Flynn Jones and asked if I could make a presentation to EB examiners about the aforementioned problems I'd noticed. I wish that I could say that my presentation had a positive effect on the way that EB examiners conducted themselves during tests, but I didn't notice any improvement. The good examiners continued to do great work while those to whom my remarks had been directed disregarded them.

The number of bring-backs I was assigned, the stress of being targeted by QAS, and the creeping cynicism in PD were taking their toll on my morale, and for the first time I began to think about retiring. Because I was in the CIA's retirement program, Central Intelligence Agency Retirement and Disability System (CIARDS), I was already eligible to retire and could not be forced out before I turned sixty, but at age sixty I would have to retire.

Life in PD was becoming worse, but my work had its compensations. For one, the job was still interesting. I still looked forward to going into the testing room and meeting a new subject, and occasionally I had some experiences that made my decision to stay on worthwhile.

One of those occasions actually involved a test that I didn't administer. The subject was a foreign national female who was marrying a CIA employee, whom I will call "Paul." When an employee submits a request to marry a foreign national, permission is granted contingent upon the foreign national being security approved. Part of the security approval is a favorable polygraph examination. On the morning of the woman's test I had run into Paul and his fiancée in PD's reception area. I had worked with Paul in Vietnam, and he introduced me to his fiancée, Mardi. Later that morning I was returning from headquarters when I ran into Mardi in the lobby. She was crying and very upset.

"Mardi, what's the matter?" I asked.

"They think I am a Communist, and Paulo will lose his job," she said.

"Mardi, why don't you come and talk to me," I said.

I took Mardi into an empty office and asked her to tell me what had happened.

"The woman who tested me says I am a Communist and that I wasn't telling her the truth," she tearfully explained. Tears can be faked, but this woman wasn't faking. "Paulo has left on a trip and won't be back for a week. And I don't know what to do," she cried. Apparently, Paul had to leave on a TDY and had been unable to wait for his fiancée to finish her polygraph test. Mardi also said that she was staying in Paul's apartment, was all alone, and didn't know anyone. To me, Mardi seemed to be on the verge of an emotional breakdown. I talked with her for over an hour and finally settled her down. I also gave her my home phone number and told her to call if she needed someone to talk to.

After Mardi left, I checked with the examiner who had tested her. "The charts are a little shaky, but I think she'll do OK the next time," was the assessment. The examiner was totally unaware of the effect that the test had had on Mardi.

The next morning I was in my office when one of PD's secretaries said, "A woman named Mardi is on the phone asking for a Mr. Sullivan." Mardi's first words to me were, "Mr. Sullivan, I am feeling so depressed. Paulo is away, and I can't call him. I don't want to alarm him, but I am going crazy." I became alarmed. Two of the psychologists assigned to PD were there that day. I asked Mardi to excuse me for a minute and went to seek their advice. I told both of them what had happened the day before and said that I now had her on the phone. I asked if one of them would listen in. One of them agreed to do so, and I went back to continue my conversation with Mardi.

I offered to pick her up and take her to talk with someone who might be able to help her. I also asked if she would like to have dinner with my family and reiterated that if I could do anything for her, she should call me. After about fifteen minutes Mardi said, "Don't worry, Mr. Sullivan, I am not going to do anything to myself. I just needed someone to talk to. Thank you very much."

In a subsequent conversation with the psychologist who had listened in on the conversation, he told me, "John, she doesn't sound like someone who is suicidal. You handled it very well." On her bring-back, Mardi had no problems, and as far as I know, she and Paul are still married. That situation gave me more satisfaction than many of the admissions I obtained from subjects.

Be that as it may, I also conducted some good tests during this period. I did bring-back tests on two applicants and obtained admissions of criminal activity that were serious enough to result in security clearance disapprovals for both of them.

One of my bring-back subjects during this period was one of the scarier people I'd ever been asked to test. The subject, a married female, had been "too nervous" to complete her first TRIP test, and I was asked to retest her. Garrett assigned me the case, saying, "John, I have a bad feeling about this lady." Garrett had been a police officer for a long time and was more than a little street smart. He went on to say that he thought the subject might have Munchausen syndrome. The subject had claimed that her baby was very ill and had been regurgitating feces. "John, anatomically, that's not possible. Babies don't eat their own fecal matter. She may be forcing the baby to eat it," Garrett said. Because this was a TRIP test, the crime issue was addressed. During the pretest, the subject was very nervous and went into great detail about the stress her child's illness was causing her. Perhaps my perception of her was influenced by Garrett's comments; in discussing her baby's illness, the subject did not come across as truthful. The same was true when I went over the lifestyle questions (crime and drugs) before testing. I thought the subject was being evasive.

When I tested her, she produced charts that were too erratic for valid interpretation. After testing on the lifestyle issues, I told the subject that she was having some difficulty with the questions and tried to establish a dialogue with her. After about fifteen minutes, the subject claimed that she was too nervous to go on. I excused myself and consulted with Garrett. "I think you're right, Cole. I think she is abusing the baby," I said, in summing up my feelings on the case. I also told Garrett that I thought the woman was a bit unstable and that this might not be a good time to go after her. Garrett agreed, and I let the woman go. The test was deemed inconclusive, but in my report I noted my suspicions. I never heard anymore about the case.

As noted before, Walters and I disagreed about whether polygraph was a science or an art. I believe polygraph to be an art, in part because on numerous occasions my colleagues and I have obtained admissions of serious wrongdoing from subjects whose polygraph charts showed no indications of deception. A good example of this phenomenon involves a test conducted by Flynn Jones. Jones had finished testing a young female applicant and brought me his charts for a quality check. Neither of us saw any problems with the subject's reactions to any of the questions, and Jones said, "I think I will let her go, but before I do, I am going to ask her, 'Are you sure there isn't something you want to tell me about using drugs?'" I tuned in to Jones's room and heard him ask the question. The young lady paused, said, "Yeah," and proceeded to admit to extensive and recent drug use.

On another occasion Garrett assigned me a bring-back on an employee who during his TRIP test had produced erratic and unreadable charts. "John, this guy is hiding something," said Garrett, as he handed me the file. "The only question we can give him is the question dealing with terrorist activity."

When I reviewed the file and charts, I agreed with Garrett that the charts didn't seem to show any reaction to the terrorism question but also asked that I be allowed to cover it when I did the test. During the bring-back test, the question that evoked the greatest and most consistent reaction was, "Since entering on duty, have you engaged in any terrorist activity?" I showed the charts to Garrett, and he told me to interrogate the subject. During the ensuing interrogation, the subject made admissions that, if I were to cite them, would reveal his identify. Let it suffice to say that his strong reaction to the question on terrorism had a good cause.

Each time I was assigned a bring-back, I reviewed the charts from the subject's initial test, and as previously noted, I often disagreed with the original examiner's decision. On occasion my disagreement was such that I took the charts to other team leaders and examiners and asked them for their assessment.

On one occasion in particular I was asked to test a female whose charts were deemed DI on the counterintelligence questions. I was in total disagreement, and I showed the charts to two team leaders and four examiners whose opinions I respected. To a person, they were unable to identify a question that had evoked a significant reaction or to which a case could be made for bringing the subject back. I then took the charts to Jonna Adams. I told her that I was very disturbed that PD was bringing this woman back and asked her to look at the charts. "I'd bring her back," Adams concluded.

"That scares the hell out of me," I replied.

My final stop before conducting the test was Flynn Jones's office. "Two team leaders and four examiners who have seen these charts don't see anything. We really shouldn't test her," I said.

"John, you're an experienced examiner; you should be able to get her through without any problem," said Jones.

During the pretest, when I tried to elicit an explanation for her reactions to the counterintelligence questions, the woman laughed—not the nervous giggle or titter of a person feeling stress, but a hearty, "you've got to be kidding" laugh. My read of her behavior supported my assessment of the charts, and I was convinced that this woman was not lying.

I conducted the test, and unfortunately, the woman's charts indicated deception. Jones was not pleased. Ultimately and DI charts aside, my DI call was overruled, and the test was deemed inconclusive. I think the DI charts were disregarded because management concluded that the subject's initial charts were NDI, and the safest call to make was inconclusive.

Less than a month later I ran into the same situation. An attractive African-American female was asked to come back for another session. Again, I disagreed with the bring-back request, and again, I took the charts and my reservations to Jones. "I think you're right, John. Let me call and tell her that we have canceled her bring-back." When Jones called, the woman had already left her office to come over for her test.

"John, when she gets here, why don't you bring her into my office, and I will explain why we are canceling her test."

I wish that I could believe that the test was canceled because of my disagreement with the call, but I think Jones's agreement with me had more to do with the subject being an attractive female than my chart interpretation.

My active disagreement with the bring-back policy didn't endear me to the powers that be, and at the twilight of my career I was beginning to doubt my decision to make a career of polygraph. My voice was lost on PD management, and it was getting to be too much to handle. By nature, I am anything but a dissenter or troublemaker. I follow the rules and resent people who don't. Those running PD and I clearly had philosophical differences and I could accept that, but those differences in philosophy made my final days in PD more stressful.

I was at a point where I felt things couldn't get much worse when Garrett asked me to conduct a RIP test on a subject that Gall had initially tested. Gall had tested the subject to resolve the crime question, which remained unresolved at the end of the subject's first-session TRIP. Gall's test results had been NDI on the crime issue. But for some reason, the Clearance Division had requested that the crime question be addressed during the test. I reviewed the charts of Gall's test and noted that the question Gall had marked as a control question evoked the strongest reaction on the test, but I didn't read the question he had used as a control.

During the pretest, when I reviewed the crime question, the subject became a bit upset and said, "That question has already been resolved. The last guy [Gall] said I was clear on that question."

I excused myself to confer with Gall. Gall wasn't in, and I went to talk with Garrett. I told Garrett what the subject had said, and he said, "Let's look at Gall's charts." Right outside of Garrett's office were some display cases Garrett laid charts on when he reviewed them. As we looked at Gall's charts and questions, Garrett said, "Bruce used a relevant question as a control to clear this guy!"

If the reaction to the control question is greater than the reaction to a relevant question, the theory or presumption is that the subject answered the relevant question truthfully. If the reaction to a relevant question is stronger than the reaction to a control question, an examiner can presume that the subject was not truthful in answering the relevant question.

I went back into the room and told the subject that we would have to revisit the crime question. I wasn't able to get readable charts from the subject, and I deemed the test inconclusive. After the test, I went to Rollins. "Grant, I just did a test on a guy Bruce tested. He used a relevant question as a control question and as a basis for clearing him, and that's wrong," I said.

"John, we let him [Gall] do some things that we don't let other examiners do," Rollins answered.

"Grant, no examiner should be allowed to do what he did," I replied. I also asked Rollins, "Who reviews Bruce's work?" The question was rhetorical; no one did. Anyone who had reviewed that test would have seen what Gall had done. Knowing that he was exempt from quality control, Gall had pulled a fast one, to say the least. Rollins went on to say that as an expert, Gall had to be given more leeway than less experienced examiners. At that point, I went a little over the line. "Grant, the *only* reason Gall is an expert is because Milenski made him one. Gall hasn't done enough tests over the last five years to maintain competence, let alone expertise," I said. I knew this because one of the schedulers who had been angry over the fact that Gall wouldn't test had recently told me, "Bruce Gall did four cases this year, and I'll bet that that is more than he did last year."

Rollins didn't answer, and then I asked him, "How many tests has Bruce done in the last year?"

Rollins told me that that was information I didn't need to know. That ended our conversation. The next day Rollins called me into his office. "Bruce was just in here. He is complaining that you are talking about that case he did, and he wants it to stop," Rollins said.

"You and Cole Garrett are the only people I have talked to about the case," I said. I also told Rollins that people were walking by as Garrett reviewed Gall's charts and probably heard his comments. Not willing to let well enough alone, I also pointed out to Rollins that we had fired some examiners for doing what Gall had done and asked him how he could defend Gall. Rollins didn't answer.

Prior to this incident Rollins and I had had only one serious disagreement. I had put Rorie Schiff in for a cash award of $1,000. She had done three very good cases: one in which a subject admitted to having sexually abused a sibling, another in which an employee admitted to having embezzled funds, and another in which an employee admitted to spousal abuse. I had worked on the third of these cases. I had concluded that the subject was abusing his son or wife or both, but I could not get an admission from him. I recommended that Schiff do the retest. She did and got the admission.

For some reason, Rollins would not sign off on my recommendation. I argued my case strenuously, and Rollins finally agreed to sign off on my request if I would reduce the recommendation to $500. I did, and Schiff got the award. I also took some heat from the panel for not recommending a larger award.

That disagreement with Rollins didn't seem to affect my relationship with him, but challenging his support for Gall did. My relationship with Gall had already deteriorated to a point of no return, but from that day on, my relationship with Rollins was never as good as it had been.

I thought the world of Rollins and still do, but I think I may have expected too much when I put him in a position of having to support me against Gall.

Personal feelings and/or political correctness aside, the charge I made against Gall was serious. I suspected that Gall had done this in other cases, and regardless of whether Rollins believed me or not, he should have done a review of Gall's work. Gall hadn't conducted many tests, and it wouldn't have taken long. However, according to Rollins, Gall was assigned only high-profile cases. If that was the case, reviewing Gall's cases might not have been politically acceptible. From that moment on, I started to look forward to retiring.

The dust had barely settled when Gall was put in charge of certifying PD's examiners. There were to be four levels of certification, Levels I through IV, with Level IV reserved for the most qualified examiners. Gall set the criteria for each level of certification. I didn't understand the purpose of certification and considered it another exercise to keep Gall busy, to keep him out of the testing rooms, and to allow him to flex his ego. My reaction to Gall's handling of the certification was much milder than Walters's. According to Gall's standards for certification, Walters was qualified only for Level II certification. Another examiner who had been the president of the American Polygraph Association and who had over twenty-five years experience as an examiner was also certified as only a Level II examiner. Walters went ballistic, and one of the people who had attended the meeting during which Gall had outlined his proposal to the branch chiefs and team leaders told me that Walters had threatened to resign. From that moment on, the disdain emanating from Walters toward Gall was palpable.

In defense of Walters, and in my opinion, there were only two true experts on polygraph in PD at that time, Walters and Pete Roberts. Each of them had forgotten more about polygraph than Gall would ever know, and although I wasn't a fan of Walters, I felt he was justified in his outrage.

Walters, in his capacity as chief of QAS, had been putting out memoranda entitled "Hopefully Helpful" in which he gave advice to examiners. In his Hopefully Helpful #31, which he entitled "Bluff Your Way," Walters excoriated Gall without specifically naming him and made the case that Gall had not only bluffed his way to expert status but was also continuing to bluff to maintain that status. Among his zingers aimed at Gall were the following:

1. Base your "Expert" status on a job title instead of on professional and technical knowledge and competency.
2. Insist that carrying the "Expert" job title immunizes you against challenge by anyone.

3. Find excuses to avoid accumulating up-to-date knowledge about polygraph research and generally accepted test techniques and test formats.

4. Create and use "designer tests" intended to produce a predetermined, desired test outcome.

5. Insist that polygraphy is an "art," not a science.

6. Convince everyone that your own personal preferences are more valid and reliable than procedures that have been objectively tested, validated, and duplicated over and over again.

7. Excuse your violations of basic polygraph principles by claiming that the people you test and the conditions under which you test them are so unique that you can do whatever you want to do.

8. Convince yourself that if you say you are an "Expert" often enough, you automatically become one.

9. Do not waste your time updating your knowledge about the polygraph profession because you already have the title "Expert."

10. Keep reminding everyone that you are an "Expert" because there really is no other way they can tell.

With the exception of #5, which I feel was aimed at me and others, all of the zingers were aimed directly at Gall, and I was amazed that the memordandum had been disseminated. Gall was the untouchable in PD, and Walters had touched him, big time.

To me, the most notable omission from Walters's memo was that no mention of testing was made. A criticism of Gall's refusal to test would have been appropriate for the memo, but for Walters to have leveled such a criticism would have left him open to being criticized for his own refusals to test.

Pablo Casals, the world's greatest cellist, was once asked, "How much do you practice?"

Casals answered, "Sixteen hours a day."

"Mr. Casals, you are the world's greatest cellist. Why do you practice so much?" was the next question.

"Because, after sixty years, I think I am finally getting someplace," Casals answered.

Similarly, Bill Russell, the Boston Celtics great, once said, "People tell me that I was a great player because I was 6'11". I was a great player because as a kid I played basketball from sunup to sundown every day I could."

Casals's and Russell's messages are clear. Practice is essential if one is to master any discipline.

When Gall convened a meeting to advise the examiners as to what the criteria for certification at each level were, he passed out a sheet of requirements. After looking at the criteria, I felt sure that I met all the requirements, as described, for Level IV certification.

After the meeting, I discussed the criteria with Flynn Jones and pointed out that, according to the guidelines, I was qualified to be a Level IV. Jones responded, "John, your experience is too outdated, and you are too old to be a Level IV."

"What are you talking about?" I asked. "I still test everyday. How can I be too old?"

Jones then told me that I could apply for Level IV certification but would not get it. A few days later I submitted my request of Level IV certification to Jones. Jones had to sign off and either approve or disapprove my request before he passed it on to Gall. Three weeks later Jones left my request for Level IV certification on my desk. Jones had refused to sign off on my request as he told me he would do. Without his support, I didn't have a chance of being approved for Level IV certification, and Gall's rejection was just a rubber stamp. I was certified as a Level III.

Part of the certification process was a procedure whereby, if a requested level was denied, Gall would meet with the requester and explain why the request had been denied. I never had that meeting.

In terms of benefits, there were none accruing to being certified at any level. Certification was nothing more than a bureaucratic exercise. However, feeling that I was qualified for Level IV status, I wanted it. Not only that, I wanted to see how far Gall would go to keep me from getting it. With a little over a year to go before I had to retire, I didn't think I had anything to lose. I went to Jones and told him that I would appeal the decision.

My first appeal was to Rollins. He rejected it out of hand. "John, you don't get any more money for being a Level IV. Why do you care? It is just a token," he commented.

"Grant, that's part of my point. If it costs PD nothing to certify me, doesn't enhance my status, and is essentially meaningless, why not certify me?" I asked. I also pointed out that I met every criterion for Level IV certification cited by Gall. When I pointed out that "Jack Lawrence" had been certified as a Level IV, Rollins took exception and told me that he was sure that Lawrence had not been certified as a Level IV. The next morning I left a Xerox copy of Lawrence's Level IV certification, which Lawrence had given me, on Rollins's desk. I did not hear back from Rollins.

When I failed to sway Rollins, I told him that I would appeal Gall's decision based on a claim of age discrimination as evidenced by Jones's "You're too old" comment. That is how I left it with Rollins.

In preparing my appeal I first reviewed my personnel file to pull together information from some of my PARs. In so doing, I found a memorandum for the record written by Garrett ten days after I submitted my request for Level IV certification. Garrett's memorandum began, "Per the request of Flynn Jones, I am writing this memorandum detailing an argument between me and John Sullivan." I immediately went to Garrett and asked for an explanation. Garrett told me that he hadn't wanted to write the memorandum but that Jones had insisted. As much as I liked Garrett, I deeply resented the fact that this was the second time he had put a memo in my file, without showing it to me and, more important, without giving me a chance to rebut it.

My memory of the incident detailed in the memo wasn't quite the same as Garrett's, but that was irrelevant. What was relevant was that Jones, in order to defend his decision not to support me for Level IV certification, was actively seeking negative incidents, real or not, that he could use to defend his position and impugn me.

I wrote a memorandum to Rollins expressing my displeasure at what I saw as unethical behavior on the part of Jones. As a result (and as the only result), the next time I went to Jones's secretary to check my file, she told me that she couldn't give it to me and that if I wanted it I would have to get it from Jones.

"What do you want it for?" asked Jones when I requested the file.

I wanted to tell him that it was none of his business, but said, "I just want to make sure you haven't sneaked any more memos in there."

Jones reluctantly gave me the file. I then confronted Jones. "Flynn, do you remember the confrontation Wanda had with Cole Garrett?" I asked. Jones said that he did.

The examiner "Wanda Carson," an African-American female, had been conducting a RIP test on a female DO officer who had reacted very strongly to one of the counterintelligence questions. Garrett, Carson's Southern white supervisor, advised Carson that the counterintelligence issue had to be resolved and that she would have to go back into the room and try to get more information. Garrett told me that Carson had refused to go back in the room to complete the test and that he ended up doing the test. This was something of a cause celebre in PD.

I had discussed with Garrett his confrontation with Carson, and Garrett said that the day after the incident he had asked Jones if he wanted a memo on his confrontation with Carson. "Flynn told me he'd take care of it," Garrett said. He added, "Flynn never asked me for a memorandum, and I never wrote one."

With that in mind, I then said to Jones, "Flynn, the only reason Garrett's memorandum was put in my file was because you ordered him to write it. You wanted to justify not supporting me for Level IV certification." Jones did not respond, and I then said, "Flynn, I will bet you $1,000 right now that you can't open Wanda's file and find a memorandum dealing with her confrontation with Garrett." Jones declined to take me up on my offer.

Ultimately, my fight for Level IV certification proved futile, and my appeal of the decision to deny Level IV certification was rejected. I hadn't expected to win this fight; I just wanted to see how far my adversaries would go to keep me from winning.

The Garrett/Carson incident was symptomatic of a growing racial tension in the office. Shortly after this incident came another that I thought was even more dramatic. On a quiet Friday afternoon I was conducting a test when I heard a very loud, "That goddamn racist!"

My subject was a bit startled. I looked out into the corridor and saw "Hilton Thomas," one of PD's African-American examiners, striding past my room, charts in hand, and mumbling to himself. I don't think there was anyone, subject or examiner, in my corridor who hadn't heard Thomas, and the words he used ("That goddamn racist"), as well as the fact that they were shouted, were a distraction. After I finished my test, I asked Garrett what had happened. "Hilton came in here with some lousy charts and wanted to let his subject go. When I told him that he had to get better charts than the ones he had before I would sign off on them, Hilton got all bent out of shape," Garret said. Thomas had clearly interpreted Garrett's instructions as being racially motivated. The upshot of the Carson and Thomas incidents was that both were assigned to another team leader within EB.

My relationship with Thomas had always been very good, and I liked him. Unfortunately, polygraph was a poor career path for him. He wasn't very good at testing. Not long after his incident with Garrett, he left PD for what he thought were greener pastures. While in his new job within the CIA, OS came up with a standardized test for all professional security officers. Thomas did not score well on the test. He then tried to come back to PD. He went to Flynn Jones and asked him how he could get back in to PD. "Go to Rollins, get down on your knees, and beg if you have to," Jones advised. Rollins turned Thomas down.

As bad as the Carson and Thomas incidents were, another incident occurred during this time that had more serious implications. "Monette Heller" was an African-American examiner who was seen by most people in PD as the examiner most likely to "go postal," i.e., come to work with a gun and wreak havoc. A senior security officer told me, "If we had seen her BI before we polyed her, we never would have hired her." Heller was a difficult person to get along with, and she had mood swings that discouraged anyone from approaching her. I never had any problems with Heller, and in that regard, I think that I was the exception in PD.

"Ellen Riordan" was a former U.S. Army nurse who had served in

Vietnam and in OMS before coming to PD. Riordan was about five feet two inches tall and slender. Heller was about five feet nine inches tall with a very athletic build. Both Heller and Riordan were assigned to the Employee Branch. On this occasion Heller complained to Rollins that Riordan had shoved her. Cole Garrett was directed to investigate Heller's charge, and he interviewed Riordan. Riordan was flabbergasted, and when talking with me after her interview with Garrett, she was on the verge of tears and very angry.

"John, Cole interrogated me as if I were a criminal. I never pushed Monette. You can ask the people who were there," she said.

Nothing of consequence happened to Riordan as a result of this incident, but Heller's charge did change the atmosphere in PD. This change in large part convinced one of our female examiners, "Freda Toll," to leave PD. On her last day in the office Toll came to me to say good-bye, and during our conversation, she said, "John, I just said good-bye to Rollins. I told him, 'Grant, you have a race problem here, and you had better take care of it.' Grant told me, 'We don't have any race problem here.' I couldn't believe he said that," she said. Toll also said that she felt like an endangered species and that, although she liked the work, she was glad to be leaving. I could sympathize with Toll, and the racial tension she mentioned gave more impetus to my thoughts of retiring.

Although much younger than I was, Rollins, even after our disagreements, took an almost paternalistic attitude toward me. Jones's attitude toward me, after our disagreements, worsened. In the first PAR I received from him after our confrontation, he criticized my interrogation skills and in so doing reversed himself on comments he had made in my previous PAR. He may have thought my interrogation skills had diminished over the period covered by the more recent of the two PARs, but that didn't stop him from suddenly assigning me some very thorny tests. These tests were usually given to me at the last minute. The following cases are two of the many examples:

On a Friday morning I came into my office and found on my desk the file on a subject whom I had tested for seven hours, over two sessions, three years previously. I had concluded that the subject had been deceitful but had failed to obtain any admissions. There had not been any acrimony between the subject and me, but I had interrogated her during both sessions. Having failed to get any admissions from her during our two previous sessions, I didn't think my chances for success on a third session would be high. Beyond my personal reservations, assigning me this case went against PD policy. An examiner who had failed to get any admissions from a subject after an interrogation was rarely, if ever, assigned to conduct another session unless the examiner had specifically requested to do the test.

When I had left work the night before, I had checked the schedule for the next day's tests, and I had not yet been assigned a case. Jones had not arrived at work at the time I saw the file on my desk, so he had to have put it there the night before. Jones could not have known about my history with this subject, and he should have discussed the case with me before assigning it to me. As soon as Jones arrived, I suggested to him that based on my history with the subject, I might not be the best person to conduct the test. Jones simply blew off my concerns.

Fortunately, the test turned out much better than I had anticipated. For reasons I still haven't figured out, the woman decided to come clean with me. She made some admissions that explained, as well as clarified, her problems with her previous tests and successfully completed her test with me. My impression was that Jones was more surprised than I.

The second test occurred under similar circumstances. I arrived in my office to find a very thick file on a subject I was scheduled to test that morning. The subject was a senior DO officer I had worked with overseas. I had been in the office until after 5:00 p.m. the day before, and at the time I left I had not been assigned that case. Again, I went to Jones.

"Flynn, this case wasn't assigned to me by 5:00 yesterday, and this is kind of short notice," I said. "I know this guy. I worked with him overseas and don't think I should test him" was my final plea.

"John, you're an experienced examiner. You can handle it," said Jones, dismissing my concerns.

I had trouble with the subject early on when the test clearly indicated that he was having a problem with the question about providing classified material to an unauthorized person. The man ultimately told me that he had passed classified information to a member of a liaison service, information that he had been specifically told not to pass. Testing subsequent to that admission resolved the issue.

This was the second time in my career that a senior Agency officer admitted that he had passed classified material to a liaison source without authorization. On the first occasion the information was deleted from my report before it was passed on. On this occasion, it wasn't, and Flynn Jones, for the first time that I can recall, actually congratulated me on having conducted a good test.

As pleased as I was that I had managed to obtain significant information from the two subjects I had tested on very short notice, these tests were exceptions and not the rule. Occasionally, I obtained some good information, but more often, my short-notice tests ended with issues still unresolved. To my knowledge, in none of these cases did a subsequent test result in the development of significant information, but that gave me little satisfaction.

My time in PD was growing short, and although I was anxious about retiring, I was looking forward to getting out of the division. I knew I wouldn't miss the work, but I would miss many of the people.

As a short timer, I was a little surprised that I had been put in to attend a counterintelligence training course. Dave Major and Rusty Capps, two retired FBI agents, had formed a company to teach counterintelligence awareness. The course lasted a week and was one of the best I took while in the Agency. At the conclusion of the course, Major suggested that I do some lecturing in some of his classes after I retired. That was the first time I gave any serious thought to a future without polygraph.

Short timer that I was, I was more or less going through the motions of my day-to-day responsibilities. As I knew it would, my appeal to the Equal Employment Opportunity commission regarding Level IV status had been denied. In and of itself, that didn't bother me, but the fact that Gall had stuck it to me did. Then came an incident that furthered my distrust in Gall.

I had been discussing the Ames case with "Brian Justice," one of PD's very fine young examiners. We were discussing Gall's and Jones's debriefing of Ames, when I coincidentally mentioned that "Mike Stepp" had received a $1,000 EPA for videotaping the debriefing. Justice's reaction was immediate and dramatic. "John, tell me that isn't so," he said.

"Yes, it is. Bruce Gall put him in for the award. The panel turned Gall's request down, but Larrabee overturned the panel's decision and Mike got a thousand bucks," I said.

"You just ruined my day. Mike didn't tape that interview; I did," Justice said. Justice went on to say that he had been the security officer at the site where Gall and Jones debriefed Ames. "Mike showed up, and he was sick as a dog. He must have eaten something that disagreed with him because he had diarrhea and was throwing up," continued Justice. Justice said that he had let Stepp lay down on the couch in his office. Stepp showed Justice how to set up and start the camera. Justice also said that he had told Jones how to start the video, and that during the lunch break, he (Justice) set the camera up for the afternoon session. Apparently, no one had actually run the camera during Ames's interview.

It occurred to me that Gall and Jones might have interviewed Ames on more than one occasion, so I asked Jones, "Flynn, how many times did you and Bruce interview Ames?"

"Just that once," Jones answered.

As far as I was concerned, Gall's request for an EPA for Stepp was fraudulent because no one actually ran the video camera. Gall's request for an award for Stepp implied that he had done a great job of running the camera. But Stepp had not made an appearance during the taping, and Gall must have known that. I told Jonna Adams what I had learned, and she saw my charge as just another example of me bad mouthing Gall. She never asked me to prove my charge and simply blew me off. I think that she felt that regardless of the veracity of my charge, PD did not need any more negative blowback from the Ames case.

Shortly after my conversation with Justice, I entered the Agency's transition-into-retirement program. Once I completed the preretirement program, I continued testing for the remainder of my time in PD.

I spent much time reflecting in those final days. The questions "Was it worth it?" and "Did I do any good?" constantly ran through my mind. During that time I often thought about the inscription on the wall in the main lobby of CIA headquarters:

"AND YE SHALL KNOW
THE TRUTH AND
THE TRUTH WILL MAKE
YOU FREE"
JOHN VIII—XVIII

For thirty-one years, I saw myself and my colleagues as truth seekers, searching for truths about America's enemies and allies that on occasion influenced policy. On two occasions information that I developed and/or verified ended up on the desk of a sitting president. One of those tests verified that a presidential candidate in a foreign country had accepted $100,000 from the Soviet Union to help with his election campaign. When the man was elected, the Soviet Union set up an embassy in his country. In the second test I learned that an assassination was being planned against an American ambassador. The U.S. president warned the perpetrator that if anything happened to that ambassador, the American government would hold him directly responsible. The attempt did not take place.

The fact that many of the truths PD examiners developed were not consistent with U.S. or Agency policy and were disregarded does not vitiate our effort. In Vietnam, many of the tests I conducted revealed information that contradicted the administration's position on the war and were disregarded. When I developed information on the extensive corruption of South Vietnamese officials, high desertion rates in the South Vietnamese military, and the North Vietnamese Army's presence in South Vietnam, that information was not acted on.

On many occasions, I uncovered incidents in which our chief liaison service in Vietnam, the Special Branch of the South Vietnamese National Police, was fabricating recruitments. I compiled a number of these incidents, submitted them to the U.S. chief of liaison, and was told that I would have to learn to live with this problem.

Sometimes, the Agency's conclusions turned out to be incorrect, despite its best efforts. The Agency's position that most of the material support for the Viet Cong went down the Ho Chi Minh trail was disputed by the army, which contended that much of the material went through the port of Sihanoukville in Cambodia. Three polygraph tests of a CIA agent in Vietnam supported the army's position and were discounted. After the United States invaded Cambodia, the Agency found out that it had been wrong.

More recently, during Iran-Contra, information developed during polygraph tests about rampant corruption in the Contra movement was disregarded. Also, a source claiming that Iraq had a viable WMD failed his only polygraph test.

Truths about Agency applicants that PD developed during polygraph tests were instrumental in keeping some bad people out of the Agency. This was very satisfying, as was identifying employees, during reinvestigation tests, who did not merit the trust we had put in them. On occasion PD's truths cleared employees of alleged wrongdoing, and that was satisfying too. In theory I understand how knowing the truth can set you free, but in so many cases the truths I found only set people free to look for other jobs.

Instances in which PD failed to identify problems, such as the Ames case, did not negate the positive work that examiners did. Such misses only showed that we examiners are human.

On August 30, 1999, I conducted my last polygraph test. The next morning I wrote up the report on that test and cleaned out my desk. Garrett, Adams, and Walters came to my office to say good-bye and wish me well.

I had wondered what it would be like when I handed my badge to the security protective officer (SPO) on the way out and was surprised that the experience wasn't very emotional. Mr. Whipple, a very senior SPO and a good friend, was on duty at the main entrance, and I turned in my badge to him. He too wished me well, and I was out the door.

Although not bitter, I was disappointed about how the last year had gone and regretted that I had not retired earlier. I also reveled in the fact that I had loved my job and many of the people I had worked with.

I was in reasonably good health, happily married, and debt free. My older son was on active duty after having graduated from the U.S. Naval Academy and my younger son was in his third year of college. The past held many more good memories than bad, and the future was nonthreatening. Who could ask for more?

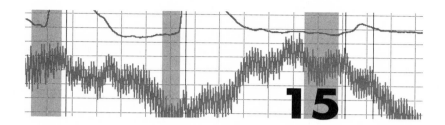

OUT TO PASTURE

No one I can think of was more reluctant about or more afraid of retirement than I was. The Agency's preretirement program, "Horizons," was excellent, but I still had much trepidation. After working at one job or another for almost fifty years, I saw retirement as being put out to pasture rather than as an opportunity to seek new challenges.

So much of a person's identity is defined by what he or she does. The first question most of us ask when we meet someone is, "What do you do?" My identity was defined by my roles as husband, father, and polygraph examiner. After August 31, 1999, one of those roles was over, and I felt that my identity had been diminished. Working for the CIA no longer has the cachet that it once did, but I always felt as though I were someone special because I worked for the CIA. After August 31, 1999, I felt less special.

Being unemployed was a new experience for me, and that too would take some getting used to. Within two months of retiring, I interviewed with eight prospective employers. Seven of the eight wanted to hire me to conduct polygraph tests. At the time I retired, I wasn't sure what I wanted to do but knew that I didn't want to conduct any more polygraph tests, and so I respectfully declined the seven offers.

Until retiring, every time I interviewed for a job, I did so because I wanted the job. In retirement I found it to be a pleasant experience to be sought after by a prospective employer and to be able to say, without being cocky or arrogant, "Thanks, but no thanks." I told my prospective employers that I was declining their job offers in part because I was writing a book. During my last year in PD, I had begun to think seriously about writing, primarily because I wanted to try to counter most of what was being written and said about polygraph. From the very beginning the idea of writing a book about polygraph seemed a bit quixotic, but I felt that I had a message to share and went ahead.

On the day after I retired, September 1, 1999, I sat down at the PC and began writing. Three hundred seventy-three days later I finished the first draft of my manuscript, which I titled *Of Spies and Lies*. I worked on the book every one of those 373 days, and on at least three days I spent more than twelve hours at the PC.

Writing the book was a continuous trip down memory lane and helped me ward off any depression brought about by my separation from the Agency. As expected, I found that I didn't miss the work, but I did miss the people. Occasionally, I called a former colleague to clarify something in the book. That helped me keep in touch, and I almost regretted finishing the book because it gave me one less reason to stay in contact with my former colleagues.

All Agency employees sign an agreement whereby they must submit any material they want to publish to the Agency's Publications Review Board (PRB). I had some concerns as to how much the PRB would ask me to delete from my manuscript and was very pleasantly surprised. Of the 106,000 words in my manuscript, the PRB deleted nine.

I submitted my cleared manuscript to the University Press of Kansas in October 2000. Michael Briggs, the managing editor of University Press of Kansas, returned the manuscript with recommended revisions in December. Briggs also suggested a subtitle for my book: "A CIA Lie Detector Remembers Vietnam."

Briggs stayed in regular contact with me throughout the process and occasionally sent me e-mails about polygraph. One of his e-mails dealt with a conference convened by the National Academy of Sciences to kick off its study of polygraph. I decided to attend the conference.

In the aftermath of the Wen Ho Lee case, the Department of Energy (DOE) had proposed that many of its scientists be polygraphed.[1] The uproar caused by that decision resulted in DOE funding an eighteen-month study on the scientific validity of polygraph. The NAS conducted the study.

I attended the first two meetings of the Committee to Review the Scientific Evidence on the Polygraph, convened by the NAS and held January 25–27, 2001. Some very strident opponents of polygraph attended the meetings, and after listening to some of them I concluded that this committee was out to disparage polygraph.

Among the most strident of the meeting attendees was Dr. Alan P. Zelicoff, a senior scientist at the Sandia National Laboratories in New Mexico. Zelicoff railed against polygraph, claiming that it was destroying careers and inhibiting qualified scientists from applying for positions that required a polygraph test. I have doubts as to how many scientists's careers were destroyed by polygraph but agree that some scientists may have been inhibited from applying for sensitive jobs. Many people are inhibited from applying to the Agency because they know they will have to take a polygraph test, but I don't see that as necessarily being a negative. Many of those are so inhibited because they know, or at least think, that they will have to lie to get a job and are afraid of getting caught.

From my experiences in testing scientists and engineers working for Agency contractors, I knew that many of them had traveled to foreign countries to participate in seminars and that many of them had provided information to their hosts that they shouldn't have provided. I know this because they told me they did, and I assumed that many DOE scientists had probably done the same thing. As I listened to Zelicoff, I couldn't help but think that fear of detection, rather than fear of a false positive, drove the resistance to polygraph testing. To paraphrase the Bard, "He doth protest too much."

At about the same time I had been attending some classes at the CICENTRE to acclimate myself to the way Major, Capps, and Associates gave presentations in order to prepare myself to give some lectures for them. During one of Major's presentations, he made the statement that CIA polygraphers had never caught a CIA spy. In what turned out to be a less than wise thing to do, I immediately took issue with the statement, citing the Scranage case as the best example. That was a bad beginning to a short-lived career as a lecturer with Major and Capps. This incident provided me with one more example of how misinformed people were about the Agency's polygraph program and added impetus to my desire to set the record straight.

Shortly after my run in with Major, an event with the potential to overshadow the Ames case occurred. On February 18, 2001, Robert Hanssen, an FBI agent, was arrested while servicing a dead drop in Foxstone Park in Vienna, Virginia. Hanssen had been spying for the Russians for years, and his arrest was a serious blow to the FBI's prestige. During the damage assessment following Hanssen's arrest, the fact that Hanssen had never been polygraphed was revealed and led the FBI to rethink its polygraph policy.

Three weeks after Hanssen's arrest John McLaughlin interviewed Dave Major of the CICENTRE and Herb Romerstein on his *One on One* TV show. During the interview Romerstein commented, in response to a question about polygraph, that Hanssen was a pathological liar and that polygraphs don't work on pathological liars. I wrote a letter to McLaughlin and Company in which I took exception to Romerstein's comment for three reasons: First, I rejected the idea that Hanssen was a pathological liar. Pathological liars lie incessantly, and none of what I had read about Hanssen supported Romerstein's assertion. Most pathological liars are very outgoing, and from what I know of Hanssen, he was a loner. Clearly, Hanssen had been living a lie, as a mole, but that doesn't qualify him as a pathological liar. Second, Romerstein's comment seemed to ignore the fact that Hanssen had been a very good spy. A pathological liar would have been a disaster as a spy. To gain the access a spy must have, he must have the confidence and trust of his colleagues. Hanssen's colleagues perceived him as strange and a loner but not as dishonest. Pathological liars whom I have known constantly overestimate their abilities and accomplishments and are usually seen by their friends and colleagues as bullshitters of the first order. Hanssen didn't fit that profile. Third, Romerstein's comment that polygraphs don't work on pathological liars was gratuitous and not based on fact. Pathological liars may not feel guilty about lying, but they do fear detection. I don't know how many of the people I caught lying were pathological liars, but I can think of at least two whom I caught who were described as pathological liars in their BIs.

Pathological liar or not, I think Hanssen would have made a good polygraph subject and would have had difficulty beating the test. Hanssen's membership in Opus Dei, I feel, was a vulnerability that a good examiner could have exploited, in the sense that questioning or challenging a member of Opus Dei's honesty would be comparable with accusing a nun of being promiscuous, and Hanssen would become defensive.

Opus Dei is an extremist Catholic organization and its members are the most self-righteous of all Catholics. A pathological liar cannot control his predilection to lie, and if Hanssen were a pathological liar, I doubt he ever would have made it into Opus Dei, because Opus Dei's background investigation of him would have uncovered his pathology.

Hanssen's ego also would have played against him. I am certain that Hanssen saw himself as very intelligent and able to outwit any interrogator. His ego would, I surmise, have led him to engage in a battle of wits with an examiner to try to explain any reactions he had during his test. Engaging a good interrogator is often a mistake.

Another factor that would have worked against Hanssen was his self-righteousness. Hanssen projected the image of the quintessential Catholic, and when push came to shove, he would have had to justify what he did. I am reasonably sure that Hanssen would not have beat me on a test, but I don't know that I would have been able to get a confession out of him. I am more confident that Pickell, Verity, Robey, Bontiempo, or Cross would have been able to get a confession out of him. The biggest problem in testing Hanssen would have been the fact that Hanssen knew that any admission on his part would send him to jail for a long time, and an examiner would have had little room to negotiate with him.

Rumor has it that the FBI polygraphed Hanssen after his arrest, and that during the test, the FBI examiner became so frustrated with Hanssen that he slapped him in the face. I can remember being frustrated by a subject, but I cannot imagine myself or any of my colleagues ever striking a subject.

During this period the media began to call me with questions about polygraph. In early March Dan Eggen, a fine reporter for *The Washington Post*, called to ask some generic questions about the CIA's polygraph program. On March 14, 2001, the *Post* published his article. It was well written but, in my opinion, a little off the mark in the sense that it seemed to imply that post-Ames Agency examiners had become much more suspicious of the employees they tested. I wrote a letter to Eggen in response to the article noting that fear of getting beat was more the driving force in the Polygraph Division than was being more suspicious of subjects. My letter to Eggen marked my entry onto the field of battle against the media's perception and portrayal of polygraph, as well as against the anti-polygraph movement in general. In his reply Eggen didn't address my concern about his article but did thank me, and told me that if he had any questions about polygraph in the future he would be in touch.

Kevin Whitelaw of *U.S. News & World Report* (USN&WR) was the next journalist to contact me. Whitelaw interviewed me over the telephone for about an hour, and on June 11, 2001, an article written by him and David E. Kaplan, titled "To Tell the Truth," appeared in *U.S. News & World Report*. Parts of Whitelaw's article were inaccurate, and I wrote a letter to USN&WR. My letter wasn't published. In my letter I took particular issue with a statement regarding CIA polygraph that Whitelaw attributed to well-known attorney Roy Krieger: "According to Krieger, one of his clients told him that a CIA examiner told him [Krieger's client] that his supervisor had told him [the examiner] to make sure he failed his test." No supervisor or anyone else in my thirty-one years in PD ever asked or even suggested that I make sure that a subject I was testing didn't pass, and I cannot imagine why any examiner would ever tell an examinee such a thing. If I were the subject of a polygraph test and the examiner told me that his supervisor had told him to make sure I didn't pass the test, my answer would be, "If that's the case, there really isn't any point in going on, and I want out."

Over the next six weeks I checked USN&WR and found no letters referring to "To Tell the Truth" in the "Letters" section of the magazine, and polygraph being as controversial as it is, I thought that strange. I wrote to USN&WR and asked why no letters about the article had been printed. On August 23, 2001, USN&WR e-mailed me and said that "space constraints" prevented them from printing any letters about the article.

Shortly thereafter, on September 11, 2001, I had just started the dishwasher when I heard Matt Lauer of the *Today Show* say, "What was that?" When I turned around to see what he was talking about, the *Today Show* cameras were focused on the World Trade Center. After the initial shock, my first thought was, "This is war!"

Four days after 9/11 I received an e-mail from a former colleague, "Steve Angel," who was a case officer assigned to the Middle East. He was absolutely bereft. "John, how could we have let this happen?" his note began. "This is what we were out here to prevent, and we failed, miserably." The sense of his guilt and abject misery came through very clearly, and I was moved. Angel was a fine officer, and his letter led me to reflect on my experiences in the Agency to see if I could come up with any answers to his question. The easy answer was that the Agency, as well as State and Defense, had ignored the warning signs of the disaster that was to come and never focused on terrorism as an international threat.

On September 12, 2001, Osama bin Laden was quoted as saying, "All we have to do is kill a few Americans, and they will run." When I read that comment, it occurred to me that bin Laden was referring to the incident in Somalia in October 1993 when nineteen American GIs were killed. Subsequently, President Clinton ordered all American troops out of Somalia. I thought then and still believe that Clinton sent the wrong message.

With the 9/11 attack, I knew that the Agency's polygraph examiners were going to be extremely busy, and I almost wished that I was back in PD. In November 2001 I took a job redacting CIA classified documents. In 2001 thousands of Agency documents were coming due to be automatically declassified because a twenty-five-year limitation was put on their classification. Prior to declassifying these documents, they had to be redacted so that material that was still sensitive was not declassified. For me and many of my former colleagues, working as a redactor turned out to be a windfall. Although I was not a warrior in the fight against terrorism, I occasionally would rub shoulders with those who were, and for a sixty-two-year-old grandfather, that was enough.

In addition to my redacting work I began a public advocacy for polygraph. Early in 2002 George W. Maschke, cofounder of the www.antipolygraph.org website, submitted a request to the CIA for a copy of my "History of the Polygraph in CIA." His request was forwarded to me; that was the first time I had heard of his website. That night I visited the website and was surprised to find my SWAG comment quoted (see chapter 14). At the prepolygraph briefings that I had given for nine years, I told the attendees that establishing a dialogue is essential for getting through a polygraph examination and also repeated my SWAG comment. Someone in the Agency who had attended the briefing had sent Maschke my comment. I later found out that Maschke had applied for a position with the FBI in 1995 and was turned down because he failed his polygraph test. Maschke was energized by this experience and became an arch adversary of polygraph.

From the statements Maschke has made about his FBI polygraph experience, I surmise that he may well have been a victim of a false positive polygraph test, and as much as I sympathize with him, I think his website does little to bolster his call for polygraph's abolishment. Maschke's website is full of anti-polygraph propaganda, provides tips on how to beat the polygraph, and from my perspective, lacks objectivity. The site includes a section in which individuals who have undergone polygraph tests are given an opportunity to describe their experiences. In one of those descriptions an individual claimed that his CIA polygraph examiner went into great detail in questioning him about his heterosexual activity, asking for details such as frequency of contacts, numbers of partners, and positions used. I doubt that *ever* happened and *know* that it didn't happen during my tenure. Periodically I pull up the website to see if anything new has been posted. I can't recall seeing a positive comment about polygraph, any mention of the Scranage or Nicholson cases, or after my book was published, any mention of it.

Several months after I discovered antipolygraph.org, in October 2002, the NAS published its findings. At the press conference called to announce the results of the study, the NAS trashed polygraph, as I had feared. Chief among the trashers was Dr. Kathryn B. Laskey, a member of the NAS Committee to Review the Scientific Evidence on the Polygraph. During the press conference Laskey interjected, out of turn and not in response to the question being discussed: "We must stress, however, that no spy has ever been caught through the use of polygraph." Laskey's comment was cited in two articles in *The New York Times*, as well as articles in *The Washington Post* and *Wall Street Journal*, and had been used by many anti-polygraph proponents as a primary basis for their recommendations to do away with polygraph. Her comment was also, at least as it applies to Agency polygraph, a misstatement of fact.

My initial response was to try to contact Laskey. I left a message on her answering machine, and when she did not return my call, I wrote her a letter. One week later Laskey called and left a message on my answering machine. Shortly thereafter, I spoke with her. When I told Laskey that her statement that no spy had ever been caught through the use of polygraph was wrong, she replied, "As soon as those words were out of my mouth, I wanted to take them back." I specifically cited the Sharon Scranage case (see chapter 9) and was amazed that Laskey hadn't heard of her. When I asked Laskey if anyone in the CIA's Polygraph Division had briefed them on polygraph tests that had resulted in admissions of acts of espionage, Laskey said, "I don't remember them doing that." Laskey also said, "I guess I will have to write a letter," and closed by telling me that the NAS panel was not out to destroy polygraph but wanted to encourage more research that would make it better. I have not heard from her since.

Next I e-mailed Shankar Vedantam, *The Washington Post* reporter who had written an article, "Can Polygraphs Detect Lies? Panel Says No, and Worries about Blemishing the Innocent," as a followup to the NAS press conference, in which he had cited Laskey's comment. Vedantam didn't acknowledge the receipt of my e-mail.

William Safire jumped on the anti-polygraph bandwagon with his op-ed piece, "Lying Lie Detectors," which appeared in *The New York Times* on October 10, 2002. In his article, Safire cited Laskey's comment and also repeated what I felt were popular misconceptions about polygraph. In his article, Safire cited the NAS study with this excerpt, " . . . and noted pointedly that 'no spy has ever been caught [by] using the polygraph.'" I sent Safire a copy of my book, and in my accompanying letter to Safire, cited the case of the Czech double agent I had caught, noting that he had been trained to beat the polygraph. Safire, in his reply, thanked me for my temperate letter but did not address any of the points I had made.

Dr. Drew Richardson, a longtime opponent of polygraph, joined the media anti-polygraph blitz with an article titled "Spies, Lies and Polygraphs," which appeared in the *Washington Times* on October 17, 2002. In it he claimed, "It was stated by various panel members very clearly and emphatically, that no spy had ever been caught as a result of polygraph [and] none would ever expect to be so revealed." My recollection is that Laskey was the only member of the panel to say that no spy had ever been caught through the use of a polygraph test, and I think the "none would ever expect to be so revealed" was Richardson's ad lib.

At a U.S. Senate Committee on the Judiciary Subcommittee on Administrative Oversight and the Courts hearing (105-431) in 1997, Richardson, in his comments on polygraph noted, "If this test had any validity [which it does not], both my own experience, and scientific research has proven, that anyone can be taught to beat this type of polygraph exam in a few minutes." Richardson's claim that "anyone can be trained to beat the polygraph" is simply not true. In my opinion, some people, but certainly not anyone, can be trained to beat the polygraph, and beating the polygraph is simply not as easy as Richardson would have people believe. In a laboratory situation, when nothing is at stake, a subject might be able to quickly learn some countermeasures, but I doubt that Richardson could train people to beat the polygraph in a real-life situation.

I have never met Richardson, but during my research, I learned that he has never been a polygraph examiner. If true, his claim that he can train anyone to beat a polygraph rings a bit hollow. I believe that Ames practiced countermeasures on his last polygraph test, but I believe just as strongly that he had not been trained in them. Nicholson was a very intelligent, well-trained, professional intelligence officer, who, after many more than a few minutes of training by the Soviets, could not defeat the polygraph.

A couple of the questions I ask people who tell me that spies can beat the polygraph are, "Who does the training? The Czechs ran the only counterpolygraph training I am aware of, and I caught a Czech intelligence officer who I believe was trained. Ames's Russian case officer told him not to worry about the polygraph, and as far as I know, Ames was not given any training. Anna Belen Montes, the DIA analyst arrested in 2001 for spying on behalf of the Cubans, claims that she asked her Cuban handler for training on how to beat the polygraph, and like Ames, was told, 'Don't worry about it.' What experience have the Soviets or Cubans had that would enable them to train someone to beat a polygraph?"

As vociferous as Richardson, Zelicoff, and the media were in their criticisms, I was disappointed that no one from the Agency or the American Polygraph Association seemed to challenge, at least publicly, the results of the NAS study, but based on my experiences with *The Washington Post*, *U.S. News & World Report*, McLaughlin and Company, et al., I also realized that the media might simply be ignoring any challenges to their reporting on the NAS study.

With the publication of my book in April 2002 and subsequent appearances on C-Span's Book World, I started giving some lectures. I also put in a lot of time reviewing classified material. My plate was full, and my anger over the comments of Laskey, Richardson, and Safire was fading.

Once my book was published I was also asked to speak at the CIA's retirement seminars on how I had coped with retirement and what I was doing with my life. My talks to these groups proved to be one of the more positive aspects of retirement. In each of my twenty or so appearances before the retirement groups, I invariably had someone come up to me and say, "You tested me." Without exception, they thanked me and told me that the experience had been better than they had anticipated. On one occasion when I was taking questions, a man raised his hand, and when I called on him, he said, "For many years, with your polygraph briefings, you put a human face on polygraph and helped a lot of us, and I just wanted to say thank you." On another occasion, a woman whom I vaguely remembered from my work with the Latin America Division raised her hand and volunteered, "We loved John in LA. His ability and integrity were unquestioned, and we had a lot of faith in him." Such moments were very gratifying.

In February 2003 the ordeal of Brian Kelley was made public on "60 Minutes." Kelley was a CIA counterintelligence expert who, prior to the arrest of FBI agent Robert Hanssen, was persecuted by the FBI in its attempts to prove that he was a Soviet mole. I know Brian Kelley and consider him to be one of the really good guys in the Agency. The mole hunt began in 1995 and was a topic of conversation in PD. I never heard Brian Kelley's name mentioned, but shortly before I retired, I recall hearing Bill Bontiempo say, "I don't care what the FBI says, I know goddamn well he is no spy." I later learned that Bontiempo was referring to Kelley.

On occasion I had tested Agency employees to clear them of allegations that had been made against them, and I took a lot of satisfaction in those tests. From what I know of the Kelley case, Kelley passed his FBI polygraph test and the FBI not only refused to accept the results of the test but also pressured the examiner, Ken Schull, to change his call. Schull publicly stated that he concurred with the "Clearly NDI" results of three polygraph tests Kelley took as part of his EOD and RIP processing, and Kelley considers Schull to be the hero in his exoneration.

Kelley's exoneration and reinstatement cheered me and things were going well until I read an op-ed piece by Dr. Alan Zelicoff, titled, "Polygraphs: Worse than Worthless," in the May 27, 2003, *Washington Post*. In his article, Zelicoff alluded to Laskey's "no spy has ever been caught" comment and again called for the abolishment of polygraph tests for government employees. In response to Zelicoff's op-ed piece I wrote an op-ed piece of my own and submitted it to the *Washington Post*. Between October 2002, when I wrote to Vedantam of the *Washington Post* and Safire of the *New York Times* and the publication of Zelicoff's op-ed piece, I had become convinced that the NAS study was seriously flawed. I also concluded that in announcing the results of the study, some NAS panel members had been intellectually dishonest.

Cases in which polygraph had caught spies were a matter of public record. A July 14, 1985, headline in the *Washington Post*, "Routine Polygraph Opened Ghanaian Espionage Probe," preceded an article about Sharon Scranage. After James Nicholson's arrest on November 16, 1996, media coverage revealed that attention had been focused on Nicholson after he failed three polygraph tests, commencing in October 1995. On March 14, 2001, Dan Eggen's article "At FBI, Polygraphs Could Stop Spies—or Careers" appeared in the *Washington Post* and noted, "Agent Harold J. Nicholson indicated deception when he said in several polygraph exams in 1995 that he had had no unauthorized contacts with foreign spies. Ten months later he was arrested on charges of spying for Russia." I felt that any research that failed to uncover such evidence was flawed.

Also in Eggen's March 2001 article, attorney Roy Krieger is quoted as saying, "Ames was walking out the [CIA headquarters'] door with grocery bags full of stuff, and he was passing his polygraphs with flying colors." This is a bit of an overstatement. Ames took only one grocery bag of classified documents, not "bags" of stuff, as Krieger contends. Krieger's comment also implies that Ames took many tests when in fact he was tested on only two occasions after he began spying for the Russians, once in 1986 and once in 1991.

Catching a couple of spies doesn't necessarily validate polygraph as a panacea for counterintelligence problems nor does missing one vitiate the process, but the smugness and satisfaction demonstrated by Laskey, Richardson, and Zelicoff in their claim that no spy had ever been caught through the use of polygraph required, if not demanded, that I try to set the record straight.

The NAS panel's failure to uncover any tests that exposed a spy suggests that its research was flawed. I submit that any high school student doing a paper on polygraph in the U.S. government would be hard pressed not to find information on Scranage and Nicholson.

Laskey's comment, "As soon as those words were out of my mouth, I wanted to take them back," speaks to the issue of intellectual dishonesty. After my conversation with Laskey, I was left with the impression that she didn't know if any spies had been caught by a polygraph test nor did she care. Based on her conversation with me, I think Laskey regretted having made the comment. If that is the case and given that her comment has been used to trash polygraph, I think it is intellectually dishonest, as well as irresponsible, for her to have failed to publicly retract her statement.

On June 9, 2003, I wrote to Dr. Paul C. Stern, study director of the Committee to Review the Scientific Evidence on the Polygraph. Laskey's comment was the main focus of my letter to Stern. I stated that Laskey, in speaking for the NAS committee, was wrong in saying that no spy had ever been caught through the use of polygraph and cited Scranage and Nicholson as examples of spies who had been caught because of polygraph. In concluding my letter, I wrote, "Doctor Stern, if you and your committee believe that no spy has ever been caught through the use of polygraph, I can suggest only that your research is incomplete, if not flawed. If, on the other hand, you are aware of cases in which spies have been caught, I think you have the responsibility to set the record straight." Doctor Stern did not reply to my letter.

I was not surprised when I was blown off by William Safire and the

Washington Post, but I was surprised that Stern didn't respond to my letter. Although I am not an intellectual heavyweight, my credentials were sufficient enough to challenge the NAS study. In my letter to Stern, I challenged the validity of the committee's research and the thoroughness, if not the integrity, of the NAS committee.

If the American Polygraph Association were looking for a spokesman, I would be very far down on any list of candidates they might choose from. I believe polygraph is more art than science, and I am deficient in my theoretical knowledge of polygraphy. Both of these factors, in conjunction with the fact that I agree with many points made by the antipolygraph faction, seem to eliminate me from any consideration for such a role. However, by default, I seemed to be taking on that role in my retirement. The publication of my book gave me some visibility, and after I appeared on C-Span's Book World, calls from the media increased. That higher visibility did not translate into any cachet with the *Washington Post* or *U.S. News & World Report*, as both chose to ignore letters that I had written rebutting articles they had printed.

Drew Richardson in his op-ed piece "Spies, Lies and Polygraphs" concluded that based on the NAS study, polygraph screening was "completely invalid as a diagnostic instrument for determining truth." In theory, Richardson's conclusion may have merit, but we don't live in a theoretical world, and in the real world, there is no better screening device than a polygraph instrument in the hands of a good examiner— "good examiner" being the operative term.

None of polygraph's detractors seems to acknowledge that the examiner's ability is a factor in the process. Apparently, acknowledging this might, if only by inference, give the polygraph process some status.

I was intensely frustrated that I could not, by myself, counter the anti-polygraph tidal wave produced by the media during this time, but my frustration was somewhat eased by a review of my book. Of the many reviews that were written, one of my favorites was published in the November 2002 issue of the U.S. Naval Institute's publication, *Proceedings*. The reviewer wrote, "The author makes a good case defending the reliability of polygraphs provided they are in competent hands." The reviewer also wrote, "It is hardly likely that any of his colleagues will question his honesty or accuracy." For Richardson, et al., there is no such thing as a good polygraph test.

The NAS study did acknowledge that polygraph is more reliable in testing on specific criminal issues than it is in general screening tests. Of course, that is true, but it is also true that CIA examiners have obtained thousands of admissions of serious criminal activity from applicants during screening tests.

Laskey, at the NAS press conference, notably did not mention any significant admissions that examiners had obtained. I know that during a visit to PD, members of the committee were provided with a large number of such admissions, and that, according to one of my former colleagues who was present, "They were blown away by the extent of the admissions we got." Apparently, without any proof one way or the other, Laskey claimed that no spy had ever been caught by polygraph, but when she was given evidence of polygraph's successes in obtaining admissions of serious wrongdoing, she chose to ignore them.

One member of the panel, Dr. Kevin R. Murphy of Penn State University, did make a positive comment about polygraph, noting, "Despite polygraph's limitations, the panel was unable to identify its equal in obtaining information." I saw no mention of Doctor Murphy's comment in any of the media reporting.

By November 2003 I had given up hope of getting a reply to my June 9 letter to Dr. Stern, and on November 13 I e-mailed NAS. In my e-mail I rehashed some of the points that I had made in my June 9 letter and said that I had been hoping that Stern would at least comment on Laskey's comment. On November 17, 2003, Stern replied to my e-mail. He claimed that he had received my June 9 letter just before he left on vacation and had misplaced it. Stern noted Laskey's comment but separated her comment from the committee's report by saying that the report itself makes no mention of whether or not a spy had been caught through the use of polygraph. I didn't see the logic in Stern's statement on Laskey's comment, but replied by noting that media reporting on the NAS study cited Laskey's comment as part of the NAS report. I asked Stern, "If you know that Laskey's comment was not based on fact or if you know that it is not true, how can you let it stand?"

Stern replied immediately. His final comment appalled me: "I have no way of judging whether Laskey's comment at the press conference is true or false. The committee's conclusions do not speak to the issue of whether polygraph has ever detected a spy." To what issue and for whom was Laskey speaking when she made her comment? Everyone at the press conference felt that her comment was based on the NAS study and was sanctioned by the NAS.

In my final reply to Doctor Stern, I suggested that if NAS did not sanction Laskey's remark, he had a responsibility to make it known. I haven't heard from him since. My letter to Stern was my last quixotic attempt to set the record on polygraph straight, and I can only hope that I have more luck with this book.

1. Dr. Wen Ho Lee is a Taiwanese-born, naturalized U.S. citizen who had been a nuclear scientist at the DOE laboratory in Los Alamos. Lee was arrested and charged with espionage in December 1999.Ultimately, fifty-eight of the fifty-nine charges against him were dropped, and Lee was released from prison.

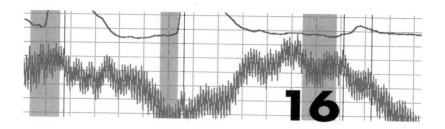

INTELLIGENCE COMMUNITY AND 9/11

Between the time I submitted my *Of Spies and Lies* manuscript in October 2001 and May 2003, when I began to work on *Gatekeeper*, I didn't think much about 9/11. I was busy revising the manuscript as my publisher requested and working full time redacting classified material. I thought the U.S. invasion of Iraq was a big mistake, and when it became apparent that Bush's "Mission Accomplished" photo op was a bit premature, criticism of the war increased exponentially. That criticism included faulting the Agency for failing to head off 9/11 and providing flawed intelligence on Iraq's weapons of mass destruction (WMD).

Without any firsthand knowledge of the Agency's operations targeting al Qaeda or WMD, I was reluctant to address these issues in *Gatekeeper* and would not be doing so were it not for Steve Angel's letter asking how the CIA could have failed so badly. (See chapter 15.)

I certainly agreed with Angel when he wrote that the CIA had failed, and although out of the loop since 1999, I can comment that the Agency experienced a thirty-year decline that took a toll on its prestige and capacity to provide good intelligence, which contributed to the disaster. That decline began with the resignation of DCI Helms on February 2, 1973. The post-Helms CIA has been characterized by escalating politicization, internal and external turf wars, and a steadily growing bureaucracy, all of which diminished the Agency's capacity to carry out its mission.

Richard Helms was the last DCI to openly challenge an administration. Helms publicly disagreed with Secretary of Defense Melvin Laird's estimation of the missile gap that existed between the United States and the Soviet Union, claiming that Laird had overestimated the gap. During Helms's tenure, the Agency also advised the Johnson and Nixon administrations that the war in Vietnam was not winnable. Helms's refusal to allow Nixon to use the Agency to help cover up Watergate was the last straw for Nixon, and Helms was pressured to resign. He wasn't forced to resign for any failure, like DCI Dulles after the Bay of Pigs, but because he refused to allow the Agency to become politicized. Helms's stand and Nixon's response forever changed the DCI's role.

The tenures of Helms's three successors—Schlesinger, Colby, and Bush—contributed to the politicization process in different ways. Schlesinger, in the five months of his tenure, made it clear that the White House was very displeased with how the Agency did business and began firing people left and right. Colby, in response to the political pressure brought on by the Church and Pike hearings, spilled the "family jewels" and in the process, exacerbated the growing antipathy between Congress and the Agency. Colby's acknowledgement of serious Agency wrongdoing confirmed many people's worst suspicions about the Agency and provided the Agency's detractors with ammunition to use in their attacks. Colby resigned in January 1976.

President Ford nominated George Bush, a good, loyal Republican and former chairman of the Republican National Committee, to replace Colby. Bush was quickly confirmed and his mantra seemed to be "Don't rock the boat." The Agency lowered its profile during Bush's tenure. This was understandable in light of the "rogue elephant" charges made during the Church and Pike hearings, and although keeping that low profile may have appeased Congress, it also weakened the prestige of the DCI and diminished the influence of the Agency. Bush grew to love the job and wanted to stay on, but when Jimmy Carter was elected in November 1976, Bush reluctantly submitted his resignation. As previously noted, Bush's tenure as DCI was unremarkable in terms of accomplishments and Turner's tenure dealt a serious blow to the Agency's morale.

Of the DCIs I served under, none was more unabashedly political than William Casey. Casey had successfully managed Ronald Reagan's 1980 campaign and was President Reagan's man. From day one as DCI, his mission was to make the Agency more an instrument of, rather than an adviser on, national policy. Hard charger that Casey was, he didn't want to influence policy only; he wanted to implement and/or change it. Casey's "bull in a china shop" approach ultimately led to Iran-Contra and another black eye for the Agency. Morale improved during Casey's tenure, but at a price of decreased support from Congress and a more negative public perception of the Agency.

For all the hard charging, Casey's tenure produced no significant successes. The defection of KGB colonel Vitaly Yurchenko in August 1985 had the potential to give the Agency's image a boost, but when Yurchenko undefected three months later, the Agency's image took another hit. Yurchenko wanted his defection to be kept as quiet as possible, and many say that Casey's attempts to make political hay of the defection were among the reasons Yurchenko undefected.

During Casey's tenure, "political correctness" became the guiding light for the way the Agency functioned. Politicization had little effect on the lower echelons of the Agency. Political correctness impacted everyone. As I have previously stated, it became politically incorrect to question the negative implications of diversity in the workplace. The CIA became one big sociology experiment, and in the name of political correctness, unqualified people were recruited, hired, and promoted. What had been a meritocracy rapidly became a mediocracy.

Morale plummeted, and working for the Agency for many became "just another job." Many of those who were eligible retired. Others just put in their time until retirement, and the stagnation that had been arrested during the first years of Casey's reign returned.

These factors, in combination with the aftereffects of Iran-Contra, made it clear that someone of stature was needed to get the Agency back on track. William Webster, the director of the FBI, filled the bill, and Reagan nominated him to be DCI. Webster's confirmation hearings took about a month, and he was sworn in on May 26, 1987.

Webster's tenure was one of introspection, and his most significant contribution was that he got the Agency back on track. He inherited the Ames problem and the paranoia that set in as agents whose identities Ames gave up were lost put DO operations in a holding pattern that lasted for years.

In May 1991 President Bush nominated Robert M. Gates to replace Webster. Gates was the first career Agency employee to become DCI since Colby. Gates's confirmation hearings were tempestuous and took four months. Although he was confirmed, problems that had come up during the confirmation hearings haunted Gates, and he never had the clout or stature with Congress that many of his predecessors had. The Agency's decline continued.

James R. Woolsey was nominated by President Clinton to replace Gates and was easily confirmed. A year after Woolsey was sworn in, Ames was arrested. In the aftermath of Ames's arrest, many fingers were pointed in trying to assess blame. There was much blame to go around, and Congress demanded that those identified as responsible for the disaster be held accountable. Woolsey refused to fire anyone. Good-bye, Jim, hello, John.

For John Deutch, the man President Clinton chose to replace Woolsey, the DCI's job was a stepping-stone to bigger and better things. Deutch wanted to be the secretary of defense and saw the DCI's job as a detour en route to the Pentagon. To get there, Deutch had to make sure that during his tenure, the Agency did nothing to make Clinton, his administration, or himself look bad. Accomplishing that meant avoiding scandals and botched operations. Thus, Deutch and his Executive Director Nora Slatkin micromanaged the DO into impotence. The pencil pushers reigned supreme, and risk taking was anathema.

When he was elected for a second term Clinton did not offer Deutch, despite his "playing it safe," the secretary of defense job, so Deutch resigned. In his short tenure, he put an onerous bureaucracy in place that left the Agency unprepared to face the challenges looming over the hill.

No DCI in the history of the Agency had as tough a row to hoe as did George Tenet when he became DCI in July 1997. The image of the Agency had been deteriorating for years, confidence in the Agency had waned, the cachet that went with being a "spook" became a thing of the past, the DO was in shambles, and morale throughout the Agency was back at the Turner levels.

In his first two years on the job Tenet seemed to reverse some of those trends. He mended fences with Congress, projected a positive image that was a public relations officer's dream, and was a hands-on leader whom Agency employees at all echelons could relate to and support. By the time I retired on August 31, 1999, it appeared that the Agency was once again in good hands.

September 11 caught the Agency and the world flat footed. Osama bin Laden and al Qaeda were very small blips on a few of the Agency's radar screens in September 2001, and sufficient resources that might have smoked out 9/11 weren't targeted against them. A memorandum for the record, written by a very senior DO officer on September 10, 2001, recommending that funds be taken from counterterrorism operations and diverted to other DO targets is one indication that the terrorist threat caught the Agency off guard. That memorandum was cited to me in November 2001 in the context of "I wonder what the *Washington Post* would do with this if they got wind of this."

With 20/20 hindsight, Helms was probably the best DCI the Agency ever had, but on a personal level, I liked Tenet more. That said, I do believe that Tenet, in supporting the administration's positions on Iraq's possession of weapons of mass destruction and on going to war in Iraq, was complicit with Bush, Cheney, Rumsfeld, Rice, et al., in misleading the American people. This was an abrogation of his responsibility as DCI and the ultimate result of the politicization of the Agency.

Hand and glove with politicization as a factor in the Agency's demise were the turf wars that raged among the intelligence community members. Fifteen agencies make up the intelligence community; three of them—the FBI, the Department of State, and the Department of Defense—seriously compete with the Agency for prestige and congressional support. Post-9/11 investigations laid much of the blame for the intelligence breakdown at the feet of the poor relationship between the Agency and the FBI. Of the agencies with whom the CIA competes, the FBI is the "main enemy." Mark Riebling in his book, *Wedge*, chillingly and thoroughly documents the historical basis for the antipathy between the two agencies and makes it very clear that this animosity seriously undermined the effectiveness of both.

The FBI's unwarranted persecution of Brian Kelley cast a shadow over FBI–CIA cooperation that is still present. Kelley is a senior Agency counterintelligence officer whom the FBI decided was a mole. But on February 18, 2001, the Bureau arrested one of their own, Robert Hanssen, as the mole they had been looking for.

A lot of lip service is paid to the idea that 9/11 brought a new spirit of cooperation to the relationship between the Bureau and the Agency. From what former colleagues and current employees have told me, it seems that initially the level of cooperation did improve, but the honeymoon was short lived. Currently, the relationship between the agencies is as bad as it ever was and is getting worse—because the FBI seems to be trying to insert itself into overseas operations, sacrosanct turf of the Agency.

Based on my experiences working with the FBI, I have concluded that running foreign agents is not the Bureau's forte and suggest that this is not a propitious time for the FBI to get into the spy business. The FBI has more than enough on its plate without adding foreign operations to its menu. FBI agents would be competing with CIA case officers, military intelligence, and DIA operatives for a limited number of overseas assets. In the process, they would only exacerbate the current acrimony.

As long as the CIA and FBI are in existence, they will fight turf battles. The best suggestion I can offer is to allow each organization to do what it does best and keep our fingers crossed.

Compared with the Agency's fights with the FBI, its skirmishes with the State Department are minor and have more to do with the inherent conflict between diplomacy and covert operations than with a real turf war. Running clandestine operations in a foreign country is a tricky business, and every ambassador fears that these operations will negatively affect diplomatic relations. On a few occasions ambassadors have refused to allow an operation to go ahead as a result of that fear. To me, this is understandable.

During Helms's tenure, an Agency asset was arrested and sentenced to death. Helms went to Secretary of State Dean Rusk and asked him to intercede on behalf of the asset. Rusk refused, and the asset was hanged.

Most of the disputes between the Agency and State before 9/11 were petty. That changed with the terrorist attacks in New York and Washington. Secretary of State Colin Powell went before the United Nations and charged Iraq with working on a WMD program. He did this, in large part, because DCI Tenet assured him that this charge was true. When Tenet subsequently called Powell to tell him that the Agency had been wrong, the State Department–CIA relationship was seriously damaged.

The WMD issue also led to a breach between Tenet and Condoleezza Rice. In Bush's State of the Union address on January 28, 2003, he included the following words: "The British government has learned that Saddam Hussein recently sought significant quantities of uranium from Africa."

After the administration acknowledged that this information was incorrect, Rice appeared on *Meet the Press* and laid the blame for the inclusion of this sentence on Tenet, telling Tim Russert that if the DCI had wanted those words out of the State of the Union address, they would have been out. In fact, Tenet had sent two memoranda to Stephen J. Hadley, Rice's deputy, advising that the claim that Hussein had been recently seeking significant quantities of uranium was erroneous. Hadley claimed that he had forgotten about the memoranda when he authorized the inclusion of the sentence in the State of the Union address and that Rice had not been aware of the memoranda. This did little to close the breach between Rice and Tenet.

Among the agencies the CIA competes with, the Department of Defense (DOD) is the only one that engages in clandestine operations similar to those of the Agency's DO. Each branch of the military has its own intelligence arm, and the DOD also has a civilian intelligence service, the Defense Intelligence Agency (DIA). The DIA has about half the manpower of the Agency, and they compete with the Agency worldwide for the same assets.

Starting with the 1979 hostage crisis in Tehran, cooperation between the Agency and the military improved greatly. I had an opportunity to observe, firsthand, the cooperation between the Agency's SOG and military personnel involved in the Desert I hostage rescue mission and was very impressed. At the lower echelons a measure of that cooperation still exists, but since 9/11 the cooperation between the two agencies has eroded dramatically from what it was, and there is almost open warfare between the Pentagon and the Agency. Rumors abound in the Agency that the Pentagon is going to take over SOG operations. SOG is the best that the Agency has to offer and to have it swallowed up in the Pentagon's bureaucracy would be a terrible mistake.

For years the DCI has been the nominal head and de facto czar of the American intelligence community. President Bush's appointment of John Negroponte to head the Department of National Intelligence is an acknowledgement of the concern over interagency turf wars and a crippling blow to the prestige of the DCI. The seriousness of the turf war was made clear in an article that appeared in the *Washington Post* on July 4,

2005. The article, headlined "CIA, Pentagon Seek to Avoid Overlap," cited a memo of understanding between Defense Secretary Donald H. Rumsfeld and DCI Porter Goss "to prevent conflicts and overlap in spying, technical collection and analysis between their two organizations." In explaining the purpose of this memo, Gen. Michael V. Hayden, the deputy director of national intelligence, noted, "We are trying to 'deconflict' the operations." The article went on to note, "Goss is concentrating on protecting the diminished role of the CIA."

Politicization and turf wars helped set the stage for 9/11, and the flawed intelligence produced by an incapacitated Agency led us into the current war with Iraq, which has become a quagmire reminiscent of Vietnam. As the war goes on, the news gets worse, and the Agency's prestige is further diminished. In the category of worst news are the stories coming out of Abu Ghraib, a prison located about ten miles west of Baghdad. When the first horrific pictures of American soldiers degrading and abusing Iraqi prisoners were made public, America's claim to the moral high ground was deeply, and I fear, permanently, damaged.

My initial reaction to the pictures was rage—rage at the depravity of the abuse, rage at the stupidity and lack of cultural awareness that would allow American soldiers to carry out such abuse, and rage that those pictures were going to get many American GIs killed. Next, I recalled a statement a military officer whom I worked for in Germany made to me in 1966. We were talking about two atrocities committed by German SS troops during World War II, the massacre of American troops at Malmedy, France, on December 17, 1944, and the "obliteration from the face of the earth" of the village of Lidice, Czechoslovakia, in June 1942, on Hitler's orders and in reprisal for Reinard Heyerdich's assassination. My boss said to me, "American soldiers will never do what those SS bastards did." At the time I agreed with him. Then came the My Lai massacre. On March 16, 1968, American troops led by 1st Lt. William Calley entered the village of My Lai in Quang Ngai province, South Vietnam; rounded up all the civilians—men, women, and children—forced them into a ditch; and began shooting them. Calley was subsequently court-martialed, convicted, and sent to prison. Nixon granted him a pardon. Seventeen years later Abu Ghraib not only demonstrated that American soldiers are capable of heinous acts but also that they could take pleasure in doing them.

My next thought was, "If those men being abused weren't terrorists or insurgents before they arrived at Abu Ghraib, they sure as hell were when they were released." Without a doubt, the pictures of the abuse that were flashed around the world had a tremendously negative impact on world opinion of the United States that outweighed the value of any information obtained from the prisoners who were being abused. It also occurred to me that if any al Qaeda or Jihadist had been having thoughts of surrendering, those pictures provided a great incentive to rethink their position and fight harder to avoid capture as well as to exact revenge.

Historically, Americans have gone to war with rallying cries on their lips. Texans engaged Santa Ana with "Remember the Alamo" on their lips. "Remember the Maine" took America into the Spanish–American War. In December 1941, recruiting offices were filled with volunteers who had been asked to "Remember Pearl Harbor." And post 9/11, recruiting offices were inundated by volunteers with "Remember 9/11" in their hearts and on their lips. I suggest that many of the enemy combatants American soldiers are fighting in Iraq may be dying with "Remember Abu Ghraib" on their lips.

Within a few days of the publication of the Abu Ghraib pictures, I began hearing from former colleagues, all of whom were appalled by the pictures. One of these colleagues told me that another of our colleagues had been hired by a civilian company to go to Iraq as an interrogator. "When he got there and saw what was going on at Abu Ghraib, he quit," summed up the e-mail note.

No positives can be derived from Abu Ghraib. At the time the pictures were made public, there didn't appear to be any Agency involvement in the abuse, and I felt a slight sense of relief. That relief was short lived.

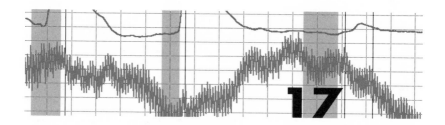

INTERROGATION AND
TORTURE

Relief I felt over the fact that there didn't seem to have been any Agency people involved in the abuses at Abu Ghraib began to evaporate when the GIs who had been involved were prosecuted. In pre- and posttrial statements, the GIs claimed that they had been acting on the orders of military intelligence officers and civilians from other government agencies (OGAs). The OGAs were the CIA and the DIA.

Any doubts I had about Agency involvement in the Abu Ghraib abuses went out the window on November 15, 2005. I was checking www.antipolygraph.org when a headline jumped out at me: "CIA Polygraph Examiner Mark Swanner Implicated in Killing." I was stunned. The headline was based on an article by Jane Mayer, titled "A Deadly Interrogation," that appeared in the November 14, 2005, *New Yorker*. Ms. Mayer's story described the capture, interrogation, abuse, and death of Manadel al Jamadi, a detainee at Abu Ghraib.

Four days later ABC News published a report titled "CIA's Harsh Interrogation Techniques Described," written by Brian Ross and Richard Esposito. In their report, Ross and Esposito claimed that the CIA authorized harsh interrogation techniques in March 2002 and went on to describe six "enhanced interrogation techniques" that were to be used on a dozen top al Qaeda targets. The report also claimed that a cadre of fourteen CIA officers had been selected to be trained in these techniques.

Unfortunately, I believe these two articles hold more than a grain of truth. Mark Swanner is a friend, and I have had a very hard time accepting the fact that he was involved in Jamadi's death, as Mayer claimed. Since reading Mayer's article, I have tried to put the interrogation she described in perspective. If what Mayer wrote is true, Jamadi was tortured and treated with depraved indifference. What was done to Jamadi violated the dictates of my interrogation training as well as my standards of personal and professional conduct.

Mayer's article did not mention whether or not Jamadi was polygraphed. I doubt that any of the detainees, particularly the high-profile al Qaeda suspects, were polygraphed. As hostile as they were, testing would have been almost impossible. I have on very rare occasions interrogated subjects without having polygraphed them, but for me and my former colleagues, interrogations were primarily conducted only after a polygraph test indicated that a subject was lying. A polygraph instrument is a tool in an interrogation that examiners hope will give an interrogator some guidelines or direction as to where to go with an interrogation. For me, interrogating without the benefit of a polygraph test would weaken the interrogation process.

My first insight into interrogation and torture came from reading Paul Gallico's book *Experiment in Terror* almost forty years ago. In the book Gallico demonstrates how the Hungarian secret police, Allamvedelmi Hatosag (AVH), extracted a false confession of espionage from an American reporter by psychologically breaking the man down until he actually believed he was a spy. The methods the AVH used to get the confession were techniques I could never imagine using.

Having grown up believing that during World War II "God was on our side" and that Americans are the good guys, it came as a shock to learn that U.S. soldiers tortured prisoners. That revelation came in the fall of 1964 while I was taking the Field Operations Intelligence (FOI) course at Fort Holabird, Maryland. My company commander was a bit of a martinet and had recently returned from a tour in Vietnam. In a private conversation with him about Vietnam, he said, "Hooking Viet Cong up to a field radio and cranking the handle was a great way to get information." He went on to say that, "After awhile, all we had to do was show a VC the wires with the alligator clips, and they would begin talking." These comments were in a private conversation, and during the interrogation phase of the FOI course, no mention of coercive interrogation tactics was made nor did any of the students ask about them.

After completing the FOI course, I was assigned to the 513th Military Intelligence Group in Frankfurt, Germany. In the fall of 1965, while attending the NATO Intelligence School in Oberammergau, I heard a Special Forces sergeant describe in detail how members of his A Team had tortured a female VC they had captured. He also mentioned that, when they followed up on the information they had tortured out of her, they were ambushed and lost three men. That was the last I heard about torture until I entered on duty with the Agency.

Working as a polygraph examiner I expected to do some interrogating, and as it turned out, I did. However, during my polygraph training, not an hour was spent on interrogation training. There wasn't much need for it as much of the information developed during PD interviews came about as a result of elicitation not interrogation. Interrogations had the potential of engendering complaints and were to be avoided. Elicitation is a process by which an interviewer/interrogator obtains information from an individual that the individual does not want to give. Interrogation is a process by which information is obtained from an individual who not only does not want to give up the information but who, through various subterfuges, is trying to hide the information.

Interrogations in PD prior to 1979, when Reid-trained examiners began testing, were interrogations in name only and were little more than enhanced elicitations. Restrictions put on examiners made real interrogations virtually impossible. Examiners were not allowed to make or even imply a threat, raise their voices, advise an applicant that he or she would not be hired if they didn't pass their tests, use profanity, or touch or get within a foot of a subject. Interrogation is an art—an art that involves acting and role playing. The restrictions put on examiners in conducting interrogations inhibited their performances.

After a year of testing, I was sent to the Agency's interrogation course. The subjects whom we interrogated were nascent case officers, and some coercion methods, including cold showers and sleep deprivation, were applied. That was it. I found the course interesting but of little use on the job.

In April 1971 Lee and I began a four-year tour in Vietnam. Those four years gave me a real introduction to interrogation, as well as some peripheral exposure to torture. Within my first month in Vietnam I was asked to conduct a very high-profile test on a Dr. Dang Tan, a North Vietnamese Army doctor who had defected in 1969. Dr. Tan was scheduled to go public at a press conference on May 11, 1971. My job was to verify the information he had provided to his CIA case officer.

Tan had been debriefed and interrogated over an extended period of time by "Ivan Serov." Serov was a DP officer and a disciple of James Jesus Angelton. He was very intense, and I could easily imagine him working for the infamous Tomas Torquemada, the first grand inquisitor and torturer of the Spanish Inquisition. He was also the only Agency interrogator I ever met who was not a polygraph examiner.

I worked with Serov for a week. He was in Tan's face for most of the time, and he was as tenacious as a pit bull. He was prepared and knew the answers to most of the questions he asked. Serov was intimidating but also a very effective interrogator. The best lesson I took away from my week of working with him was to know as much as I possibly could about a subject before undertaking an interrogation. Tan's test went well.

About a year after I arrived in Vietnam, a Professor Nguyen Van Bong was assassinated. Bong was a political opponent of President Nguyen

Van Thieu, and it was widely believed that Thieu had ordered the assassination, a charge that Thieu vehemently denied. In September 1972 two men were arrested, and they subsequently confessed to killing Bong. There was little doubt that the confessions had been obtained under duress, and the question as to whether or not the men actually killed Bong was still open to debate. I was directed to test the two men. Prior to conducting the tests, my boss informed me that I was not to be present if any physical abuse was administered to the subjects. My interpretation of that note was that if I had any indication that the subjects' captors were going to abuse them, I was to remove myself from the scene so as to avoid any complicity in the abuse.

Both subjects had been tortured. I tested them and concluded that they had in fact killed Bong. A postwar book *Gia Phong* (*The Fall and Liberation of Saigon*) and documents put out by the North Vietnamese government supported my conclusion.

Over the next two-and-a-half years, I conducted many interrogations, mostly of Vietnamese fabricators claiming to be Viet Cong or of Vietnamese claiming to have information about or access to the Viet Cong. I also conducted many tests on Vietnamese accused of theft. I cannot recall one instance when I coerced anyone I interrogated.

I do remember a test that I conducted of a maid who worked for the chief of station, Tom Polgar. Mrs. Polgar suspected that a maid had been stealing from her, and Mr. Polgar requested that the entire household staff be polygraphed. I found the thief but had trouble getting her to admit her thefts until I told her, "I know you have been stealing, and unless you tell me what you stole, I will have to turn you over to the police." The maid wrote out an extensive list of items she had stolen. When I returned to the office, "Art O'Leary," one of my bosses, suggested that I had been too harsh with the maid.

My harshest interrogation was of a VC sapper who was caught sneaking onto Danang Air Base with a load of explosives. He was a seventeen-year-old high school student who clearly hadn't spent much time roughing it out in the bush with his comrades, and I thought getting information out of him wouldn't be much of a problem. Although only seventeen, if he had completed his mission, American GIs would have died, and I went after him as hard as I ever have, before or since, to no avail. The thought of adding some physical duress to the interrogation entered my mind but only fleetingly. In my best effort at coercion I told him that, unless he gave up members of his unit, he would be turned over to the South Vietnamese Military Security Service (MSS), which was not known for its humane treatment of VC. To say my conscience is clear is trite, but at the time I rejected physical abuse, I felt that it probably would have worked. I rejected the option because I found the thought of beating information out of the young sapper repugnant.

My conscience is not so clear when I think about another Viet Cong I tested. The VC was the wife of another high-level VC. She was a peasant and very attractive, and she and her five-year-old son had been brought to Saigon by the MSS for her polygraph test. The purpose of my test was to determine if she knew the whereabouts of her husband. Testing led me to conclude that the woman did know the whereabouts of her husband. In my confrontation, I told her that I had no doubt that she had seen her husband within the last thirty days, which she denied, and I also told her that I believed that she knew where her husband was, which she also denied. At no time did I threaten or even raise my voice. When she started to softly cry, I couldn't continue the session. Neither my interpreter nor I told her MSS guards the result of my test; we said only that we would test her again the following day.

The next morning the MSS informed us that the woman had hanged herself during the night. When I saw the perfect hangman's noose around her neck, I became absolutely convinced that the MSS killed her while sexually abusing her. Thirty-two years later I still vividly remember her and her son and ask myself, "If I hadn't tested her, would she still be alive?" A couple years ago an NVA journal contained an article praising this woman's husband and her sacrifice.

My best test/interrogation in Vietnam was a three-day session with an NVA prisoner of war. I tested him to determine if he had compromised an operation for which he and several other POWs had been recruited. The interrogation never became harsh, and the POW ultimately admitted that he had revealed the details of the operation to an NVA officer in the POW camp. I think the POW confessed because he was tired of listening to me. He knew that he was lying, and he knew that I knew he was lying. I think that I just wore him down.

One of my colleagues in Vietnam, Amos Spitz, held a cocked pistol to the head of a subject as he ran a polygraph chart, and I thought that this was extremely out of line. This technique was also the closest any of my colleagues came to abusing their subjects, as far as I am aware.

When I departed Vietnam on April 10, 1975, I left knowing that I had never been a party to, witnessed, or even heard of a case in which an Agency employee engaged in torture or abuse. The only torture I had firsthand knowledge of had been carried out by the CIA's South Vietnamese liaison agencies, and I don't know what I could have done to stop it.

I returned to headquarters confident that I was a better interrogator than I had been before going to Vietnam, but I also knew that the tactics I used in my interrogations in Vietnam could not be used on the applicants I would be testing back in headquarters. That problem was addressed when I went to interrogation training at the John Reid and Associates School in Chicago. The interrogation techniques Reid taught were based on the "Reid Nine-Step Interrogation," which, as near as I can recall, involved the following:

1. Direct Positive Interrogation (DPC). Confront the subject, and make it very clear that the test and/or facts of the case do not support his/her denial.

2. Develop a theme. "You didn't intend to take [not *steal*] the money. She led you on. You are not a thief, and probably intended to give it [the missing item] back."

3. Cut off denials. The more often a person denies something, the more difficult it is to get him/her to recant.

4. Overcome objections. Try to convince the subject that it is in his/her best interest to cooperate.

5. Get and hold the subject's attention. Move closer to the subject and perhaps pose hypothetical questions.

6. Deal with the subject's passivity. Focus on the main issues to be resolved.

7. Present an alternative question. Provide the subject with two choices to explain what he/she has done. "You took [not *stole*] the money to buy food for your family" or "You took the money to party and have a good time." "Was this the first time you did this?" or "Do you do this all the time?"

8. Have the subject go over the details of what he/she did, i.e., go over any admissions obtained so as to avoid any recanting by the subject.

9. Take a written confession.

Number 9 was not applicable to the tests we conducted in headquarters, but numbers 1–8 were. Some of the steps may seem simplistic, but once I began applying them, I found out that they worked, and examiners who had undergone the Reid interrogation training had much success in obtaining admissions.

Traditional "third degree, bright light, rubber hose" interrogations were rejected out of hand during the course. Some students in the course were police officers, and some of them told me that the Reid course was good but sometimes a more direct, harder approach was necessary. I thought that this was probably true, and I was glad that I wasn't a cop.

For me, the best part of the Reid course was the material on verbal and nonverbal behaviors that can be interpreted as indications of deception or truth. Most of us are subconsciously aware of behavior that indicates truth or deception and think we can tell when someone is lying or being truthful. The Reid course made me more aware of these behaviors and, in addition, alerted me to the fact that subjects could fake behavior to undermine a test. The Reid course gave me more confidence going into an interrogation, and that confidence led to some successful interrogations

With the influx of Reid-trained examiners in PD, the length and intensity of interrogations picked up. On one occasion I wrote a report detailing the admissions I had obtained during an interrogation. The report ended up on the executive director's desk, and his assistant, "Rose Diamond," called me. Rose and I had gone through the Ops Fam course together, and I had entered on duty with her husband. "John, the Ex-Dir read your report and doesn't like that you use the word interrogation. Interrogation has a pejorative meaning, and we don't want it used," Rose said.

"But Rose, that is what we [in PD] do. I interrogated that guy," I said. I was rather surprised when she went along with me.

Rose may have been concerned because a DO officer, whose nickname was "Captain Crunch," had recently been fired for his involvement in an interrogation after which his subject had died. The case became known as the "Captain Crunch case." According to a March 2003 article in the *Atlantic Monthly*, "The Dark Art of Interrogation" by Mark Bowden, Captain Crunch had been sent to Beirut after the embassy bombing in April 1983 to find out who was responsible for the bombing. During the course of Captain Crunch's investigation, the alleged paymaster for the bombing operation was taken into custody. Captain Crunch acknowledges participating in the interrogation of this individual over a ten-day period and claims that he obtained a confession from him before he died. When this story broke, interrogation became a dirty word.

The "Captain Crunch case" is, until Mayer's "Deadly Interrogation" story in the *New Yorker*, the only incident I am aware of in which a CIA officer was alleged to have been involved in torture or prisoner abuse. Granted, other such incidents could have taken place without my knowledge, but I think that this is unlikely. My extensive involvement in DO operations, my professional and social contacts with case officers, my work with liaison services, and polygraph tests that I have conducted on DO officers make it unlikely, at least to me, that I would not have heard about some such incidents if they occurred.

In the mid-1990s much ado was made over *KUBARK Counterintelligence Interrogation*, the CIA's manual on interrogation. The manual, written in 1963, was characterized in the media, by human rights groups, and by anti-CIA people as a "torture manual" that the Agency used to train the police/torture squads of U.S. allies. At the time I was sure that we didn't engage in torture practices, and I didn't bother to read the manual. After reading the Mayer and Ross/Esposito ABC stories, I went online, pulled up the redacted manual, and read it. This was my first exposure to the manual. Chapter 9 of the KUBARK manual, "The Coercive Counterintelligence Interrogation of Resistant Sources," was required reading for anyone being trained to coerce information from a resistant or recalcitrant individual.

The Ross/Esposito ABC story claimed that a cadre of fourteen CIA officers had been selected for training in coercive techniques. If this is true, it seems to me that some of those selected would probably have been polygraph examiners because examiners are interrogators and thus would be logical candidates for the cadre. Logical though the choice may have been, I have trouble imagining any of the examiners I worked with (with maybe two exceptions) volunteering for the cadre, let alone using torture. This raises the question as to how do good men become involved in torture. Several answers come to mind.

First, abusive interrogation techniques had been given legitimacy. The torture of detainees at Guantanamo in Cuba, Bagram Air Base in Afghanistan, and Abu Ghraib in Iraq was made legitimate by declaring the detainees "enemy combatants," and not prisoners of war (POWs). According to the Bush administration, this label puts detainees outside the protection of the Geneva Convention. If detainees are outside that protection, the lines between what can and cannot be done in an interrogation are unclear and abuse may follow.

Denying detainees protection under the Geneva Convention removed accountability from the shoulders of the civilian but not the military interrogators. Military interrogators were subject to and could be held accountable for abuse under the Uniform Code of Military Justice (UCMJ).

As I read and listened to the statements made by the soldiers prosecuted for the Abu Ghraib abuses, it was clear that they believed that they had been acting on legitimate orders. It was also apparent that these individuals were being made scapegoats for a bad policy gone awry. Second, the "ticking bomb" scenario had been introduced: "These detainees have information that can prevent another terrorist attack, and we need that information now." The urgency is real and some of the detainees likely have such information. Whether or not this justifies torture is a question interrogators have to answer for themselves.

Third, the enemy had been demonized. After 9/11 and the subsequent televised killings of Americans, demonizing al Qaeda and the jihadists wasn't very difficult. Al Qaeda and the Iraqi insurgents were portrayed as religious fanatics bent on the destruction of America, and therefore, as Vice President Cheney put it, "going to the dark side" to obtain information was necessary. With the war not going as well as the administration had hoped and support for the war decreasing, the administration had to implement policies to reverse these trends. First it tried to convince the American people that al Qaeda and jihadists were, and for the foreseeable future would continue to be, a threat to the American way of life.

Fourth, the "patriotism" card had been played: "It is your patriotic duty to get information from detainees by whatever means possible. America has never been in greater danger, and you are in a position in which you can make a difference." Thomas Jefferson once said, "Patriotism is the last refuge of a scoundrel." None of my former colleagues who have conducted interrogations in Iraq is a scoundrel, and they are patriots in the best sense of the word. That said, I can see how the patriot theme might appeal to some of them.

Because insurgent and terrorists groups are so amorphous, intelligence about them is the best weapon America can use against them. Penetrating these groups has thus far seemed impossible. CIA case officers cannot travel freely in Iraq, and this makes running traditional clandestine operations virtually impossible. Case officers cannot meet, spot, assess, and recruit potential agents because they don't have access to them. Even if they did have the necessary access, the Iraqis know better than anyone how dangerous it is be seen with an American, and thus they are very difficult to recruit. Thus, the main sources of information on these groups are the detainees.

For the Agency, dealing with detainees was a comparatively new experience. In Vietnam, we dealt with POWs, not detainees, and we worked with the locals, not the American military.

Prior to 9/11, the only situation I am aware of in which the Agency had control of a detainee was the detention of Yuri Ivanovich Nosenko. Nosenko, a KGB major, who defected in 1964 . There were some inconsistencies in statements Nosenko made during his initial debriefings, and some had suspicions that he might be a double agent. Unfortunately for Nosenko, at the time he defected, another KGB defector, Anatoliy Golitsyn, who had defected in 1961, was working with the legendary Jim Angelton. After hearing Nosenko's story, Golitsyn told Angelton that Nosenko was a double agent. As a result, Nosenko spent three years in the Agency's custody, in solitary confinement.

Nosenko had been polygraphed and interrogated by "Steve Nikolaev," a Russian émigré examiner. I knew Nikolaev and didn't care for him. He had the reputation of being a rather crude, mean-spirited examiner who had never passed a Russian he polygraphed. When doubts about Golitsyn were raised, the Nosenko case was revisited, and Nosenko was repolygraphed. Steve Andros conducted the test and concluded that Nosenko was a legitimate defector. Nosenko was released from custody.

At a lecture at headquarters a few years ago, I had the privilege of meeting and talking with Nosenko. Nosenko came across as a bon vivant and was a great conversationalist. We shared a mutual dislike of Steve Nikolaev, and Nosenko told me that during his test Nikolaev had screamed, raved, and ranted; accused him of being a homosexual; and threatened him. Nosenko also told me that the isolation during his detention was very difficult for him to endure. I vividly remember how during our conversation Nosenko described how he had been told that he was a free man. Howard Osborne had gone to the detention facility to meet with him and had asked him to go with him on a walk. Nosenko told me that he believed that Osborne was taking him out to kill him and was stunned when Osborne told him that he was free.

In Iraq, the Agency is dealing with huge numbers of detainees who are under the control of the U.S. military with woefully insufficient personnel to handle them—a unique circumstance. Abu Ghraib is a primary example. The commander at Abu Ghraib at the time of the alleged abuse and torture was Brig. Gen. Janis Karpinski. General Karpinski, a reserve officer, had no previous experience in running a prison. Enlisted personnel charged in the Abu Ghraib abuse were assigned to the 372nd Military Police Company, a reserve unit. Two of the MPs had been prison guards in civilian life, and I don't believe any of them were professional soldiers. The photo of Sp/4 Lynndie England, who led a naked detainee around on a dog leash, was flashed around the world as a symbol of the chaos, cultural insensitivity, and sadism that took place in Abu Ghraib.

All of the pictures of Americans abusing prisoners at Abu Ghraib depicted enlisted personnel, and I doubt that the officers assigned to Abu Ghraib were aware of the picture-taking sessions. Had the officers been aware, I am sure they would have stopped it, not for any humane or altruistic reasons, but because if such pictures were made public, the officers who were responsible for supervising the depicted enlisted personnel could find themselves open to criticism and, more than likely, courts martial.

Mayer's story noted that Col. Thomas Pappas had shown up after Jamadi had died and had said, in referring to Jamadi's death, that Pappas wouldn't be going down alone. If true, this statement suggests that Colonel Pappas had some culpability for the conditions at Abu Ghraib, and like the enlisted personnel who were prosecuted, he should have been held accountable.

Unless the Agency has started teaching coercive interrogation techniques, I have no idea where my former colleagues might have learned these practices. The army's Survive, Evade, Resist, Escape (SERE) training teaches resistance to interrogation, and some coercive techniques used on students seem to have been applied to detainees. From what I have read about the military personnel assigned to Abu Ghraib, I doubt that any of them took SERE training, and I know of none of my former colleagues who underwent this course. The only interrogation training available to Agency employees that I am aware of is that which is available to students sent for polygraph training at DODPI. The basis for that training is the Reid Nine-Step Interrogation.

From what I have read and heard about the Abu Ghraib interrogations, none of the principles of interrogation that I learned during my time in the army, during the Agency's interrogation course or as a part of Reid training seems to have been used at Abu Ghraib. A Reid interrogation is based on the premise that the interrogator can engage his or her subject in a dialogue that will lead to a negotiation. Negotiation implies a quid pro quo. Many of the detainees at Abu Ghraib had nothing to bargain or negotiate with, and those of the detainees that did were unwilling to do so.

Again, citing the ABC News article, coercive techniques were authorized by the Department of Justice in March 2002. If this is true, the people who conducted the interrogations at Abu Ghraib, Guantanamo, Bagram, and other sites would have had less than a year of training. That might be enough time, if the interrogation instructors were qualified, but I doubt they were especially experienced. The coercive training program was set up in a knee jerk reaction to 9/11, and it was an idea conceived in confusion, born in chaos, and doomed to fail.

On December 30, 2005, Merle Pribbenow, a former colleague, e-mailed me to advise me that he had referred me to a producer on the *Hardball with Chris Matthews* TV show because the producer, Robin Goldman, had been looking for someone to discuss interrogation on the show. That same day Ms. Goldman e-mailed me a request to do an interview with Matthews, and I agreed. The interview never materialized. According to Ms. Goldman, I was preempted by the Abramoff bribery scandal, the West Virginia miners tragedy, and the Ariel Sharon stroke stories. Ulitmately Ms. Goldman told me that *Hardball* was focusing on the 2006 elections, and if the interrogation/torture issue were revisited, she would keep me in mind.

I felt that I had something to say about interrogation and torture and was a little disappointed that my interview with Matthews didn't take place. Failing with Matthews, I wrote an op-ed piece, "Mr. Bush and Torture," and after getting it approved by the PRB, I submitted it to three newspapers, none of which published it. My conclusion is that torture by Americans is too hot an issue for the media to confront.

To our shame, we have arrived at the dark side Cheney referred to, and being the eternal optimist, I can only hope that our shame will ultimately bring about a repudiation of the policies that brought us here.

EPILOGUE

During my thirty-one years as an Agency polygraph examiner, I tried to put a human face on what many perceived to be a dehumanizing process. This, and my feeling that most of the employees we in PD tested were good people, set me apart from many of my colleagues. My final heresy was my iconoclastic belief that polygraph was much more art than science. I retired from the CIA with a reputation for being Polygraph Division's Pollyanna: an eternal optimist who may have been out of touch with the real world and didn't project the image that management preferred. Even so, I went into retirement with the best wishes of the great majority of my former colleagues, many good memories, and few regrets.

My first year in retirement was spent writing *Of Spies and Lies*. I had almost completed the manuscript when 9/11 occurred. I had been out of the loop since I left the Agency, and all I knew about the attacks was what the media reported. I, like many Americans, was in a state of shock, but after the shock wore off, I returned to the manuscript and put 9/11 on the back burner. Approximately a month after 9/11, I submitted my manuscript for publication.

The sense of accomplishment that came with completing the manuscript was slightly diminished by Lee's observation that, with its submission, I was no longer a retired writer, but an unemployed retiree. Thus, I signed a contract to redact Agency classified material. Redacting Agency documents turned out to be a great way to spend time while waiting for my manuscript to be published.

With the publication of *Of Spies and Lies* in April 2002 and a subsequent appearance on CNN's Book World, I was suddenly a public voice for CIA's polygraph program. I don't think that given my iconoclastic views about polygraph, many of my former colleagues would have chosen me to speak for PD, but the choice was not theirs.

Not long after my book came out, Pete Roberts invited me to speak at Polygraph Division's annual conference. This event was my first contact with PD since I had retired, and although I was a little anxious, I was looking forward to my presentation. For three weeks I worked on a talk that would take about fifty minutes. Three days before the conference, Pete arrived on my doorstep, just as Lee and I sat down to dinner. "John, I hate to have to tell you this, but Jonna [Jonna Adams, chief of PD] told me to withdraw my invitation to have you speak at the conference," he said. He was genuinely distraught. Pete explained that Adams had invited another speaker, and the schedule did not allow enough time for both of our presentations. I am sure that Adams had invited another speaker and am just as sure that she was exacting a little payback. She and I had crossed swords on at least three occasions, and she wasn't about to give a platform to someone whose philosophy on polygraph was different from hers. That was her privilege, but in her pettiness, she put a truly decent man in an embarrassing position. I also think she deprived PD of an opportunity to hear a good presentation.

Adams may not have wanted me to speak at PD's conference, but I had invitations to speak in other venues. I was asked to lecture at Northern Virginia Community College, Michigan State University, West Point, the International Spy Museum, the National Reconnaissance Office, and several public schools and for some retirement groups, and I was enjoying myself.

A few other incidents with former colleagues led me to conclude that, as an author writing about PD, I was someone to be avoided. Two former colleagues who were also friends had agreed to let me interview them for *Gatekeeper*. I wanted to interview Ted Terrell about the Scranage case and Frank Brennan about a spy he had caught. When I tried to set up the interviews, neither of them returned my calls or e-mails. A few months later, in March 2004, an incident took place that left no doubt that I was out of favor with OS. In November 2003 I had submitted an application for a contract position with the Agency. My security clearances were due to expire in May 2004, and they would have to be updated in order for me to take the job. To update my clearances, I would have to take a polygraph test.

I had no anxiety about taking a test, but I thought it was strange that I was instructed to go to a site in Northern Virginia and not to the Agency's polygraph facility. When I mentioned this to two of my former supervisors in PD, both suggested that something was amiss, and one said, "John, they're coming after you for your book."

During the pretest of my polygraph examination, when the examiner previewed the question on removals of classified material, he qualified the question by advising me that OS wanted to know if I had removed materials to make money, either to sell classified information to a foreign intelligence service or *to write a book*. That got my attention.

The test did not go well, and I left the session thinking I would be brought back for more testing within a few days. That didn't happen, and on March 25, 2004, I had a meeting with someone from Clearance Division who, among other things, told me that I was concealing information about my book and that the results of my test were *"unresolved reactions to all issues."* This is PD speak for deception indicated to all issues. I was surprised, angry, and a little bit frightened.

At a subsequent retirement party in November 2004 that I attended at PD, I saw a former friend and colleague coming toward me. I said hello and stuck out my hand. He turned his back and walked away without saying a word.

Three months later, on February 14, 2005, I was notified that my request for a security clearance had been denied. The comments made by two former colleagues prior to my polygraph test, the way the test was conducted, the interview with the Clearance Division representative, and the incident at the retirement party left me with no doubt that OS/PD had in fact come after me for my book. I immediately appealed the decision.

Appeals of OS security clearance denials are rarely upheld, and I was completely taken by surprise when on June 27, 2005, I was notified that "the security decision to deny me a clearance had been overturned." Any satisfaction I derived from that decision is tempered by my knowledge that between the time I took my polygraph test and the time I had my clearance restored, two job offers were withdrawn, my reputation was damaged, and my chances working as an Agency contractor are slim to none.

Throughout my career I believed in and advocated the Agency's polygraph program. If my last polygraph test is an example of how PD is now doing business, I can no longer advocate the division, and that saddens me. During my thirty-one years with the Agency, I spent 2,011 days overseas on Agency business, occasionally putting myself in harm's way, and I can't help but reflect on the irony of my current situation.

Ironic though my situation may be, it has not left me bitter. My journey has been a trip, not a trek, and if I had it to do over again, I would.

INDEX

abortion: Falcone and, 72; questions on, 104

Abu Ghraib, 247–60

accountability, lack of: and Abu Ghraib, 256–57; and Ames case, 194; and Operation Bad Apple, 170

"Adamczyk, Mike," 178

"Adams, Jonna," 203, 214, 225

admissions, 3, 5, 35–36; Ames on, 188–89; bring-backs and, 207; of child molestation, 39–40, 143–44; DI call without, 20, 193; disqualification without, 79; in Employee Branch, 161; escalation of, 66; high of, 32, 103; of homosexuality, 43, 87–89; Mahle on, 192; of murder, 89; in private sector, 20; of rape, 34–35, 107; types of, 13

advance notice of test, 45, 109–10; questions on, 111–12, 125

African Americans, as examiners, 54–55

alcohol abuse, questions on, 23

Allamvedelmi Hatosag, 250

"Allen, Sara," 108, 115

alternate questions, in interrogation, 254

American Polygraph Association, 21, 31, 47, 217, 238

Ames, Aldrich (Rick), 3, 185–94; BI on, 6; debriefing of, 158–59, 188; and polygraph, 13, 189–90

Ames, Bob, 114

Ames, Maria del Rosario Casas, 185, 187

Andros, Steve, 145, 153, 258

"Angel, Steve," 232, 241

Angelton, James Jesus, 251, 257

anti-polygraph sentiment. *See* opposition to polygraph

applicant testing. *See* screening tests

Army Language School, 78

attention, in interrogation, 254

Axiton, 153

background investigations (BI): and Ames, 189, 194; misses in, 26; versus polygraph, 5–7, 22, 40, 87–88, 90–91

Backster, Grover Cleveland, Jr., 16–17

"Bagley, Frank," 197

"Banes, Janet," 143–44

"Banker," 69–71

Bannerman, Robert B., 16

"Barry, Roy," 179

"Beal, Raymond," 80

beating test, 188, 201; case officers and, 45; Dufek on, 152; MfS and, 179–80; training in, 235

behaviors, indicating deception, 7–8, 206, 254–55

Beirut bombings, 113–14, 119

Bennett, Lansing, 181

Benussi, Vittorio, 15

bin Laden, Osama, 232

blind numbers test, 4–5, 64

Bokhan, Sergei, 65

Bong, Nguyen Van, 251–52

"Bontiempo, Bill," 102–3, 115, 157–58, 162, 165, 207, 236

265

ABOUT THE AUTHOR

JOHN SULLIVAN is the son of two Irish immigrants and the author of *Of Spies and Lies: A CIA Lie Detector Remembers Vietnam*. A graduate of Albany State Teachers College, Mr. Sullivan taught for a year before enlisting in the U.S. Army in 1962. Six years later, he began a thirty-one-year career as a polygraph examiner with the CIA. He retired in 1999 as a senior examiner. Currently, Mr. Sullivan resides in northern Virginia with Lee, his wife of thirty-six years.